SPEAKING OUT

Stopping Homophobic and Transphobic Abuse in Queensland

Alan Berman and Shirleene Robinson

www.
AUSTRALIANACADEMIC**PRESS**
.com.au

First published in 2010
Australian Academic Press
32 Jeays Street
Bowen Hills Qld 4006
Australia
www.australianacademicpress.com.au

National Library of Australia Cataloguing-in-Publication entry

Author: Berman, Alan.

Title: Speaking out : stopping homophobic and transphobic abuse in
                 Queensland / Alan Berman and Shirleene Robinson.

Edition: 1st ed.

ISBN: 9781921513602 (pbk.)

Notes: Includes bibliographical references and index.

Subjects: Homophobia--Queensland--Prevention.
                 Transgender people--Violence against--Queensland--Prevention.
                 Transgender people--Crimes against--Queensland--Prevention.
                 Gays--Violence against--Queensland--Prevention.
                 Gays--Crimes against--Queensland--Prevention.

Other Authors/
Contributors: Robinson, Shirleene

Dewey Number: 306.76609943

Cover photograph by Melinda Hansen. Cover designed by Maria Biaggini.

Foreword

This important book draws attention to the social problems all too often faced by members of our lesbian, gay, bisexual, transgender, intersex and queer (LGBTIQ) community. However, *Speaking Out* is highly relevant to Queenslanders in general, and indeed all Australians. During 2009, Dr Shirleene Robinson and Dr Alan Berman gathered almost 1100 survey responses from members of the LGBTIQ community in Queensland aged over 18 years. The responses described personal experiences of homophobic and transphobic abuse, harassment and violence over lifetimes and, disturbingly, more recently. An overwhelming majority of respondents reported experiences of homophobic or transphobic abuse and harassment during their lifetimes, and 53% reported experiencing harassment or violence in the past two years. The impressive sample size of the Robinson–Berman survey demonstrates their commitment and perseverance as researchers. It also demonstrates the generosity and determination of the LGBTIQ community members who came forward in such numbers to share with the wider community their personal and distressing life experiences. The data gathered in the survey were supplemented by other useful qualitative data provided by seven focus groups conducted by the researchers across Queensland, the most decentralised and fast-growing of Australian states. Focus groups met not just in metropolitan Brisbane, but also from Cairns to the Gold and Sunshine Coasts, from Toowoomba to Townsville and in central Queensland's Rockhampton. The Robinson–Berman survey is the most comprehensive research into homophobic and transphobic abuse, harassment and violence yet undertaken in any Australian jurisdiction. But *Speaking Out* is not just a book of highly informative statistics. It is a book about the humanity of the respondents. I commend them, particularly those in the various focus groups, for their courage and generosity in sharing their stories with us. This book should convince all Australians that abuse, harassment and violence motivated by homophobia or transphobia remain a distasteful and unacceptable aspect of our society. We must do better. The recommendations in the final chapter of *Speaking Out* suggest ways in which we might. I am confident that governments in Australia, and throughout the world, will take note of this book and its recommendations in developing social policies and programs to address LGBTIQ harassment, abuse, violence and community exclusion. *Speaking Out* will help ensure our community is one where LGBTIQ members are not outsiders but true equals, free to reach their potential without prejudice and empowered to make their unique, full and rich community contribution.

The Honourable Justice Margaret A. McMurdo AC
President, Queensland Court of Appeal

Contents

List of Tables

List of Figures

Acknowledgments

Dr Alan Berman and Dr Shirleene Robinson would like to thank all those who made the publication of this book possible. Our major debt is to the members of the LGBTIQ community, who supported this project from its inception. We are both inspired by the enormous bravery that many members of this community have shown in sharing their experiences.

Funding for this project was provided by a grant from the Legal Practitioners Interest on Trust Accounts Fund (LPITAF), administered by the Queensland Department of Justice and Attorney General. We gratefully acknowledge this financial support. The grant was a joint initiative by Griffith University and Bond University and we acknowledge their assistance. Merran Lawler was involved with the project in a formative stage. The organisers of the Queensland Pride Festival and the Sunshine Coast Pride Festival granted permission for us to distribute our surveys at these venues. Maria Nordenberg provided valuable research assistance at a number of important stages. Sarah Midgley and Jacopo Sabbatini provided statistical analysis.

Shelley Argent, President of Parents and Friends of Lesbians & Gays, Paul Martin, General Manager of the Queensland Association of Healthy Communities (QAHC), Dr Wendall Rosevear, drug and alcohol abuse counsellor in Brisbane, and Vanessa Viaggio, Senior Policy Officer, Gay & Lesbian Liaison, NSW Department of Justice Crime Prevention Unit, all recognised from the outset the need in Queensland for the type of research undertaken in this project. QAHC demonstrated continuous support in a myriad of ways. The individuals employed in their offices in Brisbane, the Sunshine Coast and Cairns were especially supportive of the project. Susan Booth, the former Queensland Anti-Discrimination Commissioner, strongly supported this project, making available space in various offices of the Anti-Discrimination Commission in Queensland (ADCQ) to conduct many of the focus groups that were a key component of the qualitative research involved in this project. Ms Booth also convened a group, involving individuals representing an array of LGBTIQ community support organisations, which helped to raise awareness of this research project. The Queensland Police Service (QPS) was extremely collegial in their demonstrated willingness to discuss the purposes of the research, including especially Police Commissioner Bob Atkinson, and state-wide liaison officer Monica O'Meara. Mick Barnes, President of the Queensland Police Union, also took time out of his busy schedule to discuss the purposes of the research project.

The LGBTIQ media in Queensland, *Queensland Pride*, *Q-News*, and SameSame were all particularly supportive of this project. The mainstream press, including the ABC Radio and the *Brisbane Times* also focused attention of the general public on the research project. Darryl Scott, a social worker who had previously conducted a smaller-scale study in the Fortitude Valley of Brisbane, provided the authors with the findings of his research and provided helpful suggestions on effective ways for promoting the anonymous survey to the LGBTIQ community. Monique Forrest helped with promotion and advertising. La Trobe University's Centre for Sex, Health and Society in Victoria (particularly Research Fellow William Leonard) graciously agreed to provide constructive comments on an earlier draft of this manuscript.

Both Alan and Shirleene gratefully acknowledge the many wonderful and courageous individuals whom they had the pleasure of meeting while conducting focus groups throughout Queensland.

On a personal note, Alan would like to thank many individuals who have generously offered their time to assist in the development of various facets of this book. His father, Benny Berman, has provided personal support during the entire project. Stephen Page (family law specialist in Brisbane) and Kimberley Everton-Moore (solicitor with Legal Aid in Queensland) both provided very helpful advice on the legal aspects of this research project. Professor Gail Mason (University of Sydney Law School) was also very helpful in discussing the legal aspects of hate crimes legislation in Australia. Timothy Boyle (a fifth year student at Newcastle Law School), and Kathrin Bain (Associate Lecturer, Australian School of Taxation (Atax), Faculty of Law, The University of New South Wales) provided invaluable research assistance, and Greg Fell who generously offered to proofread the entire manuscript.

Alan also recognises the tremendous institutional support provided by the University of Newcastle in undertaking research requiring extensive interstate travel. Professor Ted Wright provided steady support of the project and sage advice on addressing many of the hurdles associated with this form of research. Jeffrey McGee (Lecturer in Law and PhD candidate at Macquarie University), Brendon Murphy (Lecturer in Law and PhD candidate at the Australian National University), Joseph Wenta and Sher Campbell (Associate Lecturers in Law), Dr John Anderson (Senior Lecturer in Law), and Hannah Robert (Lecturer in Law and PhD candidate at Sydney Law School) all provided insightful feedback and suggestions as to how the project might be developed and offered tremendous encouragement and personal support throughout the entire project.

Alan thanks the many volunteers who assisted the authors at both Queensland Pride and Sunshine Coast Pride. These volunteers helped secure an impressive number of respondents to the survey at both community events. Alan owes special thanks to many of his friends, former students and colleagues, including Kevin Carr, John Malone, Nicholas Stone, Zane Gray, James Stewart, Dana Zolis, Dr Bridget Cullen-Mandikos (Member, Queensland Civil and Administrative Tribunal), as well as Dr Angus Francis (Senior Lecturer in Law, Queensland University of Technology). Alan would also like to acknowledge the continual support of Dr William Coleman MD, who teaches paediatrics in the United States, and his wonderful wife, Julie Coleman, and daughter, Chandra Coleman, who have provided unwavering affirmation of every aspect of his life.

Long-time colleague Michael Gill from the United States suggested helpful ways of promoting the survey through social networking sites. Mike Lake and Alex Gertsen, also from the United States, Sue Kirby, and recently deceased Judge John Goldring of the District Court of New South Wales were especially supportive of this research. Alan acknowledges the administrative assistance provided by Kath Murri-Jones (Research Grants Officer, Griffith University), Kathleen Boo (Financial Consultant, Griffith University), Sabrina Rashid (Research Communications Officer, Griffith University), and Debra Willett (University of Newcastle).

Shirleene would like to extend particular thanks to Bond University for administrative support. On a more personal note, she would like to thank Shana Engelhart Cavalcanti, for enthusiastically promoting the project in many different ways throughout its duration, Nicola Curtis for Pride Day, Melinda Hansen for her beautiful photography, Maria Nordenberg for patience and encouragement, Nik Ranger for input, Peter Rohde for Pride Day and public speaking and Jacopo Sabbatini and Emily Wilson, who provided support throughout, coupled with invaluable assistance on the Sunshine Coast. Yorick Smaal was very generous with his time at an important stage. Angela White has heard a lot about statistics. Such a project would not have been possible without the support of such friends.

Shirleene would also like to record an extra special thank you to Sarah Midgley, who was there every step of the way on this project, from extreme early morning starts at Pride Days to incredibly late nights spent proof-reading. Sarah has always believed in the importance of this project and her commitment, encouragement, cheerful support and intelligent feedback has been invaluable. Mostly, her love has been a constant reminder of all that is good in this world and is without measure.

Introduction

After outlining an incident of homophobic abuse he had experienced, one Queensland man noted that he had not reported this harassment to authorities because 'it's hard to explain to someone who isn't gay how it feels to be abused because of your sexuality'. Throughout the course of 2009, the two authors of this book undertook a comprehensive investigation, exploring the ways that homophobic and transphophic harassment and violence impact on the LGBTIQ (lesbian, gay, bisexual, transgender, intersex and queer) community.[1] By the time the survey concluded at the year's end, 1,094 LGBTIQ people from Queensland had taken the time to describe their experiences. Such a response rate makes this study the largest exploration of homophobia and transphobia ever embarked on in Queensland. Indeed, it is one of the largest such studies undertaken in Australia. Many of the respondents outlined very traumatic experiences and recounting them took enormous courage. It is our hope that their strength in recording these experiences will assist others in similar situations and help to reduce homophobic and transphobic abuse, harassment and violence in Queensland.

   Speaking Out: Stopping Homophobic and Transphobic Abuse in Queensland is part of a growing body of national and international literature that explores the incidence, effects and societal costs of homophobic and transphobic abuse. The book demonstrates categorically that this form of prejudice is a significant problem in Queensland. Fifty-three per cent of those who responded to the survey upon which this book is based wrote that they had experienced homophobic or transphobic abuse within the past two years. The rate of abuse experienced over the course of a lifetime was even higher. Many respondents had experienced multiple cases of verbal abuse in the course of their lifetime, with more cases of verbal abuse being reported than there were survey respondents. Twenty-three per cent of respondents had experienced physical assault without a weapon. Fourteen per cent had experienced sexual assault without a weapon. These figures are all significantly higher than crime figures recorded for the broader community. Most forms of abuse that members of the LGBTIQ community experienced were accompanied by homophobic or transphobic language, making it clear that these attacks were motivated by prejudice and should be considered hate crimes.[2] Moreover, just as members of the LGBTIQ community in other Australian states experience constant low-level non-violent abuse and harassment, so to do members of Queensland's LGBTIQ community.

As both a range of international and national studies have found, the majority of cases of homophobic and transphobic abuse are not reported to authorities.[3] This study supports those conclusions. Many respondents to this Queensland study wrote that they found it very difficult to report the abuse they had sustained as a result of their sexuality or gender identity. This book explores both the extent to which harassment and violence affect members of Queensland's LGBTIQ population and the reasons why LGBTIQ people are less likely than heterosexual people to report abuse.

As this book demonstrates, this form of prejudice is a major problem that reduces the quality of life of many individuals. Homophobia and transphobia reduce the health and wellbeing of LGBTIQ people, undermine the human rights and dignity of both the victims and perpetrators of the violence and lead to economic and social losses as a result of LGBTIQ people's reduced social and workforce participation. This book aims to:

- explore the ways in which homophobic and transphobic abuse impact upon the lives of LGBTIQ people resident in Queensland
- provide information that may assist individuals currently experiencing homophobic or transphobic abuse, harassment and violence
- increase the rate of reporting of homophobic and transphobic incidents and create greater partnerships in crime prevention between law enforcement and the LGBTIQ community
- improve access to justice by facilitating more effective service delivery for those who are victims of homophobic or transphobic abuse, harassment and violence
- suggest legislative and social reform that will reduce the incidence of homophobic and transphobic abuse, harassment and violence
- promote diversity in all its forms.

After outlining the extent to which homophobia and transphobia impact on the LGBTIQ population of Queensland, the concluding chapter of the book then considers primary prevention and suggests ways in which homophobia and transphobia can be addressed. In doing so, it sets forth a practical model that will reduce the future incidence of the ongoing types of non-violent abuse and harassment that continue to afflict LGBTIQ individuals. It will also address the less frequent incidence of actual severe physical violence. The concluding chapter also explores ways that the rates of reporting homophobic and transphobic abuse, harassment and violence to relevant authorities can be increased. These include legislative, educational, policing and social reforms on the part of the government, the police, the criminal justice system, and allied professional groups. The book also suggests increased funding initiatives for future research in this area to examine 'best practice' models within different jurisdictions in Australia, with a view to establishing a national framework for reporting and seeking professional assistance following incidents involving homophobia and transphobia. The authors hope this may lead to greater future efforts to address homophobia and transphobia, not only in Queensland, but also throughout Australia.

Homophobia and Transphobia

Prejudices against sexual minorities predate the rise of the gay and lesbian rights movement of the 1970s. It can be stated that:

> the language to describe 'homophobia' emerged subsequent to, and in large part as a result of, the gay liberation movement. It is clear, however, that homophobia as an identifiable set of prejudices was inextricably linked to a growing public discourse surrounding same-sex sexual identity from the late nineteenth century onwards, and was deeply intertwined with the consolidation of ideas about gender and domesticity that occurred at this time.[4]

From the 1970s onwards, LGBTIQ communities in a variety of western nations were able to gain both an increased public profile and growing recognition from mainstream society.[5] Within Australia, the first Gay and Lesbian Mardi Gras, which was held in 1978, served as a protest against sexual oppression and marked the increased public visibility of non-heterosexual identities. Since that era, the LGBTIQ movement has achieved a variety of gains, often in spite of conservative opposition.[6]

As the public profile of the LGBTIQ community grew, a number of psychologists became increasingly interested in exploring the prejudices that some individuals and institutions held against LGBTIQ individuals. In 1972, the American psychologist George Weinberg used the term 'homophobia' for the first time academically to describe:

> [A] phobia about homosexuals ... It was a fear of homosexuals which seemed to be associated with a fear of contagion, a fear of reducing the things one had fought for — home and family. It was a religious fear and it had led to great brutality as fear always does.[7]

The psychological model proposed by Weinberg, which viewed homophobia as a type of individual fear and dread of non-heteronormative sexualities, has since been joined by other models that have attempted to explain the origins of both homophobia and transphobia. These include theories that link violence against LGBTIQ people to the policing of heteronormative constructions of gender and in particular masculinity (gender normativity), and structural accounts that understand violence and discrimination against LGBTIQ people as a means of securing and maintaining heterosexist authority and privilege.[8]

Weinberg's definition of 'homophobia' has attracted criticism from some academics, who point out that the term 'heterosexism' more accurately describes an 'ideological system that denies, denigrates and stigmatises any non-heterosexual form of behaviour, identity, relationship or community'.[9] While it is certainly important to recognise the structural forms of compulsory heterosexuality that negatively impact on LGBTIQ individuals, the term 'homophobia' has broadened since Weinberg's initial definition. As Gail Mason points out, the currency that homophobia has acquired in public discourse means it is more widely understood than the term heterosexism, particularly outside of sexuality studies and academia.[10] Consequently, this study uses the term 'homophobia' to describe anti-homosexual policies, practices and behaviours, both overt and covert.

As broader awareness about transgendered and transsexual individuals has also developed, recognition of the prejudice these people experience has also grown.[11] The term 'transphobia' used to denote 'fear and hatred of transgender [and transsexual] persons'.[12] While there have always been transgendered people throughout history — individuals whose gender identity did not match their birth identity — society has been slow to recognise the existence and rights of these people.[13] In 1966, the German endocrinologist Harry Benjamin published the book, *The Transsexual Phenomenon*, which outlined how some individuals were born with a biological sex that did not match their gender identity.[14] In contemporary society, the terms transgendered and transsexual are used to describe individuals in such a position. The term transgendered is generally used to describe those who have not had medical treatment to align their biological sex and gender identity, while those individuals who have undergone medical treatment often prefer to be known as transsexual.[15]

Theories linking homophobia and transphobia to the policing of heteronormative constructions of gender identity and masculinity help explain the operation of these prejudices. As Elaine Craig points out:

> Because gender is constructed in societies which strongly embrace static, binary conceptions of gender, and in which social, familial, occupational, and sexual interactions are heavily influenced by gendered social scripts, gender expressions which are ambiguous, or which have changed since a prior interaction, or which are strongly incongruent with normative understandings of the correlation between gender and biology, are typically experienced by others as at least uncomfortable, and often actually disruptive. The dominant social response to disruption is an ultimately futile effort to reinforce a gender binary.[16]

This dominant gender binary reinforces constructed ideas of masculinity and femininity. Men are expected to define themselves in opposition to that which is perceived to be unmanly or effeminate.[17] A significant number of historians and academics have pointed out the links between these gender pressures and sexism.[18]

As Patrick D. Hopkins asserts, within a system that socially constructs gender roles, heterosexuality is rigidly enforced. He maintains:

> Masculinity assumes, essentialises, naturalises and privileges heterosexuality. A violation of heterosexuality can be seen as a treachery against masculinity, which can register as an affront to a man's core sense of self, a threat to his (male) identity. There could be no fear or hatred of gays and lesbians if there were no concept of a proper gender identity and a proper sexual orientation.[19]

Michael Kimmel has pointed out that 'masculinity as a homosocial enactment is fraught with danger, with the risk of failure and with intense relentless competition'.[20] Other academic writers such as Robert Connell have also pointed out the limitations and pressures that masculinity places on men in western societies.[21] Thus homophobia can be viewed as a prejudice that is used to secure and maintain heterosexist authority and privilege.

During the course of her research on transphobia, Elaine Craig has pointed out that rigid understandings of gender identity also lead to prejudice against transgendered individuals. Tarryn Witten and Evan Eyler concur, asserting that:

> interpersonal violence and abuse against transsexual, transgendered and cross-dressing persons (hereafter referred to as anti-transgender violence unless otherwise qualified) represents a form of gender terror-

ism whose underlying motivation is the maintenance of a social system in which males dominate females through emotional, verbal and physical acts of force, and in which the line between the genders must be rigidly maintained in support of this social schema.[22]

Craig argues that 'individuals who transgress gender norms are among the most despised, marginalised and discriminated against members of any societies'.[23]

International research into homophobia and transphobia has chartered the damaging impact these prejudices have on society and individuals.[24] As Warren Blumfield notes, prejudices against minorities on the basis of sexuality or gender identity 'serves the dominant group by establishing and maintaining power and mastery over those who are marginalised or disenfranchised'.[25] It leads to victimisation and violence and stigmatises and oppresses people. It is not, however, only sexual minorities who are demoralised by such prejudice. The dominant group itself suffers from its disavowal of difference and diversity. As Blumfield points out, such prejudice can prevent some heterosexual individuals from seeking close friendships with others of the same sex, provides implicit permission to treat others badly, restricts contact with a segment of the population and limits tolerance.[26]

Research exploring homophobia and transphobia in Australia is a recently emerging field of study, but a number of pivotal works have been authored in this field that have assisted in the production of this text. The 1997 collection, *Homophobic Violence*, edited by Gail Mason and Stephen Tomsen, outlined the impact of homophobic violence, particularly in the southern states of Australia.[27] Mason's 2002 text, the *Spectacle of Violence*, explored the broader causes of violence and hostility towards gay men and lesbians.[28] The edited collection, *Homophobia: An Australian History*, which was released in 2008, traced the historical evolution of homophobic prejudice in an Australian context.[29]

A number of other important studies have been released in report form. In 1994, the Victorian group Gay Men and Lesbians Against Discrimination (GLAD) released the first study that gauged the extent to which violence affected an Australian gay and lesbian community.[30] Other particularly important studies conducted since then include the 1999 survey conducted by the University of Sydney, entitled *The Pink Ceiling is Too Low*, which explored homophobia in the workplace.[31] In 2003, researchers from La Trobe University in Victoria released a nationwide study, *Private Lives: A Report on the Health and Wellbeing of GLBTI Australians*.[32] Also in 2003, the Attorney General's Department of New

South Wales released the study, *'You Shouldn't Have to Hide to be Safe':*
A Report on Homophobic Hostilities and Violence Against Gay Men and
Lesbians in New South Wales.[33] Michael Flood and Clive Hamilton's
2005 report, *Mapping Homophobia in Australia* explored attitudes
toward homosexuality across the nation by polling almost 25,000 heterosexual Australians.[34] In 2008, researchers at La Trobe University released
the report, *Coming Forward,* which explored the underreporting of heterosexist violence and same-sex partner abuse in Victoria.[35]

Impact

A range of broad studies have documented the damaging impact of
homophobia and transphobia on Australian residents. The poorer health
of non-heterosexual people has also been linked to the discrimination,
marginalisation and violence that these individuals encounter.[36] A 2006
study conducted across Australia by researchers from La Trobe University
exploring the experiences of non-heterosexual Australians found that
49% of male respondents and 44% of female respondents experienced at
least one of the two main criteria for a major depressive episode.[37] This
study also found that 16% of all survey respondents had experienced
suicidal thoughts in the two weeks prior to completing the survey.[38] A
2007 study, also conducted by researchers from La Trobe University,
found that the health of transgendered people in Australia and New
Zealand is slightly lower than the average recorded in a 2006 study of
the non-heterosexual community.[39]

The experiences of same sex attracted youth (SSAY) are particularly disturbing. An Australia-wide survey conducted in 2005 found that 38% of
1,745 respondents aged between 14 and 21 had experienced unfair and
unlawful treatment on the basis of their sexuality at work and school.[40]
Furthermore, the same survey found that SSAY were more than four times
as likely as their heterosexual counterparts to commit suicide.[41] The recommendations that feature in Chapter Ten consider strategies that can address
the impact of homophobia and transphobia on SSAY.

It is also important to note the impact of internalised homophobia on
members of the LGBTIQ community. Internalised homophobia occurs
when non-heterosexual individuals are unable to reconcile their sexuality
with social pressures of heterosexism and homophobic and transphobic
prejudices. As Gregory Herek, Jeanine Cogan, Roy Gillis and Eric Glunt,
who have studied this problem from an American perspective, point out,
internalised homophobia is associated with a decreased sense of connection

to the LGBTIQ community, lower self-esteem and significantly higher depressive symptoms.[42]

Homophobia and transphobia also often see members of the LGBTIQ community engage in behaviour modification and efforts to hide their sexuality or gender identity. The 2006 national study conducted by researchers at La Trobe University found that over 67% of participants modified their daily activities as a result of a fear of prejudice or discrimination.[43] While comparatively little work has considered this in an Australian context, this book explores this issue as one aspect of the most damaging effects of homophobia and transphobia.

This book outlines the situation with regard to homophobia and transphobia in Queensland and its similarity to the situation across Australia. These prejudices impact on members of this state's LGBTIQ population in a myriad of intersecting and detrimental ways. While abuse itself occurs, the fear of abuse and associated societal heterosexism, also cause enormous distress to LGBTIQ individuals.

The Queensland Context

Although Queensland is currently one of Australia's fastest growing states, primary research about the extent to which homophobic and transphobic abuse occurs is limited. Indeed, this study is the first to explore homophobic and transphobic abuse across the entire state. Prior to this study, the only research into abuse against LGBTIQ individuals that had been conducted was Darryl Scott's 2004 report, *Everyone Has the Right to be Able to Walk Safe Within Their Community.*[44] Scott's study limited its scope to the abuse in the Fortitude Valley geographical location, a section of Brisbane that is home to many of that city's LGBTIQ nightclubs and is also a popular residential area for LGBTIQ residents of Brisbane. Despite the limited geographical scope of his study and an accordingly small number of respondents, Scott found that over 44% of LGBTIQ respondents had experienced verbal abuse in the last three months and 11% had experienced some level of violence, physical attacks or sexual assault.[45]

Scott's study indicated that abuse is a problem that impacts disproportionately on LGBTIQ residents in Queensland. Similarly, their 2005 research exploring homophobic attitudes among heterosexual Australians, Michael Flood and Clive Hamilton pointed out that Queensland and the Northern Territory were the most homophobic of all Australian states or territories.[46] Indeed, according to this study, when male and female respondents were combined, there was a 9% difference in rates of homophobia between Victoria — ranked as Australia's least homophobic state — and Queensland.[47] Queensland's recent history provides an indication of why this is the case.[48] From 1968 to 1987, Queensland was governed by right-wing premier Joh Bjelke-Petersen, a politician who frequently used homophobia as a political strategy.[49] During his time in power, police officers frequently entrapped gay men in sexual situations before arresting them and gay men and lesbians were prevented from taking up employment as teachers.[50] At various points, Bjelke-Petersen's government also debated criminalising lesbianism and making gay bars illegal. Due to this regressive government, Queensland was the second last Australian state to decriminalise male-to-male sexual intercourse in 1990.[51] The legacy of this official homophobia is still strongly felt by many contemporary LGBTIQ Queenslanders.

Mapping Homophobic and Transphobic Abuse: Methodology

This study, as the first to explore the way homophobia and transphobia impact on Queensland's LGBTIQ population, has benefitted enormously from preceding studies undertaken in other states. In particular, it owes a considerable debt to the 2003 *You Shouldn't Have to Hide to Be Safe* report from New South Wales, Daryl Scott's 2004 Fortitude Valley report and the 2008 *Coming Forward* report from Victoria.[52] The research teams behind these studies generously provided permission for the authors of this Queensland study to use their methodology and questions. This provided a sound methodology and an approach that elicited both quantitative and qualitative data.[53] This also serves the purpose of allowing for comparisons between Queensland and other states to be drawn.

The questionnaire used for this Queensland study also featured a number of questions designed by the two researchers involved in this study. An online website was established in 2009 (www.stopgayhatenow.com), which allowed for respondents to log on and fill out their responses to this survey anonymously. The researchers involved in this project used methodology designed to recruit and promote the survey across the breadth of Queensland and to capture both urban and rural respondents from a variety of backgrounds.

Recruitment occurred through a variety of mediums and was limited to respondents aged over 18 years. Online methods used to attract respondents included the establishment of a Facebook group that was set up by the authors, and postings made on a range of other LGBTIQ community websites. The Facebook group attracted over 250 members. Personal and community email networks were also utilised. The authors publicised the survey through media releases and interviews, both in print, such as the *Brisbane Times, Q-News, Queensland Pride* and SameSame.com.au, and on radio stations, including the ABC and *Queer Radio*, Brisbane. We also relied on the expertise of a promotions expert, who helped to arrange press advertisements in the LGBTIQ press, online advertisements on commercial LGBTIQ sites and publicity via nightclubs and pubs. A transgender consultant helped us to email and reach transgendered participants. We also printed out posters, drink coasters and other promotional material. This material was displayed at heterosexual and LGBTIQ venues and university campuses throughout the state. Over a third of responses were drawn from PDF versions of the survey filled out in person at LGBTIQ community events, such as the Brisbane Pride Festival and the Sunshine Coast Pride Day. The responses to the PDF versions of the survey were manually entered by a research assistant under the supervision of the authors.

Respondents who filled out the surveys were given the opportunity to fill out a second survey which asked if they wished to participate in focus groups to discuss further the issue of homophobic and transphobic violence in a small-group setting. At community events, the individuals were given two sets of printed survey forms and they were filled out and placed into separate boxes.

Focus groups provide an excellent means of supplementing the raw data provided in the heavily quantitative surveys.[54] Seven focus groups were held across Queensland in locations chosen to provide a wide sampling of regions. Focus groups were held in Brisbane, Cairns, the Gold Coast, the Sunshine Coast, Rockhampton, Toowoomba and Townsville. These focus groups provided valuable qualitative information that added further elucidation to the statistical information. Due to the small populations in some of these regions, it was not possible to hold separate focus groups for members of different racial groups or members of the transgender community. Instead, mixed groups were held that reflected the composition and diversity of the LGBTIQ population as much as was possible from the numbers of individuals available. The questions discussed in focus groups are attached as an Appendix to this book and followed the same format as the NSW 2003 focus group questions.

On the basis of this quantitative and qualitative research, this book is able to present a comprehensive overview of the extent to which the LBGTIQ community in Queensland is affected by homophobic and transphobic abuse. It is also able to use data gathered to suggest positive steps than can be taken to reduce this considerable social problem.

Shirleene Robinson was primarily responsible for the Introduction, and Chapters 1, 2, 3 and 4. Chapter 6 was co-written by Alan Berman and Shirleene Robinson. Alan Berman was primarily responsible for Chapters 5, 7, 8, 9 and 10.

When considering the way homophobia and transphobia impact on individuals, it is important to have a solid understanding of the population demographics that have informed the study. Chapter 1 sets out the demographic characteristics of those who responded to the survey. It finds that the survey managed to attract a solid sample of the LGBTIQ respondents from a variety of different ages. The regional locations of respondents tended to reflect the broader population distribution of the state of Queensland.

Chapter 2 focuses on the way LGBTIQ individuals experienced homophobic and transphobic harassment and violence over the course of a lifetime. This provides a comprehensive overview of the way homophobic and transphobic abuse has shaped, impacted upon and otherwise affected respondents. It finds that most survey respondents had experienced some form of abuse in the course of their lifetime in a variety of contexts, including, but not limited to, while in public, at the workplace, and in the educational sector, with more incidents of verbal abuse being recorded than there were survey respondents.

Chapter 3 explores the way homophobic and transphobic abuse has impacted on respondents over the past two years. By limiting its focus to the past two years, it is able to make observations about the relatively recent prevalence of homophobic and transphobic harassment and violence to be drawn. It finds that more than of half of respondents suffered from a form of abuse in this time period. The psychological, physical and other impacts of such abuse are outlined in this chapter.

A concept of which groups and individuals are more likely to perpetrate homophobic or transphobic abuse is essential if those perpetrators are to be stopped and their behaviour altered. Chapter 4 uses the data collected in the course of this survey to provide a profile of those who are most likely to perpetrate this type of abuse. It finds that the majority of perpetrators are likely to be young males with no prior relationship to the victim. This conclusion matches research that has been conducted nationally and internationally, raising questions about the links between homophobic and transphobic abuse and insecure concepts of masculinity on the part of offenders. It is pointed out that homophobic and transphobic abuse can be conducted by other offenders, including women and those in positions of authority.

Having considered previously the extent to which homophobic and transphobic abuse impact on the LGBTIQ population, Chapter 5 considers the numbers of respondents who have sought assistance and the effectiveness of the assistance that they sought. As outlined in preceding chapters, the impact of homophobic and transphobic abuse can be damaging in a multitude of ways. An awareness of the avenues available to those affected by homophobic and transphobic harassment and violence is important if better support is to be provided to those who have suffered in this way. The chapter also makes some observations about factors that would improve support services used by those who seek help after being abused.

The majority of people who suffer from homophobic or transphobic abuse do not report it to authorities. The rate of reporting from the LGBTIQ community is much lower than the rate of reporting among the broader community. Chapter 6 explores the numbers of respondents who do not report harassment or violence, outlining the major factors that act as barriers to reporting. It suggests factors that would lead to the greater reporting of homophobic and transphobic harassment and violence.

Chapter 7 considers the experiences that members of the LGBTIQ community have had with the police in the aftermath of homophobic and transphobic harassment and violence. It finds that the legacy of past homophobic and transphobic police practices is still felt by a number of respondents. A relationship of trust and understanding between members of the LGBTIQ community and police officers would clearly increase the numbers of victims reporting forms of abuse and help to combat homophobic and transphobic abuse, harassment and violence. The LGBTIQ liaison program operated by the Queensland Police Service (QPS) clearly has potential to act as a means of building a better relationship between the QPS and members of the LGBTIQ community. This chapter thus explores the extent to which members of the LGBTIQ community are aware of these officers and impressions of their effectiveness. This chapter also explores the liaison programs in other jurisdictions within Australia with a view to reshaping the liaison program in Queensland so as to achieve the objectives of the program and hopefully lead to an increased emphasis on some of the objectives of the liaison programs in New South Wales and Victoria. These include creating more trust and confidence in the QPS to create greater partnerships in crime prevention, increase reporting of prejudice-motivated violence, reduce the incidence of crime, harassment and fear within the LGBTIQ community and ensure a supportive workplace for LGBTIQ employees of the QPS and as liaison officers.

Some instances of homophobic and transphobic harassment and violence have proceeded to the judicial system. Anecdotal evidence suggests that many respondents find the prospect of being involved in this system quite upsetting. Chapter 8 maps the experiences of respondents who have moved within the judicial system, considering police responses within a legal context, the court system and overall impressions that respondents had of the judicial system.

Homophobia and transphobia are not only limited to abuse and attacks. These prejudices also have the impact of forcing respondents to alter and modify their behaviour and their openness about their gender identity and sexuality. Chapter 9 explores the extent to which homophobia and transphobia cause respondents to engage in behaviour modification. It considers the perceptions respondents have about homophobic and transphobic abuse and the steps they take to modify their behaviour in the hope of avoiding such abuse. This provides a further indication of the extent to which members of the LGBTIQ community are affected by these prejudices.

Having set out the extent of homophobic and transphobic harassment and violence and the way that respondents deal with this abuse, Chapter 10 sets out recommendations of legal, educational and social reforms that can be taken to address this serious problem. The ability to a live a life free from discrimination, harassment and abuse on the grounds of gender identity and sexual orientation is a basic human right. While homophobic and transphobic abuse, harassment and violence have clearly eroded this right for many Queenslanders, this is an issue that can be addressed and solutions can be implemented that will allow members of the LGBTIQ community to live a life that is open, authentic and free from such incidents.

Notes

1 This book uses the inclusive term LGBTIQ throughout to describe the lesbian, gay, bisexual, transgender, intersex and queer community. When the authors are referring to other organisations that use different acronyms to describe this community (for example, GLBT), those different acronyms are adopted in the context of discussing such organisations.

2 Gail Mason, 'Body Maps: Envisaging Homophobia, Violence and Safety', *Social and Legal Studies*, Vol. 10, No. 1 (2001); and Gail Mason, 'Not Our Kind of Hate Crime', *Law and Critique*, Vol. 12, No. 3 (2001).

3 E.g., Elizabeth Peel, 'Violence Against Lesbians and Gay Men: Decision-Making in Reporting and Non-Reporting Crime', *Feminism and Psychology*, Vol. 9, No. 2 (1999); Gregory Herek, Jeanine Cogan and J. Roy Gillis, 'Victim Experiences in

Hate Crimes Based on Sexual Orientation' in Barbara Perry, ed., *Hate and Bias Crime: A Reader* (New York: Routledge, 2003); Attorney General's Department of New South Wales, *'You Shouldn't Have to Hide to Be Safe': A Report on Homophobic Hostilities and Violence and Gay Men and Lesbians in New South Wales* (Sydney: New South Wales Attorney General's Department, 2003); Sam Dick, 'Homophobic Hate Crime: The Gay British Crime Survey 2008', Stonewall, 2008 <http://www.stonewall.org.uk/documents/ homophobic_hate _crime_final_ report.pdf> (accessed 24 January 2009) and William Leonard and others, *Coming Forward: The Underreporting of Heterosexist Violence and Same Sex Partner Abuse in Victoria* (Melbourne: The Australian Research Centre in Sex, Health and Society, La Trobe University, 2008).

4   Shirleene Robinson, 'Introduction' in Shirleene Robinson, ed., *Homophobia: An Australian History* (Annandale, New South Wales: Federation Press, 2008), p.4.

5   Barry Adam, *The Rise of a Gay and Lesbian Movement* (New York: Twayne Publishers, 1995), pp.81-108.

6   Graham Willett, *Living out Loud: A History of Gay and Lesbian Activism in Australia* (St. Leonards, New South Wales: Allen & Unwin, 2000)

7   George Weinberg, *Society and the Healthy Homosexual* (Garden City, New York: Anchor Press, 1972). See also Gregory M. Herek, 'Beyond 'Homophobia: Thinking About Sexual Prejudice and Stigma in the Twenty-First Century', *Sexuality Research and Social Policy*, Vol. 1, No. 2 (April 2004).

8   Martin Kantor, *Homophobia: The State of Sexual Bigotry Today*, 2nd edition (Westport, Connecticut: Praeger, 2009)

9   Gregory Herek, 'Psychological Heterosexism in the United States' in Anthony R. D'Augelli and Charlotte J. Patterson, eds., *Lesbian, Gay and Bisexual Identities Over the Lifespan: Psychological Perspectives* (New York: Oxford University Press, 1995), p.321.

10 Gail Mason, *The Spectacle of Violence: Homophobia, Gender and Knowledge* (London: Routledge, 2002), p.7.

11 David Valentine, *Imagining Transgender: An Ethnography of a Category* (Durham: Duke University Press, 2007)

12 Jody Norton, '"Brain Says You're A Girl, But I Think You're A Sissy Boy": Cultural Origins of Transphobia', *International Journal of Sexuality and Gender Studies*, Vol. 2, No. 2 (1997), p.139.

13 Susan Stryker and Stephen Whittle, eds., *The Transgender Reader* (New York: Routledge, 2006).

14 Harry Benjamin, *The Transsexual Phenomenon* (New York: The Julian Press, 1966). See also Stryker and Whittle, eds., *The Transgender Reader*.

15 Robert J. Hill, 'Editor's Notes' in Robert J. Hill, ed., *Challenging Homophobia and Heterosexism: Lesbian, Gay, Bisexual, Transgender and Queer Issues in Organizational Settings* (San Francisco: Jossey-Bass, 2006), p.3.

16 Elaine Craig, 'Trans-phobia and the Relational Production of Gender', *Hasting Women's Law Journal*, No. 18 (2007), p.138.

17 Michael S. Kimmel, 'Masculinity as Homophobia: Fear, Shame, and Silence in the Construction of Gender Identity' in Harry Brod and Michael Kaufman, eds., *Theorizing Masculinities* (London: Sage, 1994), p.120.

18 See particularly Suzanne Pharr, *Homophobia: A Weapon of Sexism* (Little Rock: Chardon Press, 1988) and Lisa Heldke and Peg O'Connor, *Oppression, Privilege, and Resistance: Theoretical Perspectives on Racism, Sexism and Heterosexism* (New York: McGraw-Hill, 2004).

19 Patrick D. Hopkins, 'Gender Treachery: Homophobia, Masculinity, and Threatened Identities' in Lisa Heldke and Pat O'Connor, eds., *Oppression, Privilege, and Resistance: Theoretical Perspectives on Racism, Sexism, and Heterosexism* (New York: McGraw Hill, 2004), p.244.

20 Kimmel, 'Masculinity as Homophobia', p.120.

21 R.W. Connell, *Masculinities* (Crow's Nest, NSW: Allen and Unwin, 2003).

22 Tarynn M. Witten and A. Evan Eyler, 'Hate Crimes and Violence Against the Transgendered', *Peace Review*, Vol. 11, No. 3 (1999), p.461.

23 Craig, 'Trans-phobia and the Relational Production of Gender', p.137.

24 See particularly, G.D. Comstock, *Violence Against Lesbians and Gay Men* (New York: Columbia University Press, 1991); W.J. Blumfield, 'Introduction' in Warren J. Blumfield, ed., *Homophobia: How We All Pay the Price* (Boston: Beacon Press, 1992); Gregory M. Herek, ed., *Stigma and Sexual Orientation: Understanding Prejudice Against Lesbians, Gay Men, and Bisexuals* (London: Sage Publications, 1998); Douglas Janoff, *Pink Blood: Homophobic Violence in Canada* (Toronto: University of Toronto Press, 2005).

25 Warren Blumfield, 'Introduction' in Blumfield, ed., *Homophobia: How We All Pay the Price*, p.8.

26 Ibid.

27 Gail Mason and Stephen Tomsen, eds., *Homophobic Violence* (Annandale, New South Wales: The Hawkins Press, 1997).

28 Mason, *The Spectacle of Violence*.

29 Robinson, ed., *Homophobia: An Australian History*.

30 Gay Men and Lesbians Against Discrimination, *Not a Day Goes By: Report on the GLAD Survey into Discrimination and Violence Against Lesbians and Gay Men* (Melbourne: GLAD, 1994).

31 J. Irwin, *The Pink Ceiling is Too Low: Workplace Experiences of Lesbians, Gay Men and Transgender People* (Sydney: Australian Centre for Lesbian and Gay Research, University of Sydney, 1999).

32 Marion Pitts and others, *Private Lives: A Report on the Health and Wellbeing of GLBTI Australians* (Melbourne: The Australian Research Centre in Sex, Health and Society, La Trobe University, 2003).

33 Attorney General's Department of New South Wales, '*You Shouldn't Have to Hide to Be Safe*'.

34 Michael Flood and Clive Hamilton, 'Mapping Homophobia in Australia', The Australia Institute webpaper, http://www. unilife.curtin.edu.au/sexualdiversity/documents/MappingHomophobiainAustralia.pdf> (accessed 23 January 2010).

35 Leonard and others, *Coming Forward*.

36 I. Meyer, 'Prejudice, social stress, and mental health in lesbian, gay, and bisexual populations: Conceptual issues and research evidence', *Psychological Bulletin*, Vol. 129, No. 5 (2003), pp.674-697.

37 Marian Pitts and others, *Private Lives*.

38 Ibid., p.8.

39 M. Couch and others, *TranZnation: A Report on the Health and Well-being of Transgender People in Australia and New Zealand* (Melbourne: Australian Research Centre in Sex, Health and Society, La Trobe University, 2007), p.24.

40 Lynne Hillier, Anne Turner and Anne Mitchell, *Writing Themselves In Again: 6 Years on — The second national report of the sexual health and well being of same sex attracted young people in Australia*. Melbourne: The Australian Research Centre in Sex, Health and Society — La Trobe University (2005), available at <http://www.latrobe.edu. au/arcshs/download_reports.html> (accessed 7 January 2010).

41 Ibid.

42 Gregory M. Herek, Jeanine C. Cogan, J. Roy Gillis and Eric K. Glunt 'Correlates of Internalized Homophobia in A Community Sample of Lesbians and Gay Men', *Journal of the Gay and Lesbian Medical Association*, Vol. 2 (1997), p.17.

43 Pitts and others, *Private Lives*.

44 Darryl Scott's findings were written up into the 2004 report, *Everyone has the Right to be Able to Walk Safe in Their Community*, Valley Walksafe Project (report provided courtesy of author).

45 Scott, *Everyone has the right to be able to walk safe in their community*, p.27.

46 Michael Flood and Clive Hamilton, 'Mapping Homophobia in Australia' in Robinson, ed., *Homophobia: An Australian History*, p.22.

47 Ibid.

48 For a comprehensive overview of Queensland's LGBTIQ history, see Clive Moore, *Sunshine and Rainbows: The Development of Gay and Lesbian Culture in Queensland* (St Lucia, Queensland: University of Queensland Press, 2001).

49 Shirleene Robinson, 'Homophobia as Party Politics: The construction of the "homosexual deviant" in Joh Bjelke-Petersen's Queensland', *Queensland Review*, forthcoming, March 2010.

50 Ibid.

51 Ibid.

52 Attorney General's Department of New South Wales, *'You Shouldn't Have to Hide to Be Safe'*; Leonard and others, *Coming Forward*.

53 For more on the benefits yielded by combining both methods, see David L. Morgan, 'Practical Methods for Combining Qualitative and Quantitative Methods: Applications for Health Research', *Qualitative Health Research*, Vol. 8, No. 3 (1998).

54 David L. Morgan, *Focus Groups as Qualitative Research* (Thousand Oaks, California: Sage, 1998).

CHAPTER 1

Demographics of Respondents

In total, 1265 people responded to the *Speaking Out* survey between 21 May 2009 and 17 November 2009. Some of these respondents sit outside of the scope of this analysis, with non-Queensland residents (51 respondents) and heterosexuals (119 respondents) being excluded from the analysis. A further 52 respondents did not specify their sexuality and were thus excluded. After removing these data, the total number of responses considered in the analysis was 1094.

The sheer geographical reach of Queensland is awe inspiring. It encompasses a total area of 1,852,642 km², more than seven times the size of the United Kingdom. Although the geographical scope of the state is enormous, this survey managed to attract respondents from all regions. There were respondents who lived as far south as the coastal border town of Coolangatta and those who lived far beyond the northern tropical city of Cairns. There were respondents from small towns, large towns and rural regions. There were respondents from an enormous variety of cultural and ethnic backgrounds. Aboriginal and Torres Strait Islander respondents were well-represented. In summary, the respondents who participated in this study reflected both the variety of the state and the diversity of the LGBTIQ community.

Throughout this book, percentages are rounded to the nearest per cent. As Figure 1.1 demonstrates, out of the sample of 1094 respondents, 480 (44%) were male, 573 (52%) were female, 13 (1%) were male to female transgender (M2F), 11 (1%) were female to male transgender (F2M) and 17 (2%) selected 'Other'.

Common themes recurring in the 'other' category included respondents who identified as gender queer, transgendered and intersex. One respondent wrote that they were 'born and still in a female body but [were] feeling as though [they] might be male'. Another respondent noted they were 'intersex and diagnosed male but [were] living as a female'.

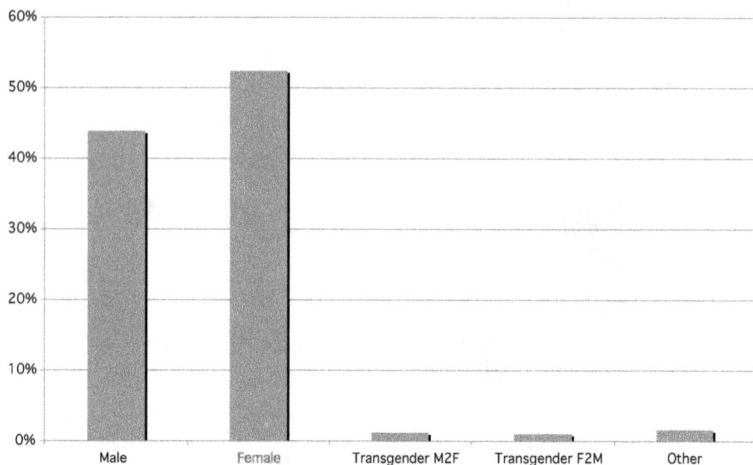

Figure 1.1
Gender identity of respondents.

There were more female than male respondents, which contrasts with both the 2003 'You Shouldn't Have to Hide to be Safe' study from New South Wales and the 2008 Coming Forward survey from Victoria, which both recorded more male than female respondents.[1] While it has been observed that men are more likely to fill out online surveys than women, anecdotal evidence from the researchers of this survey found that women were more likely to fill out surveys when approached in person. The researchers believe that this is the most probable explanation for the greater proportion of female respondents.

As Figure 1.2. shows, out of the total number of respondents, 478 (44%) identified as gay, 439 (40%) identified as lesbian, 123 (11%) identified as bisexual and 54 (5%) identified as other. It is important to note that the 44% of gay people consists of 92% male respondents, 7% female respondents and 1% transgender female-to-male (F2M) respondents.

Descriptions used by respondents who selected the 'other' category included 'queer', 'asexual', 'pansexual', 'fluid', 'transsexual', 'omnisexual', 'intergender', 'queer as partner is transitioning' and 'sex worker'. Some respondents resisted the use of pre-existing labels, with one writing 'I don't identify with any of these imposed labels. I am all and none of them'. Another wrote they would prefer to be known as 'human', rather than placed into a category of sexuality.

....

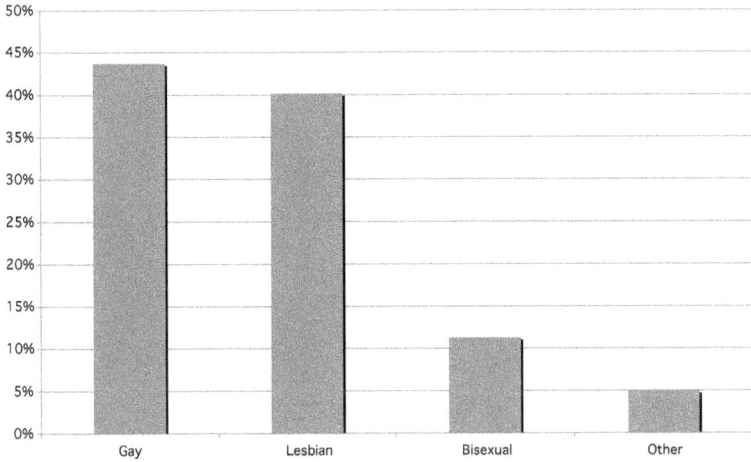

Figure 1.2
Sexuality of respondents.

Figure 1.3 displays the residential locations of respondents. Out of the total respondents to the survey, 324 (30%) lived in the Greater Brisbane area. This includes the inner-Brisbane suburbs of South Brisbane and New Farm, each home to 37 respondents (3%), while a further 24 respondents (2%) lived in the Fortitude Valley. 378 (35%) resided in the remainder of South-East Queensland. This distribution of respondents is also reflected in the map below (Figure 1.4).

The Gold Coast was home to 102 (9%) respondents, while 66 (6%) respondents were from the Sunshine Coast. North Queensland was home to 50 (5%) of respondents. Central Queensland was home to 35 (3%) of survey respondents, while South-West Queensland was home to 32 (3%) of respondents.

The significant number of responses from the Greater Brisbane area can be attributed to three main factors. First, according to Queensland government statistics, 25% (rounded to the nearest percentage for consistency) of Queensland's population lives within the Brisbane region.[2] Second, it is also evident that a disproportionate number of homosexual and transgendered Queenslanders also live in Brisbane. As discussions in regional focus groups revealed, many rural Queenslanders are attracted to Brisbane because of a perception that the city provides greater opportunities to meet other LGBTIQ individuals, and an increased acceptance of LGBTIQ identities.

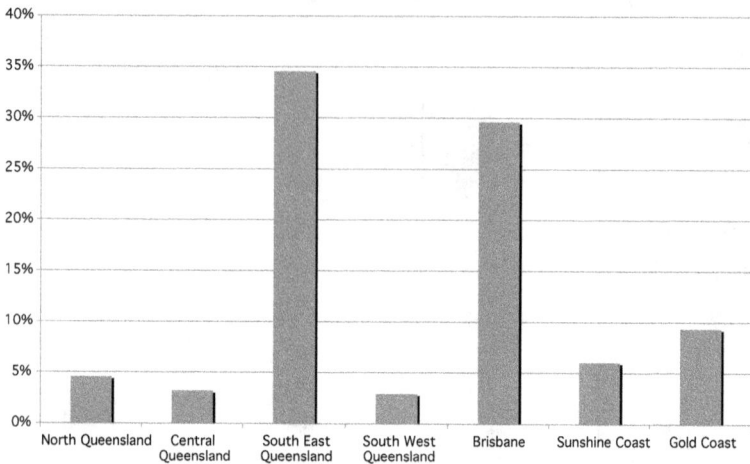

Figure 1.3
Residendial location of respondents.

Finally, the methodology of the survey would have attracted more Brisbane respondents. Four hundred and fifty-three paper surveys were filled out at the Brisbane Pride Festival on 13 June 2009. Although not all of these respondents would have lived in Brisbane, it is reasonable to conclude that a significant proportion would have resided in or near the Greater Brisbane area. A map providing a visual image of this data is provided as Figure 1.4.

Figure 1.5 displays data for the 890 respondents who provided their ages. Two hundred and seventy-five respondents (31%) were aged between 25 and 34 years and 241 (27%) were aged between 18 and 24 years. A further 206 respondents (23%) were aged between 35 and 44 years. One hundred and sixteen respondents (13%) were aged between 45 and 54. Finally, 52 respondents (6%) were aged over 55 years. The average age of all 890 respondents was 33. The average age of females was 32, the average age of males was 36, the average age of transgender F2M was 29, the average age of transgender M2F was 43, the average age of those who answered 'other' was 30. The oldest person surveyed was 76 years of age. People under the age of 18 were not able to participate in the survey.

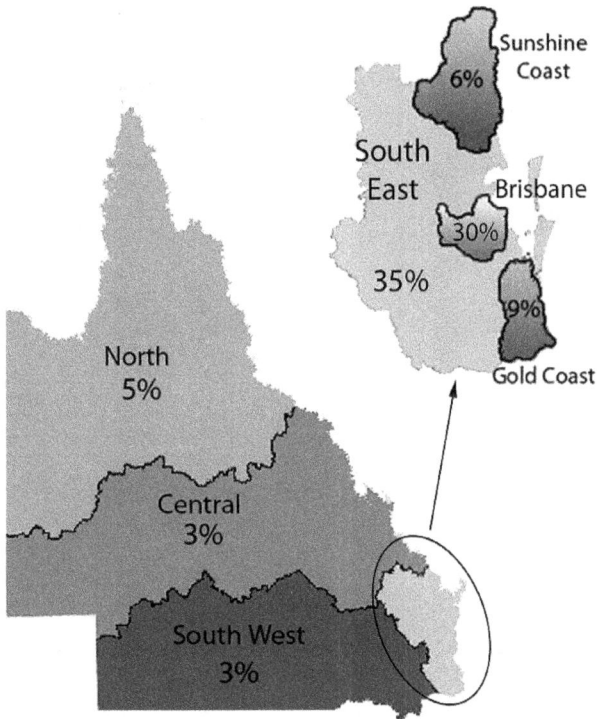

Figure 1.4
Map of residential location of respondents.

Country of Birth

Out of the 1,094 people who answered the survey, 899 (82%) were born in Australia. One hundred and ninety-two respondents (18%) indicated they were born elsewhere. This is very similar to broader Queensland population statistics from 2006, which stated that 17% of the broader Queensland population were born overseas.[3] Three respondents to this survey did not indicate whether or not they were born in Australia. Out of the 192 people born overseas, 184 people specified a country of birth. Fifty-nine (5%) respondents were born in the United Kingdom, 45 (4%) were born in New Zealand and 13 (1%) were born the United States of America. Respondents came from a further 35 other countries, including Brazil, Canada, Denmark, Fiji, France, Germany, India, Italy, Malaysia,

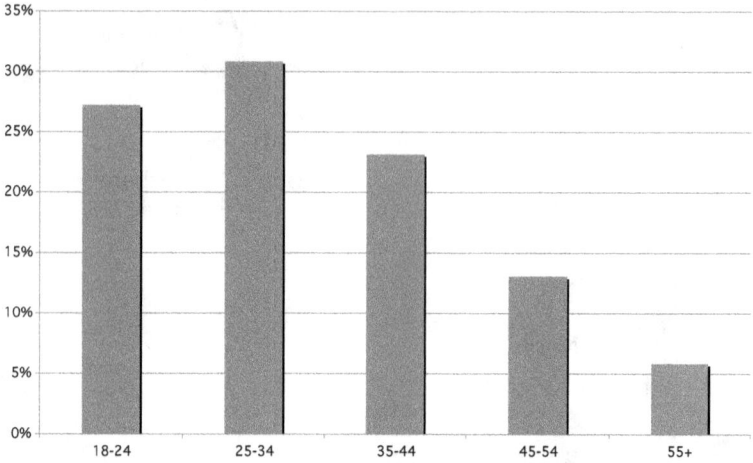

Figure 1.5
Ages of respondents.

Papua New Guinea, the Philippines, Singapore, South Africa, Sri Lanka, Sweden and Vietnam.

These figures indicate that the LGBTIQ population in Queensland is comprised of more diverse nationalities than the LGBTIQ population of Victoria. The *Coming Forward* report undertaken in Victoria in 2008 found that 88% (rounded to the nearest per cent for consistency) of respondents were born in Australia, with 14% being drawn from a range of 21 countries.[4]

In Queensland, 82 respondents (7%) reported that they spoke another language apart from English at home, with 61 respondents listing their other language; 987 respondents (90%) did not speak any language other than English at home and 25 respondents (2%) did not specify. Spanish was the most prevalent language apart from English spoken, with nine individuals noting they spoke this language at home. Six individuals spoke German and five individuals spoke French. Four respondents noted that they could communicate via Auslan, the Australian sign language of the deaf community. Respondents listed another 22 languages, ranging from Cantonese to Vietnamese, bringing the total number of languages spoken apart from English to 27.

Ancestry

Seven hundred and seventy-six respondents out of 1094 (71%) who answered this question described their ancestry as being 'Anglo'. This was followed by 70 respondents (6%) who wrote their ancestry as 'German' and 41 respondents (4%) who described their ancestry as 'Italian'. Thirty-six respondents selected multiple ancestries.

Aboriginal and Torres Strait Islanders

Out of the 975 people who answered the question, 'Are you of Aboriginal descent?', 38 people (4%) said yes. Nine hundred and thirty-seven people (96%) said they did not identify as Aboriginal. The percentage of non-respondents to this question was 11%.

Out of the 1017 people who answered the question, 'Are you of Torres Strait Islander origin?', seven people (1%) said yes. One thousand and ten (99%) said they did not identify as Torres Strait Islander. The percentage of non-respondents to this question was 7%.

In total, 5% of survey respondents who answered these two questions identified as being Aboriginal or Torres Strait Islanders. Queensland government statistics from 2006 show that the Aboriginal and Torres Strait Islander population of this state forms around 3.5% of the total Queensland population.[5] Thus, statistics indicate that the survey was extremely successful in reaching Indigenous respondents.

Religion

Out of the 1094 survey respondents, 620 respondents (57%) who answered this question reported having no religious affiliation. 465 respondents (43%) specified a religious affiliation and nine survey respondents (1%) did not provide an answer to the question. One hundred and forty-six respondents identified as Catholic and 84 identified as Anglican (Church of England). Seventeen respondents identified as 'spiritual', while another six respondents simply noted that they 'had their own beliefs'. The corresponding percentages are shown Table 1.1.

Out of those 465 respondents who specified a religious affiliation, 147 respondents (32%) reported that they actively participated in their religion. Three hundred respondents (65%) reported that they did not actively participate in their religion. Eighteen respondents (4%) of those who specified a religion did not indicate whether they actively participated in their religion.

Living Arrangements

Figure 1.6 displays the data about the living arrangements of respondents. The most common living arrangement for survey respondents was to reside with a partner, with 460 respondents (42%) selecting this option. Respondents were not asked to identify if their partner was the same sex or the opposite sex to them. By cross-comparison analysis though, it was found out that out of the 465 respondents who live with their partner 429 respondents were in a same-sex relationship, 28 respondents were in an opposite-sex relationship and three respondents did not specify the details of their relationship. Living with housemates/friends was the next most popular living arrangement, with 267 (25%) of respondents selecting this option. Another 171 (17%) of respondents noted that they lived with parents/relatives. One hundred and sixty-nine respondents (16%) wrote that they lived alone. Another 84 respondents (8%) lived with children. A further 31 respondents (1%) selected the 'other' option. Eighty-eight respondents (8%) selected multiple categories. For example, some respondents lived with both their partner and children.

....
Table 1.1
Religious Affiliation of Respondents

Religious affiliation	Percentage
No religion	57
Catholic	13
Anglican (Church of England)	8
Buddhism	3
Uniting Church	3
Wicca	2
Christian	2
Spiritual	2
Judaism	1
Baptist	1
Pagan	1
Agnostic	1
Metropolitan Community Church	1
Lutheran	1
Own beliefs	1
Other	4

....

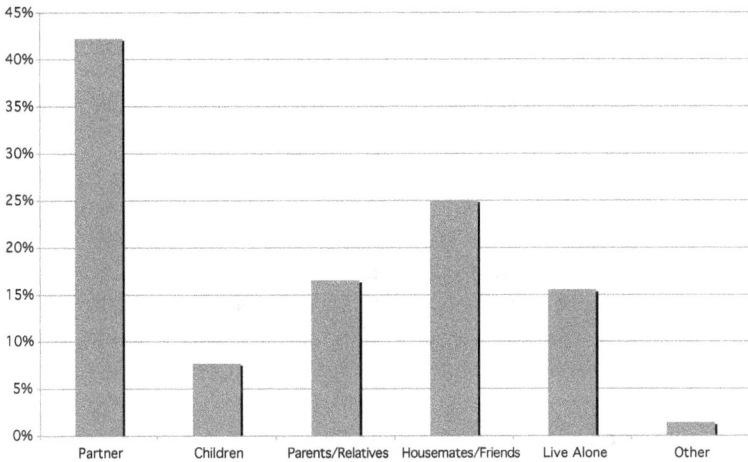

Figure 1.6
Living situations of respondents.

Some of the living arrangements described by respondents who selected the 'other' option included 'I am the carer of a disabled person', 'I live with my two partners who are married to each other', 'I live in college', 'I live alone in a hotel complex I am part-owner of', 'I live with a gay father figure' and 'I live with a gay son figure'.

Disability

Out of the 1052 individuals who answered the relevant question, 119 survey respondents (11%) reported having one or more disabilities. Nine hundred and thirty-three (89%) reported not having any disabilities. Forty-one respondents (4% of all survey respondents) did not provide an answer to this question.

The general rate of disability recorded by survey respondents was lower than that recorded in Queensland population statistics in 2005, which showed that 22% of Queenslanders had at least one disability.[6] This is probably attributable to the fact that the general population of Queensland would include a greater proportion of elderly people than did this survey. Queenslanders aged over 75 years are the group most likely to suffer from disabilities, the majority of which are age-related.[7] As is outlined in Figure 1.7, mental health-related issues impact more significantly on LGBTIQ than heterosexual individuals.

One hundred and nineteen respondents reported that they had at least one disability, while some noted that they had more than one. The most common type of disability was physical, with 54 respondents (45% of 119 respondents) writing this response. Fifty respondents (42%) reported that they had psychiatric disabilities and 15 respondents (13%) wrote that they had cognitive disabilities.

Thirty respondents (25%) wrote that their disability fitted into the 'Other' category. Written responses in this section included HIV/AIDS (3% of 119), deafness (3%) or hearing impaired (3%), Aspergers syndrome (3%), depression (3%), stress and post-traumatic stress disorder (2%) and anxiety or panic attacks (2%). Some single respondents indicated they suffered from blindness in one eye, hepatitis, diabetes, bipolar disorder, degenerative disc disorder and agoraphobia.

It is important to note that levels of psychiatric and psychological disability are much higher amongst Queensland's LGBTIQ population than amongst the state's broader population. As the Queensland Association for Healthy Communities has previously pointed out, 27% of LGBTIQ Queenslanders have experienced depressive illnesses and 40% have experienced anxiety disorders, a much greater rate than that of the heterosexual community.[8]

Out of the 1094 respondents to this survey, 59 people (5%) outlined some form of chronic psychiatric disability. It should be noted that 4% of

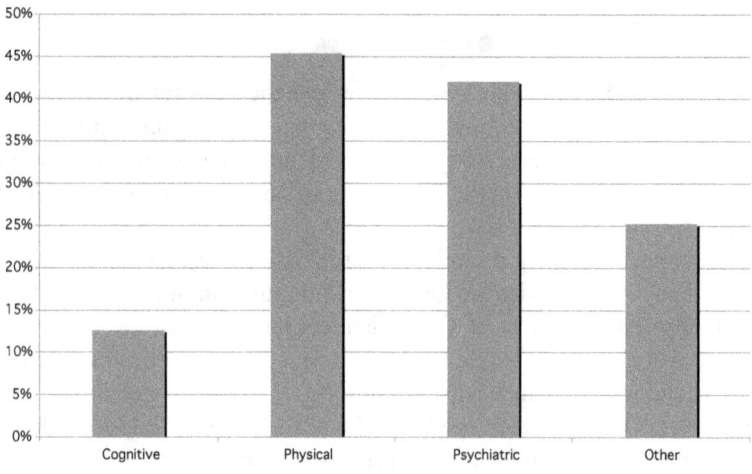

Figure 1.7
Types of disabilities.

survey respondents did not specify whether they had a disability, so this percentage of people with a psychiatric disability could be slightly higher.

Education and Occupation

Figure 1.8 provides information about those respondents who are currently in the education system. Three hundred and eight respondents (28%) out of the 1094 survey respondents indicated that they were currently attending a school or educational establishment. Nineteen respondents (2%) did not provide an answer to this question and the remainder of the survey respondents (70%) indicated that they were not attending a school or educational establishment. Out of the 296 respondents who specified their mode of study, 180 respondents (61%) were in full-time study, while 116 (39% of the people studying) were in part-time study. 12 respondents (4% of those studying) did not indicate the mode of study.

Two hundred and twenty-seven respondents (77%) were attending a university or higher education institution, 36 respondents (12%) were attending a technical or further education institution and six respondents (two per cent) were attending secondary school. Twenty-seven respondents (9%) recorded their type of educational institution. Figure 1.8 also shows the percentage of full-time and part-time students studying across the four types of institutions.

Figure 1.9 describes the highest educational qualification of respondents. One hundred and thirty-nine (13%) of survey respondents had a postgraduate degree as their highest qualification, while 267 (24%) had a university degree as their highest qualification. Two hundred and forty respondents (22%) had a tertiary diploma or trade certificate. Two hundred and fifty-eight respondents (24%) recorded secondary school as their highest level of formal education, while 92 respondents (8%) listed partial secondary schooling as their highest level qualification. Eleven respondents (1%) reported having no formal schooling. Eight-seven respondents (8%) did not provide a response to this question. These figures show that members of the LGBTIQ population in Queensland are more likely to have a postgraduate qualification than members of the broader Australian population. Census statistics from 2001 show that 7% of Australians had a postgraduate qualification.[9]

Employment

Eight hundred and seventy respondents (80%) wrote that they were currently employed. Two hundred and four respondents (19%) noted that

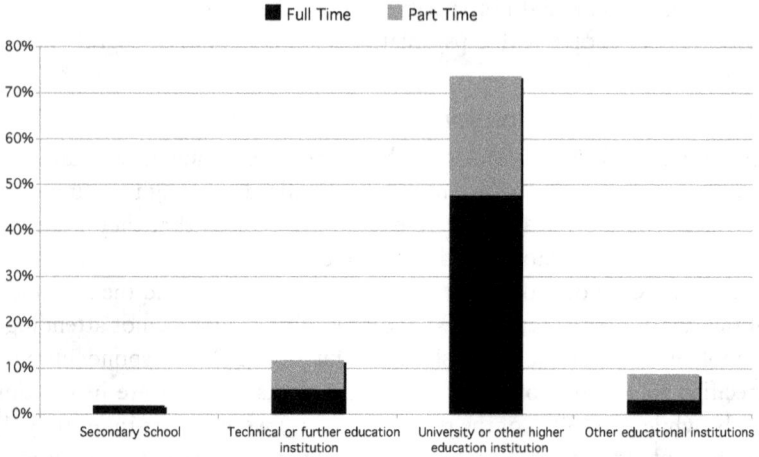

Figure 1.8
Institution attended by those still in education system.

they were not employed. Twenty respondents (2%) did not answer this question. For those who specified 'yes' to being employed, 578 respondents (66%) were in full-time employment. One hundred and eight respondents (12%) were in part-time employment. One hundred and seventy-three (20%) were in casual employment. Eleven respondents (1%) did not specify the nature of their employment. Table 1.2. displays the occupational categories of respondents.

Pensions and Benefits

Two hundred and thirty-five survey respondents (21%) reported currently receiving a benefit or pension. Sixty-nine respondents (31% of the 220 respondents who indicated the type of pension or benefit) were receiving Newstart allowance from Centrelink. Sixty-two respondents (28%) were receiving Youth Allowance from Centrelink. Fifty-four respondents (25%) were receiving a Disability Support Pension. 30 respondents (14%) were receiving a Parenting/Family Allowance from Centrelink, 29 respondents (13%) were receiving the Aged Pension and 22 respondents (10%) were receiving the Parenting Pension. Other respondents mentioned receiving Abstudy, a carer's allowance, personal support, a scholarship and foreign pensions. Several respondents were receiving more than one form of pension, with 69 multiple responses to the question.

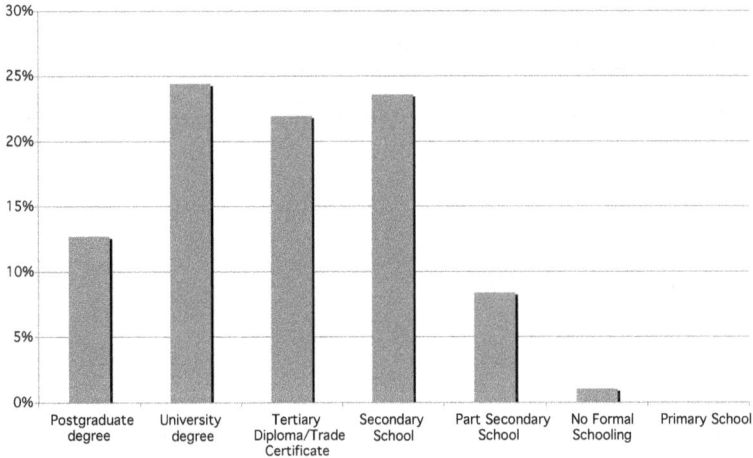

Figure 1.9
Highest educational qualifications of respondents.

Relationship History

Six hundred respondents (55%) reported currently being in a relationship with a member of the same sex. Female respondents were more likely to be in this position, with 367 female respondents (64%) currently being in a same-sex relationship. This echoes the findings of the *Coming Forward* report from Victoria.[10] 221 male respondents (46%) reported that they were currently in a same-sex relationship. Two male-to-female transgender respondents (15% of the male-to-female transgender respondents) were currently in relationships with someone of the same sex. Two female-to-male transgender respondents (15% of the female-to-male transgender respondents) reported being in relationships with people of the same sex.

Two hundred and seventy respondents (25%) reported that they had previously been in a married/de facto relationship with someone of the opposite sex. Fifty-eight respondents (5%) reported that they were currently in a married/de facto relationship with someone of the opposite sex. Seven hundred and fifty-three respondents (69%) had never been in an opposite-sex married/de facto relationship and 13 respondents (1%) did not provide an answer to the question.

Conclusion

Respondents were drawn from a variety of different circumstances, occupations and locations. A wide variety of ages are represented. The statis-

Table 1.2
Occupational Categories of Respondents

Occupation	Percentage
Professional	24
Manager	15
Sales	12
Education	9
Clerical/administration	8
Technical/trade	7
Community/personal service provider	5
Hospitality/bar work	4
Labourer	2
Self employed	2
Machinery operator/driver	1
Health	1
Other	10

tics show that the LGBTIQ population of Queensland is as culturally and demographically diverse as the broader population of the state. The sample size and the geographical, gender and age diversity of the respondents enables this study to make solid observations about the way that homophobic and transphobic violence have impacted on Queensland's LGBTIQ population.

Endnotes

1 New South Wales Attorney General's Department, '*You Shouldn't Have to Hide to be Safe*': *A Report on Homophobic Hostilities and Violence Against Gay Men and Lesbians in New South Wales* (Sydney: New South Wales Attorney General's Department, Crime Prevention Division, 2003), p.27; William Leonard and others, *Coming Forward: The Underreporting of Heterosexist Violence and Same Sex Partner Abuse in Victoria* (Melbourne: Australian Research Centre in Sex, Health and Society, La Trobe, 2008), p.12.

2 Office of Economic and Statistical Research, 'Queensland Regional Profiles', <http://statistics.oesr.qld.gov.au/report-viewer/run?__report=qld-reg-profile.rpt design&sessionid= 7C7DE96133B38058E043A18F39298058&__format=pdf> (accessed 6 January 2010).

3 'Diversity Figures: A Statistical Snapshot of the Diversity of Queensland's Population', Multicultural Affairs Queensland website <http://www.multicultural. qld.gov.au/media/diversity_figures_brochure.pdf> (accessed 2 March 2010).

4 Leonard and others, *Coming Forward*, p.14.

5 Queensland Government, Department of Local Government, Planning, Sport and Recreation, *Queensland's Aboriginal and Torres Strait Islander Population* (Brisbane: Queensland Government, Department of Local Government, Planning, Sport and Recreation, 2006), p.7.

6 Queensland Government, Disability and Community Care Services, 'Disability — A Queensland Profile, 2005', <http://www.disability.qld.gov.au/information/documents/disabilities-queensland-profile-2005.pdf> (accessed 28 February 2010).

7 Ibid.

8 Queensland Association for Healthy Communities, 'Mental Health and Well-Being in Lesbian, Gay, Bisexual and Transgender Communities', QAHC website http://www.qahc.org.au/files/shared/Mental_ Health_LGBT_factsheet-w.pdf> (accessed 3 March 2010).

9 Australian Bureau of Statistics, 2001 Census of Population and Housing Australia, 'Level of Education — Count of Persons Aged 15 and Over With a Qualification', Australian Bureau of Statistics website <http://www.census data.abs.gov.au> (accessed 3 March 2010).

10 Leonard and others, *Coming Forward*, p.14.

CHAPTER 2

Experiencing Homophobic
and Transphobic Violence
and Harassment Over a Lifetime

After conducting a study involving nearly 25,000 heterosexual Australians in 2003 and 2004, Michael Flood and Clive Hamilton concluded that Queensland and the Northern Territory were the most homophobic parts of Australia.[1] As mentioned previously, there was a 9% gap between overall rates of homophobia between Queensland and Victoria, which ranked as Australia's least homophobic state.[2] Consequently, it is not surprising that this study finds that the set of prejudices grouped together as homophobia and transphobia have significantly impacted on the lives of LGBTIQ individuals in Queensland. As the statistics reveal, homosexual and transgendered individuals residing in Queensland are more likely than not to experience harassment or violence simply as a result of living a life that is appropriate and authentic for them.

Throughout the course of this survey and its associated focus groups, respondents and participants showed considerable bravery, reliance and spirit in conveying the ways these prejudices had impacted on them. Although many had experienced significant trauma, they told the authors of this book that they were prepared to share their experiences in the hope that documenting what had happened to them would assist the legal system to better understand this prejudice and reduce future incidents.

Types of Homophobia/Transphobia Experienced in a Lifetime
Throughout the survey, respondents were given the opportunity to identify any types of homophobic or transphobic violence or harassment they had experienced in their lifetime. Fifteen major types of abuse, including verbal abuse, written threats, physical assault with or without a weapon, sexual assault with or without a weapon, vandalism and deliberate

32

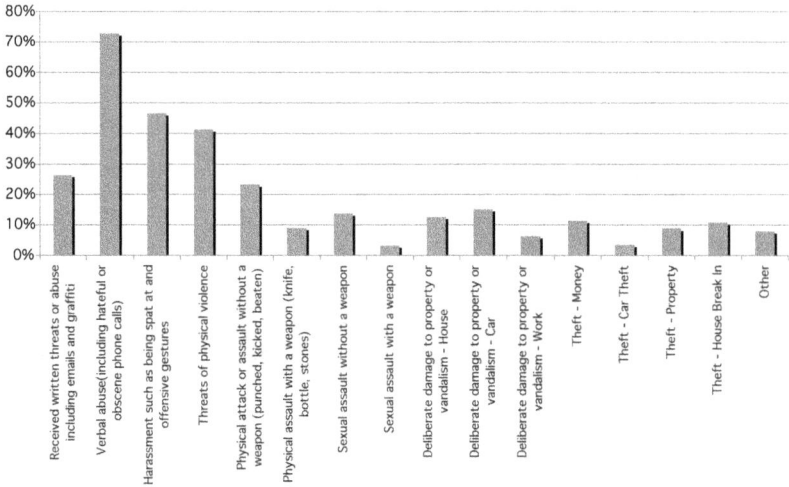

Figure 2.1
Types of abuse experienced over a lifetime.

damage to property and theft were listed on the survey. Respondents were also provided with an 'other' option so that they could describe in their own words any other types of homophobic or transphobic abuse they had experienced. This information is summarised in Figure 2.1. They were also asked if they had experienced this abuse alone, as a couple or as part of a group and this data is shown in Figure 2.2.

Over the course of a lifetime, verbal abuse was the most common form of homophobia or transphobia. This result matches both the findings of the 2003 New South Wales report, *'You Shouldn't Have to Hide to be Safe'* and the 2008 Victorian report, *Coming forward*.[3] Continual low-level harassment was also identified as the most prevalent form of abuse in Queensland. As shown in Figure 2.1, 796 respondents to the *Speaking Out* survey (73%) recorded that they had experienced verbal abuse in their lifetime. This statistic shows that being the subject of verbal abuse is a very common occurrence for LGBTIQ people. Furthermore, Figure 2.2 reveals that many respondents experienced verbal abuse both on their own and with others. Five hundred and sixty-six respondents (52% of survey respondents) recorded that they had experienced verbal abuse on their own, 419 (38%) had experienced this as a same-sex couple and 327 respondents (30%) had experienced this as part of a group. As many respondents had experienced verbal abuse

Alone As a same-sex couple In a group

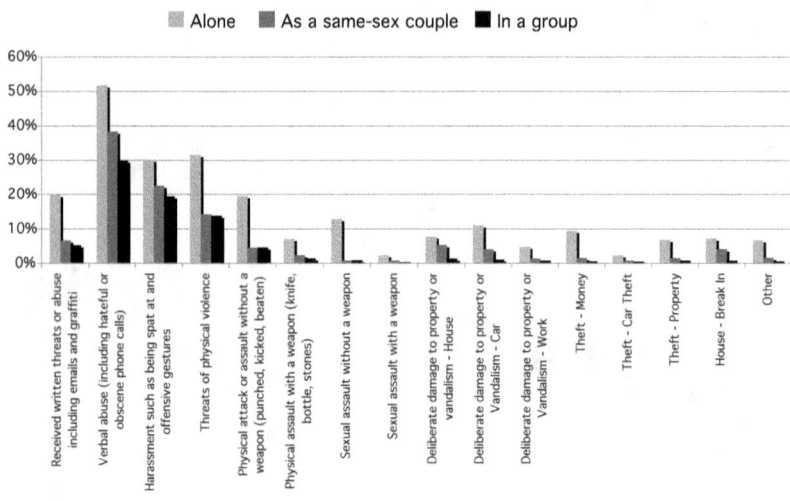

Figure 2.2
Who respondents were with when each type of abuse occurred (over a lifetime).

both alone and with others, the total number of responses to these questions exceeded the number of respondents to the survey.

One Queensland lesbian respondent described her experience of being asked 'inappropriate verbal questions, verbally being asked to stop displaying "lesbian behaviour" in a public place'. Another lesbian respondent was told that she 'should never have female children in case [she] fell in love with them'. A gay male respondent described entering an elevator with his male partner when another man and his female partner 'gave us a filthy look and said "faggots". I asked him if he had a problem and then he went off yelling about the gay mafia, saying "You dirty lot, I'm going to kill the lot of you"'.

S, a male who participated in the Cairns focus group, described how he was verbally abused within the workplace and outlined that verbal abuse extended into the broader community. He recalls that 'I had members of my staff who would make all these comments and they would be getting their children as well to make these comments. If I went into the supermarket, I was verbally abused not only by adults but by their children as well'.

One male respondent described an experience where a 'casual male acquaintance started screaming at me without provocation in front of a party about how "homosexuals aren't normal, that there's something wrong with their brains"'. The respondent said that when he tried to defend himself, the perpetrator told him he 'was not normal and [was] less than human' because of his sexual orientation.

One respondent wrote that verbal abuse had been a daily occurrence in their life. 'They say very hurtful and rude remarks based on sexual orientation, the way I look, dress, etcetera, and talk loudly so everyone stops and stares and they all begin to laugh.' As Linda Garnets, Gregory Herek and Barrie Levey argue, having studied both the causes and impact of such incidents, verbal assault should not be dismissed as a 'minor' form of harassment. It can be deeply upsetting for some individuals and it 'challenges the victim's routine sense of security and invulnerability, making the world seem more malevolent and less predictable'.[4]

Harassment (including Spitting and Offensive Gestures)

Following verbal abuse, the second most common form of homophobic or transphobic abuse experienced was being spat at or being the subject of offensive gestures. Figure 2.1 shows 510 respondents to the survey (47%) experience this form of abuse in their lifetime. In New South Wales, this was also identified as the second most prevalent form of homophobic or transphobic abuse, with 61% of respondents in the 'You Shouldn't Have to Hide to be Safe' report describing this as a form of abuse that they had experienced in their lifetime.[5] As depicted in Figure 2.2, 331 respondents (30% of survey respondents) had experienced this alone, 247 respondents (23%) as a same-sex couple and 212 respondents (19%) had experienced this in a group.

In Queensland, one respondent described 'being confronted by thugs at the local shopping centre who called us names and then spat on both me and my partner'. Another respondent reported 'having had my car spat on before and after being called names' by the perpetrator. A transgendered respondent from north Queensland described being 'spat on twice by a bikie with a mouth full of rum and coke. The first time I confronted him with the security. Second time I called the police who had to pick me up from the rear of the pub for my own and their safety'.

Threats of Physical Violence

The third most prevalent form of abuse identified by Queensland respondents was threats of physical violence. Figure 2.1 indicates that 452 respondents to the survey (41%) experience threats of physical violence in their lifetime. In Figure 2.2, 346 respondents (32% of survey respondents) had experienced this alone, 155 respondents (14%) had experienced this as a same-sex couple and 151 respondents (14%) had experienced this in a group.

One female respondent described such an incident, when she was walking with her ex-partner through Brisbane's West End, when 'a drunk man followed us, yelling abuse and threatened us'. Another lesbian respondent reported that 'we were verbally abused ... called derogative names like "fucking filthy dykes" and threatened with [them saying] "we will show you how to really fuck"'. A male respondent reported 'guys yelling "faggot" at me for putting my arm around my mate [and telling me] they'd "kick my head in"'.

Written Threats and Abuse

Threats of physical violence were immediately followed in prevalence by written threats or abuse (including email or graffiti). As shown in Figure 2.1, 287 respondents (26%) experience this form of abuse in their life-time. In Figure 2.2, 217 respondents (20% of survey respondents) experienced this alone, 72 respondents (7%) as a same-sex couple and 57 respondents (5%) in a group.

One respondent described receiving 'written emails using harassing and derogatory language'. Another described how her partner 'described a threatening email saying that if she went to my parent's house for Christmas, they would call child services and have our daughter taken off us'. Another respondent received 'emails from a Christian group constantly trying to "make me better"'. Another described receiving 'extreme abuse and stalking via the internet'. One female participant in the Sunshine Coast focus group, who was employed at a university in a diversity support role, received emails saying 'you queers shouldn't be on campus, you should all be barred'.

Physical Attack or Assault (without a weapon)

The fifth most common type of homophobic or transphobic harassment or violence was physical attack or assault without a weapon (including being punched, kicked our beaten). Two hundred and fifty-four survey respondents (23%) reported this form of abuse. This figure is comparable with that recorded in the 'You shouldn't have to hide to be safe' survey, which found that 25% of New South Wales respondents had experienced physical attack or assault without a weapon.[6] The figures describing the levels of physical attacks or assaults on the LGBTIQ population of Queensland are a striking deviation from broader population statistics from the year 2000, which declared that 7.6% of 'mainstream' Queenslanders had been the victim of assault.[7] This means that members of the LGBTIQ population are approximately three times more likely than 'mainstream' Queenslanders to experience physical violence. If figures from respondents who indicated they had experienced physical assault with a weapon (9% of survey respondents) are also included, then members of the Queensland LGBTIQ population are more than four times more likely to experience physical assault than all Queenslanders.

The data from this survey also provided insight into whether victims were alone or in company at the time of the physical assault without a weapon. The survey found that 213 respondents (19% of survey respondents) had experienced physical attack or assault alone, 49 (4%) had experienced this as part of a same-sex couple and 50 respondents (5%) had experienced this as part of a group.

Such physical attacks took place in a range of different forums. One younger respondent described 'life-threatening school fights [where] half of the school came to see the fights'. A number of researchers have written about physical homophobic violence in Australian schools and the impact that this has had on young LGBTIQ people in their formative years.[8]

In some instances, perpetrators unleashed physical violence after reading cues which they perceived to be 'homosexual' or 'unmanly'. In one such instance, a male respondent, who was wearing drag after attending a fancy dress party, described being 'punched and kicked and told that I needed to know what it was to be a real man'. Another male, leaving his work premises in Brisbane was walking home when:

... three young drunk men who had been on Caxton Street drinking after a football match approached. One hit me in the stomach, the other slapped my backside, tousled my hair, waved me goodbye as they ran. Called me something akin to 'gay' as they ran.

Another male was hit in the face with a metal pole and suffered a broken nose and nerve damage. Another respondent described how he was 'attacked from behind, spun around, elbowed in the face'. Another described how he was:

... beaten to a pulp [with his] face smashed in, unconscious, teeth missing, jaw broken in five places, five metal plates and screws to hold jaw together, jaw wired shut for 4 months, infections in the face, reconstructive surgery needed and braces needed for a further 4 years to realign teeth.

Although the overwhelming majority of homophobic and transphobic violence was conducted by males who appeared to identify as heterosexual, one respondent described an incident when he experienced homophobia in a same-sex encounter. He reported:

> They picked me up for sex, came home, saw my medication and then physically threatened me, and verbally degraded me for being HIV positive. They called me a 'dirty fucking faggot' [and said] 'you should be shot'. Coming from other gay men, I found this hard to understand. I assume they are still in the closet.

The events outlined by the respondent point to a perpetrator dealing with internalised homophobia.[9] Although this study did not explicitly address internalised homophobia, this topic was briefly addressed in the Introduction to this book and it is clear that this is also a problem that weights heavily on LGBTIQ individuals.[10]

Deliberate Damage or Vandalism to Property (Car)

The sixth most common type of homophobic or transphobic harassment or violence was deliberate damage or vandalism to property (car) with 164 survey respondents (15%) indicating that they had experienced this form of abuse in their lifetime. One hundred and twenty-one respondents (11% of survey respondents) had experienced this alone, 44 (4%) as a same-sex couple and 12 respondents (1%) had experienced this in a group. One transgendered respondent outlined how her 'work car was trashed with trannie slurs written all over it'. Another respondent described 'walking back to our car when we noticed someone writing on it'.

Sexual Assault (without a weapon)

The seventh most prevalent form of abuse was sexual assault without a weapon. One hundred and fifty survey respondents (14%) experienced this. One hundred and forty-one respondents (13% of survey respondents) were sexually assaulted without a weapon on their own, eight (1%) as a same-sex couple and 10 respondents (1%) as a group. One respondent described being 'sexually assaulted while sleeping and [then waking] up to them doing it'. Another described how a group of perpetrators 'beat and raped' her. Another respondent from regional Queensland, who had transitioned from male to female, described a deeply traumatic, violent sexual attack that occurred before her transition. She wrote:

> In 1999, on my 19th birthday (I was still living as a man) I was tricked into leaving a nightclub with newly met friends (four people) who

started teasing me about being a faggot. This later became violent and they hit and kicked me to the ground. After being overpowered, they stripped me, tearing clothes off and raped me on the bonnet of a car, one after the other, egging each other to 'fuck the fag out of the faggot'. Somewhere I lost consciousness but woke to a beer bottle being shoved in my anus.

Later, this respondent went to hospital, where she lied about her injuries due to the deep distress associated with this extremely violent assault. She said, 'Needless to say, this event caused me to hide my feelings and not trust others, even still to this day'.

Deliberate Damage or Vandalism to Property (House)

The eighth most common type of abuse was deliberate damage or vandalism to property (house). One hundred and thirty-seven survey respondents (13%) experienced this form of abuse. Eighty-five respondents (8% of survey respondents) experienced this on their own, 57 respondents (5%) experienced this as part of a same-sex couple and 14 respondents (1%) experienced this as part of a group. One respondent described how a 'tenant had set fire' to their house and another had 'allowed water to continuously run through a house for three months without telling us' as a result of the respondent's sexuality.

Theft of Money

The ninth most prevalent type of homophobic or transphobic abuse was the theft of money. In total, 124 people, or 11% of overall survey respondents had experienced this. One hundred and three respondents (9%) reported that this had happened to them alone, 17 (2%) as part of a same-sex couple and six (1%) as a group. One respondent described an incident where 'money was taken from two wallets from our bedroom while we were in the house by a casual visitor'.

House Break-Ins

Respondents identified house break-ins as the 10th most common incidence of abuse. A total of 118 respondents, or 11% of survey respondents, reported that this had happened to them. Seventy-nine individuals (7%) experienced this on their own, 45 (4%) as part of a same-sex couple and nine (1%) as part of a group. One respondent noted how he 'came home. House [was] broken into. Homophobic slurs [were] written on walls. Items [were] stolen'.

Physical Assault (With a Weapon)

The 11th most prevalent form of homophobic and transphobic abuse was physical assault with a weapon (knife, bottle, stones). Overall, 98 individuals, or 9% of overall survey respondents, noted that they had experienced this. Seventy-eight respondents (7%) experienced this individually, 26 (2%) as part of a same-sex couple and 16 (1%) as part of a group.

Property Theft

Property theft was ranked as the 12th most common form of homophobic or transphobic abuse. Overall, 96 individuals, or 9% of survey respondents, noted that they had experienced this. Seventy-five respondents (7%) noted that this had happened to them on their own, 17 (2%) reported that it had happened to them as part of a same-sex couple and nine (1%) wrote that they had experienced property theft as part of a group. One respondent described an incident where it was raining and an individual took their umbrella without asking. 'I asked for it back and derogative terms were used against me. I did not retaliate and left the issue alone and later found my umbrella broken and in the bin'.

Damage to Property (Work)

The 13th most common type of homophobic or transphobic abuse was deliberate damage to property or vandalism (work). In total, 68 respondents, or 6% of survey respondents reported this abuse. Fifty-two respondents (5%) reported this had happened to them alone, 14 as part of a same-sex couple (1%) and eight as a group (1%). One respondent described how 'offensive abuse and [a] threat [were] etched into [a] glass window' at their workplace. This followed an incident where a housemate (who was drunk) had perpetrated 'extreme verbal abuse and physical assault' at the respondent's house. Following this, the respondent had been evicted. The damage to the respondent's window at work was subsequent to this incident. Another respondent outlined how their 'queer business had been broken into'.

Car Theft

The 14th most prevalent type of abuse was car theft. This meant that 39 individuals, or 4% of survey respondents, were impacted by this type of incident. Twenty-six individuals (2% of overall survey respondents) experienced this alone, nine as part of a same-sex couple (one per cent) and five (under half of 1%) as part of a group.

Sexual Assault (With a Weapon)

Sexual assault with a weapon was ranked as the 15th most common type of abuse experienced by respondents. This meant that 36 respondents in total, or 3% of all survey respondents experienced this form of violence. 26 respondents (2%) experienced this alone, eight (1%) experienced this as part of a same-sex couple and four respondents (under half of 1%) experienced this as part of a group. One responder described three offenders with 'makeshift weapons threatening us with sexual violence outside our home'.

Other Experiences

Eighty-six individuals (8%) used the 'other' option to describe their experiences of homophobic or transphobic violence. Seventy-three respondents (7%) in this category reported that they had experienced homophobic or transphobic abuse on their own, 18 (2%) as part of a same-sex couple and six (1%) as part of a group.

Respondents used this option to describe a wide variety of incidents. One man described an incident where a homophobic attack quickly turned back on the perpetrator. He reported:

> As I was walking past [the] Louis Vuitton [store] on the Gold Coast one morning when Indy was on, a rather large (fat) straight male [in his] mid-40s was yelling at me, calling me a fag and [saying] 'Oh, you want that handbag don't you, you faggot'. I replied, 'Nah mate, I got enough at home', then he [said] 'Well fuck off fag or I will make you' as he rose his fist to me. (There was a security guard at the front of the shop who I heard calling for more security.) I replied 'Come on you fat old c-nt, bring it!' and chased him. He took off and the security guard laughed, cancelled backup and said 'well done'.) About five minutes later, I ran into him again and he mouthed off at me again so I said 'That's it, you're fucked now', and chased him, and he ran into his hotel foyer.

Although this perpetrator of homophobia was not able to physically harm this man, other respondents described instances where they felt severely threatened. One male Brisbane respondent described:

> Walking home from the Sportsman's Hotel on the night of the Pride march. I had to walk past the Normanby Hotel. It had closed and there were a few strangers waiting for cabs. Two men called me a 'faggot, fucking poofer', started circling me, then (oddly) politely

asked me if I 'had any crack' [cocaine]. I said 'no'. When they heard my voice, they decided I must be a lesbian, threatened to rape me, threatened to 'stick' a bottle inside my 'c-nt'. Threatened to bash me.

One respondent wrote that their backpack 'was hit with a large knife and things inside were destroyed'. A female respondent described how she had been stalked and reported to Centrelink. A male respondent who chose this option described how a nurse in a hospital had refused to treat him because he was gay. A female respondent described 'rape, discrimination and harassment at work'.

Another wrote that their partner was 'murdered because of our same-sex relationship'. Although this was the only response that mentioned homicide related to sexuality, it is worth noting that the survey was set out to record individual experiences of homophobic and transphobic violence and thus there was no means for respondents to outline incidents of homophobic and transphobic murders of which they may have been aware.

Stephen Tomsen, who has studied anti-gay homicide in New South Wales between 1980 and 2000, proved that homicide was indeed a crime that disproportionately impacted on the gay community in that state.[11] It is perhaps worth concluding this consideration of anti-homosexual and anti-transgender homicide with a quote made by Miller and Humphreys in a 1980s American study. These authors made the point that:

… an intense rage is present in nearly all homicide cases involving gay male victims. A striking feature … is their gruesome, often vicious, nature. Seldom is the homosexual victim simply shot. He is more apt to be stabbed a dozen times, mutilated and strangled.[12]

Gender and Abuse

Data gathered in the course of the survey revealed that there a number of differences in the way that LGBTIQ people of different gender identities experienced homophobia or transphobia. As shown in Table 2.1, male respondents were more likely than female respondents to be the victims of all forms of assault, with the exception of sexual assault without a weapon. This finding is consistent with the results of the *You Shouldn't Have to Hide to be Safe* report from New South Wales.[13]

Gail Mason has also pointed out that although, like gay men, lesbian women are most likely to have harassment or violence perpetrated against them by men previously unknown to them, there are some characteristics that are:

Table 2.1
Types of Abuse by Gender Identity

Form of abuse	Male	Female	Transgender M2F	Transgender F2M	Other
Received written threats or abuse including emails and graffiti	35%	18%	54%	27%	29%
Verbal abuse (including hateful or obscene phone calls)	76%	69%	92%	55%	82%
Harassment such as being spat at and offensive gestures	50%	42%	54%	45%	94%
Threats of physical violence	54%	29%	62%	64%	53%
Physical attack without a weapon (punched, kicked, beaten)	32%	15%	46%	36%	35%
Physical assault with a weapon (knife, bottle, stones)	12%	6%	38%	9%	12%
Sexual assault without a weapon	12%	14%	46%	45%	24%
Sexual assault with a weapon	4%	2%	15%	9%	0%
Deliberate damage to property or vandalism — House	14%	10%	46%	18%	24%
Deliberate damage to property or vandalism — Car	19%	12%	31%	9%	6%
Deliberate damage to property or vandalism — Work	8%	4%	23%	9%	6%
Theft — Money	15%	7%	38%	9%	12%
Theft — Car theft	5%	3%	8%	0%	0%
Theft — Property	11%	6%	23%	0%	12%
Theft — House break-in	14%	8%	23%	9%	12%
Other	7%	8%	15%	0%	24%

... rarely evident in violence against gay men. The most significant differences between anti-gay and anti-lesbian violence are that lesbians are more likely to experience violence committed by older men, men acting alone, and men who are acquainted with the woman.[14]

Men are more likely to report violence in a public place. Mason has pointed out that the statistical differences between women and men with regard to harassment and violence in public might be explained as a result of a number of factors that include:

The greater visibility of gay men, especially in gay identified areas of large cities; the fact that women sometimes modify their behaviour to avoid victimisation; and ... the high level of violence against women generally makes it difficult for lesbian women to determine the motive in many instances of victimisation. It is also important to note that overseas research indicates that lesbians are subject to higher rates of verbal harassment by family members than gay men and report greater fear of violence.[15]

Statistics from 2008 compiled by the Australian Institute of Criminology, show that young men more broadly are more likely than women to be the victims of violent attacks in Australia.[16] The findings of this report, which suggest men are more likely to experience physical (non-sexual) assault, are consistent with this. There is also a possibility that male respondents were not reporting sexual attacks. This point was made by a respondent in the Sunshine Coast focus group, who said that men were not likely to report sexual attacks due to 'the shame and stigma that goes along with that in a crisis of masculinity'.

Significantly, male-to-female transgendered individuals were the group most likely to experience violence and abuse in all categories. D, a participant in the Cairns focus group who had transitioned from male to female, was in a pub in the town of Moranbah when she experienced transphobic harassment that was accompanied by transphobic language. She was sitting down watching a football game on television when a man spat rum and coke on her. When she confronted the man, he at first blamed his spitting on asthma before saying 'Fuck off, you fucking fruit'. About half an hour later, the same man again spat rum and coke on her. D complained to the manager and police were called to the venue.

As Tarynn Witten and Evan Eyler have argued, hate crimes against transgendered people represent 'a form of gender terrorism whose underlying motivation is the maintenance of a social system in which males dominate females through emotional, verbal and physical acts of force, and in which the line between the genders must be rigidly maintained in support of this social schema'.[17]

Male-to-female transgendered respondents were also substantially overrepresented in the sexual assault categories (both with and without weapons). Fifty-six (12%) of male respondents reported sexual assault without a weapon, with 19 (4%) experiencing sexual assault with a weapon. Seventy-nine (14%) of female respondents reported sexual assault without a weapon, with 14 (2%) experiencing sexual assault with a weapon. Six (46%) of male-to-female transgendered respondents reported sexual assault without a weapon, while two (15%) experienced sexual assault with a weapon. Five (45%) of female-to-male transgendered respondents reported sexual assault without a weapon, while one (9%) experienced sexual assault with a weapon.

Witten and Eyler argue that sexual violence against transgendered individuals is similar in a number of ways to anti-female violence.[18] They contend that many male perpetrators who commit violence against women attempt to justify this as their right 'as an intimate partner in control of the relationship (and thus the woman), or as being a reasonable action to take against a woman who is transgressing social restraints' (perhaps by being out at night unescorted by a male companion) who is 'asking for [sexual assault]'. They conclude:

> Sexual violence against transgenders often receives similar justification by its perpetrators: a genetic male who dresses in women's clothing accepts [de facto] the 'woman's role', and is thus a legitimate target for sexual assault. In other cases, male-to-female cross-dressers and transgenders are simply mistaken for women and attacked as such.[19]

As Table 2.2 shows, when types of abuse by sexuality are considered, male gay respondents seem more likely to be the victim of violent physical attacks, with or without weapons. Lesbian respondents are more likely to be the victims of sexual attacks, both with or without weapons. They were also more likely to describe insidious forms of harassment and homophobia, such as family and other relationship pressures and work place homophobia.

Some respondents provided more information about the way that their sexuality impacted on the type of homophobic or transphobic abuse they encountered. One bisexual female respondent noted that, after she explained her sexual orientation to a man she was in a relationship with:

> ... he flew into an irrational rage, accompanied by verbal abuse. This barrage of obscenities and insults continued whenever the subject was raised. It was often cited as a reason why I 'wasn't good enough for him' and accompanied by other insults relating to sexual promiscuity and 'worth'. It also contributed to the eventual relationship breakdown.

Table 2.2
Types of Abuse by Sexuality

Form of abuse	Lesbians	Gay	Bisexual	Other
Received written threats or abuse including emails and graffiti	19%	32%	23%	35%
Verbal abuse (including hateful or obscene phone calls)	71%	76%	63%	81%
Harassment such as being spat at and offensive gestures	43%	48%	41%	76%
Threats of physical violence	31%	52%	29%	57%
Physical attack without a weapon (punched, kicked, beaten)	15%	30%	18%	39%
Physical assault with a weapon (knife, bottle, stones)	7%	10%	7%	20%
Sexual assault without a weapon	14%	11%	18%	28%
Sexual assault with a weapon	3%	4%	2%	6%
Deliberate damage to property or vandalism — House	9%	14%	11%	28%
Deliberate damage to property or vandalism — Car	13%	18%	11%	13%
Deliberate damage to property or vandalism — Work	4%	8%	3%	11%
Theft — Money	6%	16%	11%	17%
Theft — Car Theft	3%	5%	2%	2%
Theft — Property	6%	11%	8%	11%
Theft — House break-in	8%	13%	9%	17%
Other	8%	6%	8%	19%

Alone or With Others

As previously outlined, the data presented in Figure 2.2 reveals that all types of homophobic or transphobic harassment are more likely to occur when victims are alone rather than in a couple or in a group. It can be argued that this occurs because perpetrators are more likely to engage in homophobic or transphobic harassment or violence when they perceive that they have an advantage in terms of numbers. This finding is similar to the conclusions of 2008 *Coming Forward* report from Victoria, which found that non-physical abuse, physical abuse, theft and sexual assault were all more likely to occur when the victim was on their own.[20]

There were also many instances where respondents in focus groups outlined out being in public spaces with their same-sex partners could cause homophobic comments. K, a middle-aged participant in the Gold Coast focus group, described how walking with his partner early in the morning around Surfer's Paradise could raise comments from others walking by. He said offenders were likely to say '"Oh, look at the two queens walking together". You know that if you back-chatted or anything, you know you'd be in trouble'.

Attacks when respondents were in groups were also outlined. K said:

You could be walking down the street with a group of guys and because one might walk in a mince and be picked on, you can also be picked on by another person passing by and included in that group as well. It's quite easy just by association to be ... picked out.

A male respondent described walking down the street with another male who 'was a little more flamboyant' when a group of males asked them for a cigarette. He wrote 'then they worked it and decided it was okay to punch me in the head and knock me to the ground'. J, a female participant in the Gold Coast focus group, said it 'was absolutely [the] same with females. If you're walking along the beach and you're with a stereotype ...'. These respondents felt that by being with a partner or a group, they were more likely to be perceived to be gay or lesbian and thus the subject of abuse or harassment.

Abuse by Association

A number of respondents and participants in the focus groups mentioned that family and friends and associates had received abuse as a result of their association with LGBTIQ individuals. One male participant from the Gold Coast focus group who had a religious background described how his children had been subjected to homophobic abuse. The issue of abuse being directed towards children was flagged as a matter of concern by a number of focus group participants. One female participant in the Sunshine Coast focus made a particular point of saying how important protecting her children from homophobic abuse was to her when she was confronted with harassment.

Another participant from the Toowoomba focus group, who worked with her aunt in a hospital, said that her aunt often received comments from a male co-worker, who told her that 'all gay people should die' and 'it's a choice'. One lesbian woman noted that the verbal abuse her parent's neighbour continued to reiterate was stressful not just for her but also for her elderly parents, who were aged in their 80s. She described how he 'mentions their sick daughter whenever he gets the chance. This is hurtful to them (as they are fully supportive towards me and my partner)'. She asserted that 'although he has attacked us directly, the effects have also been felt indirectly through their impact on my parents'.

Homophobia and Transphobia Within the LGBTIQ Community

Although it was outside of the parameters of this survey, some respondents and participants in the focus group did mention that they felt homophobia and violence could be problems within the LGBTIQ community. A number of transgender respondents felt that the LGBTIQ community was not always accepting of them. One transgender woman described the use of verbal abuse within the transgender community when 'I had someone that I assumed was a friend, another trans girl. I did something that she didn't approve of and she withdrew her gender recognition of me'. The woman described feeling really hurt when the other woman would not refer to her as a woman.

One female respondent described how 'another lesbian told me I wasn't a lesbian because I didn't look like one and she hadn't seen me out at gay events/places. She was quite mean about it'. Instances of same-sex partner abuse and violence within the LGBTIQ community were considered in the 2008 Victorian report, *Coming Forward* and there is scope to consider these issues in a further Queensland study in the future. It should be mentioned that these types of abuse are forms of internalised homophobia and transphobia and are products of a broader system that marginalises and oppresses difference.[21]

Location

Previous academic studies have tended to provide data that indicate that men and women experience homophobic and transphobic violence in different settings.[22] Kevin T. Berrill, who explored homophobic violence in the United States, found that men were more likely to be assaulted in public spaces or 'gay identified spaces', while women were more likely to experience homophobia in non-gay spaces and in the workplace and home.[23] This is a difference that has also been noted in an Australian context by Gail Mason.[24] Respondents to this survey reported homophobic and transphobic attacks occurring in a wide array of locations, although on average, male respondents tended to describe more violent public attacks than women.

Some respondents felt that Queensland as a state was not a safe environment to reside in as a member of the LGBTIQ community. One middle-aged male participant in the Brisbane focus group said that:

> I don't personally feel very safe anywhere in Queensland and I think Queensland overall is a hostile state to live in. But there are some spots more dangerous than the ordinary hostile spots, for example, Ipswich and certain areas in the country.

The tendency to describe rural locations as more homophobic than larger cities was often reiterated in focus groups. S, a male participant in the Cairns focus group, who moved to the Atherton Tablelands area five years previously, observed that, 'I think it's in these regional communities that homophobia is even more intense and it was honestly like going back a hundred years. It was like going back in time'. He added that in his experience, some individuals in this rural region were members of the:

> ... religious right and ... it was almost like, well, 'We're going to keep the world out because we're going to preserve what we've got', and it's like, 'Well, that doesn't happen here. We don't have gays here. They have it done there, down south, but not up here"'.

S, a young female participant in the Toowoomba focus group emphasised that she felt less vulnerable to harassment and violence living away from the regional town of Goondiwindi, where she was originally from. She said, in Goondiwindi, 'If I was to hold hands with a girlfriend, I would be a piece of meat dead on the concrete'. She also described an incident where a male friend was physically attacked in this rural town for 'wearing a pink shirt'.

Homophobia and transphobia were not limited to rural locations. Urban streets in large cities could also be sites where and harassment and violence occurred. One respondent, who worked as a delivery driver described:

> ... stopping at a set of traffic lights and as I waited for them to change, a large sedan pulled alongside the windows were down and

the occupants in the car started with the verbal insults and abuse, also the threats, and as I wound up my window, I received an egging and some dents from eggs thrown and punches given to my car. I believe it was started by the Rainbow sticker on the back window of my own car. I finished the delivery I was on where the customer asked if I was okay. I went back to work and quit for the night, I was scared and frightened and shocked that this could happen.

Many respondents walking on foot described attackers driving past and abusing them. One woman described how she was 'walking along the street, going to eat [when a] group of four to five testosterone filled males yelled "fucking dyke" as I passed them'. Another respondent wrote that 'we were walking home and guys in a car drove past us a few times and then got out of their car and started throwing objects at us and we ran'. A male respondent described walking home from a train station, whereupon he was 'yelled at from a car. They parked, got out and punched and kicked me to unconsciousness'.

Some respondents changed their movements to avoid areas where they felt homophobic or transphobic attacks were more likely to occur. D., a transgendered participant from the Cairns focus group, outlined some of the strategies she had used to attempt to avoid violence and harassment while in a 'redneck town'. She said, 'I'd always walk home along the streets where they were lit, never take a shortcut through a back block or anything like that, it just wasn't worth it'.

Some areas of towns and particular streets were avoided by LGBTIQ individuals due to fears of homophobic and transphobic attacks. E, a transsexual person from the Townsville focus group, said:

> ... there are some places I would not walk as a transsexual person and places I would not go, like Oxford Street [in Townsville] for argument's sake. I would not walk up there at certain times of the day because the chances of being harassed would be such that it would be provoking my safety and I wouldn't do it.

Public venues such as restaurants were also mentioned a number of times by respondents. One person described how they were eating dinner at a restaurant with their partner when they 'were asked if we were gay since we were having dinner together. We replied "yes" and just received some homophobic slurs'. Another respondent described how they had 'been at restaurants with my partner when others start making jokes amongst themselves and pointing, etcetera. [We] have had to get up and leave the restaurant'. Another respondent described how she and her partner were dining at a restaurant in inner-Brisbane:

At first, service was warm and thorough but once I kissed my lover at the table, we were consistently ignored, shrugged off and made wait an inordinate amount of time for food, which was cold. It was made obvious by the waiters that we were not welcome because we were obviously a couple.

Spaces perceived to be 'gay', such as beats and LGBTIQ venues, were also mentioned as locations where prejudice was frequently expressed. The New South Wales *You Shouldn't Have to Hide to be Safe* report also mentioned locality as a contributing factor to abuse.[25] Stephen Tomsen and Kevin Markwell, who have explored safety and hostility at and around gay and lesbian public events, have found that LGBTIQ individuals are often exposed to homophobia and transphobia when they leave such events.[26]

A number of respondents outlined experiences where they were harassed or they were the subject of violence at LGBTIQ events or places. Many of these incidents took place in the Fortitude Valley precinct, which is home to most of Brisbane's LGBTIQ venues. The tendency for this area to host homophobic and transphobic violence was noted by Darryl Scott in 2004, when he coordinated the Valley Walksafe Anti-Violence Campaign and wrote a report, *Everyone has the Right to Walk Safe in Their Community*.[27] Two years later, in 2006, anti-homosexual violence in the Valley received further public attention when David Graham, a popular contestant on the reality television program Big Brother, revealed that he had been 'gay bashed' in this area.[28]

Evidence provided by respondents to this survey indicates a substantial proportion had experienced violence in this precinct. One Brisbane respondent described an incident where 'three males and a female' came to the outside of the Wickham Hotel. He reported that they 'threatened physical violence through the fence, they abused people verbally and then waited outside to threaten/follow/stalk individuals once they left. I was followed, so I crossed a busy street where I ran down an alley. They followed but I made my way into a busy car park where they couldn't find me'.

Another Brisbane respondent described walking about a block between two LGBTIQ nightclubs, the Beat nightclub and the Wickham Hotel. He noted 'there [were] many intoxicated members of the public walking from one club to another. Seeing that I'd come from the Beat nightclub, they presumed that I was gay and verbally harassed me for it'. One female respondent reported that she and her girlfriend at the time 'were verbally harassed and spat at by a group of intoxicated heterosexual males and females as we left our local gay bar and were heading back to the car to go home'.

One male participant from the Sunshine Coast focus group outlined how a gay venue called Crush used to attract heterosexual men from a nearby shopping centre who would be 'jeering and stuff' at the patrons of the bar. 'A lot of young guys would hang out outside and bash up whatever gays they could find and all that sort of stuff. They would sit there and wait, just to pick them off.'

Some members of the Brisbane focus group expressed a similar sentiment, explaining that there was a perception that certain Brisbane suburbs were known as 'gay areas' and attracted groups of youths who were intent on 'gay bashing'. One female respondent said, 'If you want to bash someone, you go to Spring Hill, or the Valley or New Farm, the three gay suburbs [and] drive around until they see someone who looks [gay]'.

N, a participant in the Cairns focus group, found he was most often verbally questioned and harassed about his sexuality outside of parties and gay venues. 'Certainly in town I've had people come up to me after our parties, these half-drunk men [saying] "Are you a homosexual? Are you gay?" It's only their girlfriends that stop them, yell at them in horror and embarrassment.'

Gay beats — areas frequented by gay men looking for sexual contact — were also mentioned as dangerous locations. J, a participant in the Gold Coast focus group, said that 'beats are probably the most dangerous place you could go. I think that's just a given'. K, a male participant in the same focus group, agreed. 'I think night time especially on a beat would be extremely dangerous. Phillip's Park and all that sort of thing would be just lethal.'

Even homes, which should serve as a place of utmost safety, were sites of homophobic and transphobic violence. One Brisbane respondent described how he experienced a 'series of harassing phone calls, sms messages, emails and buzzing at my apartment on George Street. [The perpetrator/s] gained entry to my apartment and threw some of my belongings off the balcony of my 36th floor apartment'.

A respondent from regional Queensland, who participated in a focus group, outlined her situation of being violently attacked in her own home when her father found out about her transgender status. 'In 2007, my stepfather found out I was transsexual. He kicked me out of the house I was renting off him and he did this with a beating'. The respondent noted that, apart from court cases and domestic violence protection orders, she has not had contact from her family since this incident.

Contributing Factors Other than Sexuality

Race was identified by some respondents as a factor that made them more susceptible to homophobic or transphobic harassment and violence. One respondent described walking out of a bar to a taxi rank and 'immediately [being] harassed by two guys sitting in the mall. At first it was racial and then my sexuality'. Another respondent described being out when a 'group across the street started hollering comments that were homophobic. They also did seem to have a problem with me being Indian'.

E, an Indigenous participant in the Cairns focus group, felt that he and his partner were more likely to be subject to homophobic abuse because his partner was non-Indigenous and they were in a 'mixed' relationship. He said, 'I actually feel very unsafe when we're together ... it screams out gay or it screams out something ... why is a white guy standing with a black guy, so close to each other?' He felt that 'just because my partner and I are together, we're just a little bit different from everyone else and that's what makes people even pay attention more'.

N, a 41-year-old male respondent from the Cairns focus group, identified racism as a factor that might play into homophobic attacks. He felt that he was 'probably safer than most because of my age ... and I think because of my race, because I'm white and because I'm sort of middle class. I think I'm probably more...safer from violence generally'.

One young male respondent from the Sunshine Coast focus group spoke of links between homophobic violence and sexism. He said that public violence was:

> ... about the traditional use of space as well. That space is always for middle and working class white men, it's not for women who don't go out at night on their own and you know, I assume that's pretty much the case for most people unless you are kind of groups of young guys roaming the streets in packs.

Apart from racism and sexism, some respondents felt that contributing factors might have been their appearance, clothing or presentation, which may have attracted the attention of the perpetrator/s. One respondent described being 'accosted by a man abusing me because I was wearing a World AIDS Day t-shirt. His abuse was based entirely on assumption as I hadn't said anything or even looked in his general direction'. Presentation and appearance were also mentioned as a contributing factor by respondents to the New South Wales study, *You Shouldn't Have to Hide to be Safe*.[29]

Injuries and Impact

The evidence that was provided in focus groups and in surveys about the impact of homophobic and transphobic abuse indicates that most victims experience a significant degree of trauma as a result of their experiences. International and national studies have charted a range of ongoing psychological and physical issues that are experienced by the victims of homophobic and transphobic abuse and harassment.

Violence against members of the LGBTIQ community can be particularly insidious as, unlike victims of racially based hate crimes, members of this community often do not know other individuals who share their sexuality/gender identity. Furthermore, as Gail Mason points out, to receive support after abuse, victims must often disclose their sexuality to others, which can be a process that some individuals are not comfortable with.[30]

Mason describes psycho-physiological indicators of stress, including 'higher levels of depression and withdrawal, increased sleep difficulties, anxiety, and loss of confidence. For some lesbians and gay men violence may reinforce existing vulnerabilities regarding their sexuality'.[31] One respondent summed up the experiences of many when they described how they had 'experienced intense feelings of hurt, anger, resentment, hopelessness' in the aftermath of abuse.

The psychological impact of abuse and harassment was outlined by a number of respondents. One person reported verbal harassment that:

> ... was quite a while ago and wasn't a major incident but it did cause me to be upset for a while. Myself and my girlfriend were walking along the street holding hands and a group of guys in a car passed us and one of them yelled out 'Dykes!' It didn't bother my girlfriend but it bothered me.

One respondent, who had experienced verbal abuse over the telephone, wrote that 'it was over the phone so not much could happen but it really upset me because I feel everyone has rights. It also hurt because I am still having trouble with my family and friends accepting my sexuality'.

A female participant from the Sunshine Coast focus group described how verbal abuse at the point when she was just 'coming out' about her sexuality made her 'step back in for a while ... if I didn't have a supportive network of older lesbians, I could have actually still stayed in'. The impact of both homophobic and transphobic violence in behaviour modification is considered in further detail in Chapter 10.

....

E, a transsexual woman from the Townsville group said that:

The big problem is the mental problems that go with it. If you get totally rejected every day of the week, you feel that you are not worth being there, you're not worth living, you're not worthy of anything because everyone hates you. If everybody hates you, what's the point of living? Why should I bother? I'm knocking my head against a brick wall.

Some respondents did not feel comfortable sharing public affection after abuse. One respondent described enjoying a romantic evening on her partner's birthday, sharing a hug 'when a mother and her partner yelled at us to stop what we were doing because there were children around and she didn't want them to have to see gay shit. She told us we were disgusting and made us feel humiliated'. The respondent wrote that this 'ruined a beautiful evening and after that we no longer hold hands in public. Even now, I have a phobia about public displays of affection'. A female participant in the Brisbane focus group also made this point. 'My girlfriend now, she's had eggs thrown at her when she was going out with her ex. So they're all traumatised. They can't hold your hand because they've all been abused.'

Even individuals who managed to physically wield off homophobic abuse found the aftermath of the scenario difficult to deal with. One young male respondent successfully managed to fight off 'a chump and his mate' who had made homophobic comments to him and his partner in the Fortitude Valley Night Owl convenience store. The perpetrator challenged him to a fight, which they lost, although the respondent did lose the ball-bearing in his earring and sustained damage to his ear. He regretted that the incident had happened and felt 'sad for my boyfriend who witnessed it'.

Although the psychological aftermath of homophobic and transphobic abuse is clearly harrowing, the situations of some victims were compounded by physical injuries, which also caused ongoing trauma. Some horrific injuries, including broken bones, infections and ongoing disabilities, which took years to heal, were an ongoing concern for many victims. One respondent described injuries that required four years to be healed. As outlined earlier, emotional and psychological scars in some instances could not be healed.

Conclusion

This chapter has outlined the way that homophobia and transphobia impacted on Queensland individuals over the course of their lifetimes.

It found that an overwhelming majority of LGBTIQ individuals had experienced abuse and harassment in the past. Seventy-six per cent of male respondents, 69% of female respondents, 92% of male-to-female transgendered respondents and 55% of female-to-male transgendered respondents reported receiving verbal abuse. Thirty-two per cent of male respondents, 15% of female respondents, 46% of male-to-female transgendered respondents and 36% of female-to-male transgendered respondents had experienced physical assault without a weapon. Twelve per cent of male respondents, 14% of female respondents, 46% of male to female transgendered respondents and 45% of female-to-male transgendered respondents had experienced sexual assault without a weapon.

As the largest study of homophobic and transphobic harassment and violence undertaken in this state, this study was uniquely poised to illuminate the scale to which LGBTIQ lives have been affected by prejudice. It has revealed deplorable statistics that emphasise the urgent need for preventative strategies to be adopted to reduce homophobia and transphobia. Some of the means by which this might be achieved are outlined in Chapter 10.

Notes

1   Michael Flood and Clive Hamilton, 'Mapping Homophobia in Australia' in Shirleene Robinson, ed., *Homophobia: An Australian History* (Annandale, New South Wales: Federation Press, 2008), p.22.

2   Ibid., p.21.

3   New South Wales Attorney General's Department, *'You Shouldn't Have to Hide to be Safe': A Report on Homophobic Hostilities and Violence Against Gay Men and Lesbians in New South Wales* (Sydney: New South Wales Attorney General's Department, Crime Prevention Division, 2003), p.35-36; William Leonard and others, *Coming Forward: The Underreporting of Heterosexist Violence and Same Sex Partner Abuse in Victoria* (Melbourne: Australian Research Centre in Sex, Health and Society, La Trobe, 2008), p.24.

4   Linda Garnets, Gregory Herek and Barrie Levey, 'Violence and Victimization of Lesbians and Gay Men: Mental Health Consequences', in Gregory Herek and Kevin Berill, eds., *Hate Crimes: Confronting Violence Against Lesbians and Gay Men* (Newbury Park, California: Sage Publications, 1992), p.215.

5   New South Wales Attorney General's Department, *'You Shouldn't Have to Hide to be Safe'*, p.35.

6   Ibid.

7   Office of the Government Statistician, *Crime and Justice Statistics Queensland 1999-2000* (Brisbane: Office of the Government Statistician, 2001), p.8.

8   See, for example, Lynn Hillier and Lyn Harrison, 'Homophobia and the Production of Shame: Young People and Same Sex Attraction', *Culture, Health and Society*, Vol. 6, No. 1 (January-February 2004).

9   Martin Kantor, *Homophobia: Descriptions, Development, and Dynamics of Gay Bashing* (London: Praeger, 1998), pp.50–62.

10 Gregory M. Herek and others, 'Correlates of Internalized Homophobia in a Community Sample of Lesbians and Gay Men', *Journal of the Gay and Lesbian Medical Association*, Vol. 2 (1997), p.17.

11 Stephen Tomsen, 'Hatred, Murder and Male Honour: Anti-homosexual Homicide in New South Wales, 1980–2000', *Australian Institute of Criminology Research and Public Policy Series*, No. 43 (2002).

12 B. Miller and L. Humphreys, 'Lifestyles and Violence: Homosexual Victims of Assault and Murder', *Qualitative Sociology*, Vol. 3, No. 3 (1980), p.179.

13 New South Wales Attorney General's Department, *You Shouldn't Have to Hide to be Safe*, p.36.

14 Gail Mason, 'Sexuality and Violence: Questions of Difference' in Chris Cunneen, David Fraser and Stephen Tomsen, eds., *Faces of Hate: Hate Crime in Australia* (Annandale: Hawkins Press, 1997), p.123.

15 Gail Mason, 'Violence Against Lesbians and Gay Men', *Crime Prevention Today*, No. 2 (Canberra: Australian Institute of Criminology, 1993), p.5.

16 Australian Institute of Criminology, 'Crime Victimisation', Australian Institute of Criminology website http://www.aic.gov.au/publications/current%20series/facts/ 1-20/ 2008 /3%20crime%20victimisation.aspx (accessed 5 January 2010).

17 Tarynn M. Witten and A. Evan Eyler, 'Hate Crimes and Violence Against the Transgendered', *Peace Review*, Vol. 11, No. 3 (1999), p.461.

18 Ibid, p.466.

19 Ibid.

20 Leonard and others, *Coming forward: The underreporting of heterosexist violence and same sex partner abuse in Victoria*, p.28.

21 See, for example, Herek and others, 'Correlates of Internalised Homophobia in a Community Sample of Lesbians and Gay Men'.

22 See Krishten Kuehnle and Anne Sullivan, 'Patterns of Anti-Gay Violence: An Analysis of Incident Characteristics and Victim Reporting', *Journal of Interpersonal Violence*, Vol. 16 (2001), p.940.

23 Kevin T. Berrill, 'Anti-Gay Violence and Victimization in the United States: An Overview', *Journal of Interpersonal Violence*, Vol. 5 (1990), p.280.

24 See, for example, 'Sexuality and Violence', p.128.

25 New South Wales Attorney General's Department, *'You Shouldn't Have to Hide to be Safe'*, p.42.

26 Stephen Tomsen and Kevin Markwell, 'When the Glitter Settles: Safety and Hostility at and around Gay and Lesbian Public Events', *Australian Institute of Criminology Research and Public Policy Series*, No. 100 (2009).

27 Darryl Scott's findings were written up into the report 2004, *Everyone has the right to be able to walk safe in their community, Valley Walksafe Project* (report provided courtesy of author).

....

28 *Sunday Mail* [Brisbane], 30 April 2006, p.7.

29 New South Wales Attorney General's Department, *'You Shouldn't Have to Hide to be Safe'*, p.42.

30 Mason, 'Violence Against Lesbians and Gay Men', p.5.

31 Ibid.

CHAPTER 3

Experiencing Homophobic and Transphobic Violence and Harassment Within the Past Two Years

One female respondent to the *Speaking Out* survey, writing with palpable frustration, described the sheer frequency of homophobic abuse she and her partner experience. She reported that 'almost every time my partner and I go out in public, whether it be to a shopping centre, walk down the beach etc we always have AT LEAST one or more people scream DYKES out at us'. Furthermore, she noted that '… if we are out drinking someone will always come up and try and start a fight with us for being "faggots" or we are told by men all we need to sort ourselves out is [to have] their "dick in us"'. Summing up the frequency of abuse, she concluded, 'You take your pick, this happens nearly every time we leave the house'.

Statistics indicate that the frequency and prevalence of homophobic and transphobic violence and harassment is an issue of major concern to Queensland's LGBTIQ community. Fifty-three per cent of those individuals who participated in this study (583 respondents) reported that they had been harassed or abused within the last two years on the basis of their sexuality or gender identity. By considering homophobic and transphobic experiences that respondents have undergone in the last two years, this chapter is able to build on the previous chapter, which explored the prevalence of these forms of abuse over a lifetime. Within the data set exploring homophobia and transphobia over the past two years, respondents were also asked to describe their most recent experience of homophobic or transphobic harassment or abuse. A consideration of harassment and abuse over the past two years provides a more specific level of information about its level of occurrence.

Types of Homophobia/Transphobia Experienced Within the Past Two Years

The statistics regarding the types of harassment and violence that members of the LGBTIQ community have experienced over the last 2 years showed similar trends in the prevalence of the different types of abuse that respondents reported receiving over the course of their lifetimes. This is consistent with the findings of the 2008 Victorian report, *Coming Forward*.[1] The five most predominant forms of abuse and harassment remained the same both over the lifetime of respondents and within the past two years. Verbal abuse, spitting and offensive gestures, threats of physical violence, written threats and abuse and physical attack or assault (without a weapon) were still the most likely forms of harassment or abuse respondents were likely to experience.

The most significant shifts were that a decreased number of respondents were likely to report abuse occurring in the last two years than over a lifetime. This is an obvious result as more abuse would accumulate over a lifetime than during a limited two-year window. Figure 3.1 summarises the types of abuse experienced. Figure 3.2 shows whether respondents were alone, in a same-sex couple or group when each type of abuse occurred. Again, respondents were more likely to suffer all types of abuse on their own.

Verbal Abuse (including hateful or obscene phone calls)

Verbal abuse was once again the most predominant form of abuse. In total, 473 respondents (43%) reported that they had experienced verbal abuse in the last two years. Three hundred and twenty-eight respondents (30%) indicated that they had experienced this alone, 240 respondents (22%) said that they had experienced it as a same-sex couple and 172 respondents (16%) as part of a group. Again, this finding is consistent with previous studies undertaken in New South Wales and Victoria.[2] The power of verbal abuse to disrupt and affect LGBTIQ individuals should not be minimised. A growing body of evidence has shown that verbal abuse can cause enormous disturbance to individuals.[3] Again, this points to the conclusion that ongoing verbal abuse is a constant issue for members of the LGBTIQ community.

Many respondents outlined their recent experiences of verbal abuse. About one and a half years before he attended the Townsville focus group, S, who is aged in his 50s, was with his partner, walking away from the West End Hotel when three men came towards them, calling

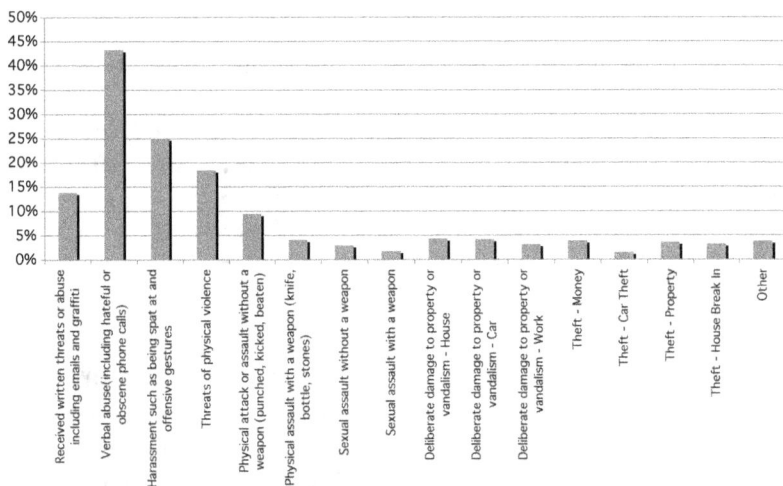

Figure 3.1
Types of abuse experienced within the past two years.

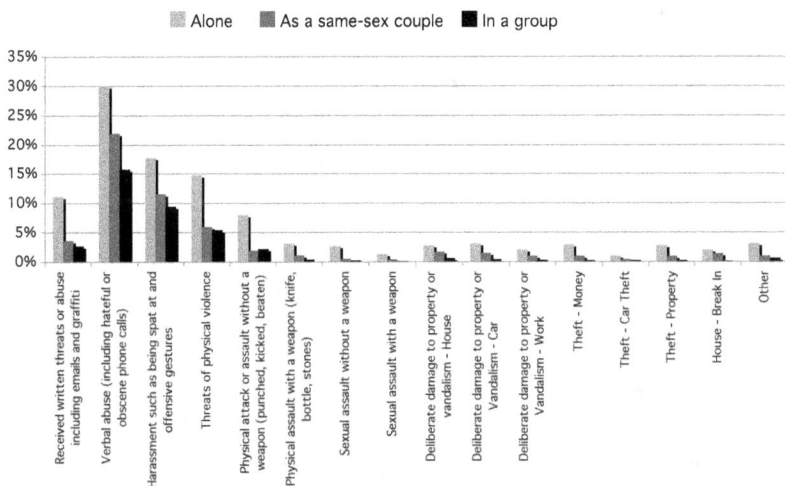

Figure 3.2
Who respondents were with when each type of abuse occurred (within the past two years).

he and his partner 'fucking poofters'. S felt that that this homophobic language would have served as a precursor to an attack, had he and his partner not been able to take shelter in the nearby Midtown Hotel before police arrived.

One female respondent described experiencing 'general homophobic comments from (presumably) heterosexual men in the street when with my partner'. A male respondent reported receiving 'general homophobic abuse when I went for dinner with my partner'. One male respondent described receiving 'verbal abuse by groups of young guys looking for trouble'.

Harassment (including Spitting and Offensive Gestures)

Overall, 274 respondents (25%) had been harassed in the last two years, including being spat at or had been the subject of offensive gestures. One hundred and ninety-four respondents (18%) reported they had been spat at or had been the subject of offensive gestures alone, 126 (12%) of respondents had experienced this as a same-sex couple and 103 (9%) respondents had experienced this as a group.

One respondent articulated what many noted they had experienced by describing being the subject of 'offensive gestures and name-calling'. Another described holding hands with a partner when they were 'spat on and told we were disgusting'.

Threats of Physical Violence

In total, 201 respondents (18%) indicated that they had been the subject of threats of physical violence within the past two years. One hundred and sixty-one respondents (15%) reported that they had been threatened with physical violence alone in the past two years, 65 respondents (6%) had been threatened as a same-sex couple and 59 respondents (5%) had been threatened as part of a group.

One lesbian respondent described how her 'ex boyfriend accused me of engaging in lesbian relationships/being a lesbian — with threats and violence'. A male respondent reported a perpetrator telling him 'I will track you down and slit your throat, you gay c-nt'. One male respondent described an incident that also included threats of sexual violence. He wrote that:

I was walking home from a night out with friends and I was alone. A taxi full of drunken males stopped the taxi and some got out and started running towards me (I thought they were going to bash me). They stopped just before getting to me (some pushed me around) and [started] yelling 'Hey faggot, want to suck some real cock?' and then some others got out of the taxi and ran over towards me (I really thought I was going to be bashed) but they stopped the others by dragging them back to the cab. I ran for the petrol station (about 100m down the road) and ironically I called a taxi myself.

Written Threats and Abuse

Written threats and abuse (including email or graffiti) remained the fourth most prevalent form of abuse and harassment. Overall, 151 respondents (14%) reported that they had received written abuse and threats within the past two years. One hundred and twenty-two respondents (11%) noted that they had received written threats and abuse alone, while 39 respondents (4%) received them as a same-sex couple and 29 respondents (3%) received them as a group.

One respondent described receiving anonymous emails stating that their lifestyle was 'not what god intended'. Another described receiving 'continuous hurtful emails over several days'. One female respondent reported that she had 'received a text saying that I was a "stupid leso" and that "all lesbians and gays deserve to die because they cause AIDS". It also threatened physical abuse, saying I should watch over my shoulder'. After receiving a series of threatening letters in the workplace, one respondent eventually quit their job and went back to study at university.

Physical Attack or Assault (without a weapon)

Overall, 103 respondents (9%) reported that they had been the victim of a physical attack or assault within the last two years. This is higher than the Queensland average, based on the most recent available statistics from 2005. According to these statistics, the general rate of assault (with or without a weapon) amongst the broader state community was 5.7%.[4] 87 respondents (8% of survey respondents) reported that they had been physically attacked or assaulted alone, while 21 respondents (2%) were attacked as a same-sex couple and 24 respondents (2%) were attacked in a group.

One male respondent described how in Fortitude Valley in Brisbane 'last June myself and my partner were physically attacked on the streets by one main offender while his six or seven friends cheered him on. I ended up in hospital with a dislocated shoulder'. Another described a perpetrator punching him in the stomach and face. One female respondent outlined an incident where:

> I was called a 'dyke' and was pushed to the ground, kicked in the side by one person and punched in the face by the other. I managed to overpower them and get away as they were intoxicated.

Deliberate Damage or Vandalism to Property (House)
In total, 47 people (4%) had experienced deliberate damage to property (house) in the last two years. Thirty respondents (3%) reported that they had experienced this alone. Nineteen (2%) had experienced it as part of a same-sex couple and six respondents (1%) had experienced it as part of a group.

Deliberate Damage or Vandalism to Property (Car)
As a whole, 46 respondents (4%) reported that their car had been damaged or vandalised in the last two years. Thirty-four respondents (3%) reported that they had experienced vandalism or damage to their car alone, 16 (1%) had experienced this as a same-sex couple and four respondents (under half a per cent) in a group.

One respondent described finding 'scratches along side of my car and also a milkshake thrown all over it'. A female respondent reported that someone had written the word 'les' on her car. Another respondent articulated how some forms of homophobic and transphobic violence could overlap, in an incident where 'my car was egged and damaged with me in the car. [This was] coupled with threats of violence and verbal abuse by a car full of people in their early 20s, a mixture of both men and women'.

Physical Assault (with a weapon)
In total, 44 respondents (4%) had been physically assaulted with a weapon in the last two years. Thirty-four respondents (3%) reported they had been physically assaulted with a weapon in the last two years alone, 12 (1%) respondents as a same-sex couple and four respondents (under half a per cent) as a group. One respondent described such an incident when he reported being hit over the head from behind with a bottle by a passerby while he was drinking at a popular gay venue.

Theft of Money

Theft of money in the last two years was experienced by 42 respondents (4%). Thirty-two respondents (3%) reported they had experienced the theft of money alone in the last two years, 11 respondents (1%) as a same-sex couple and two respondents (under half a per cent) as a group.

Property Theft

Overall, 39 respondents (4% of survey respondents) had experienced property theft in the last two years. Thirty respondents (3% of survey respondents) reported that they had experienced property theft alone in the past 2 years. Ten respondents (1%) reported that they had experienced this as part of a same-sex couple, while six (under half a per cent) reported that they had experienced this as part of a group.

One respondent simply noted that their 'bag was stolen' as a result of their sexuality. Another described an incident where a 'person approached me and asked for sex and when I refused he stole my car keys and phone'. This seems to be an incident where internalised homophobia may have been a motivating factor in the theft.[5]

House Break-Ins

In total, 35 respondents (3%) had experienced a house break-in during the last two years. Twenty-two respondents (2%) reported that they had experienced house-break ins during the last two years alone, 15 respondents (1%) as part of a same-sex couple and one respondent as part of a group.

Damage to Property (Work)

Thirty-four respondents (3%) had experienced this in the last two years. Twenty-three respondents (2%) reported that they had experienced damage to property (work) alone in the past two years. Eleven respondents (1%) reported that they had experienced this as part of a same-sex couple, while three (less than 1%) experienced this as a group. One respondent who had experienced this described how their 'queer business had an attempted break-in. I was there at the time and the police responded swiftly'.

Sexual Assault (without a weapon)

In total, 32 respondents (3%) had been sexually assaulted without a weapon in the past two years. Twenty-nine respondents (3%) reported that they had been sexually assaulted without a weapon on their own, five respondents (under half a percent) had been part of a same-sex couple and two respondents (under half a percent) had been part of a group. Very few respondents wished to outline the trauma of their experiences. One female respondent reported she had 'been beaten and raped'.

The level of sexual assault experienced both with and without a weapon is much higher among the LGBTIQ community than the broader Australian community. In 2005, 0.3% of the broader community experienced sexual assault either with or without a weapon.[6] When the statistics for sexual assault without a weapon and with weapon against LGBTIQ people are combined, in Queensland the victimisation rate is 5%.

Sexual Assault (with a weapon)

In total, 19 respondents (2%) had been sexually assaulted with a weapon in the last two years. Fourteen respondents (1%) reported that they had been sexually assaulted with a weapon, while alone, in the last 2 years. Four respondents (under half a per cent) had been sexually assaulted with a weapon as part of a same-sex couple and one respondent had been attacked in this way as part of a group.

Car Theft

Overall, 16 respondents (1%) had experienced car theft in the past two years. Eleven respondents (1%) reported that they had experienced car theft alone in the past two years. Four respondents (under half of one per cent) reported that they had experienced this as part of a same-sex couple, while two respondents (under half of one per cent) reported they had experienced it as part of a group.

Other Experiences

Forty-one respondents (4%) wrote that they had experienced 'other' types of homophobic or transphobic harassment or violence in the last two years. Thirty-four respondents (3%) noted they had experienced this alone, 11 respondents (1%) as a same-sex couple and seven respondents (under 1%) as a group.

....

Although the 'other' category was used to describe a variety of different occurrences, the majority of write-in responses revolved around workplace discrimination. One respondent reported that they 'received different treatment at work [and were] not given same training or opportunities'. Another respondent noted of similar workplace discrimination, reporting that they were the subject of 'workplace bullying — snide comments, "backstabbing", [were] ignored during meetings, verbally abused, put down in front of others [and received] negative comments about sexuality'. Another respondent described being 'outed', with the perpetrator informing the victim's friends and family about their sexual preference.

Abuse Within the Last Two Years by Gender Identity

Gail Mason has cautioned against not recognising the difference that gender can have on experiences of homophobic violence.[7] As a result, data from this survey considered the way that gender and gender identity impacted on the way survey respondents experienced homophobic or transphobic violence.

As mentioned previously, 53% of survey respondents reported that they had experienced homophobic or transphobic harassment or violence within the last two years. When data from the past two years is arranged by gender, 245 males (51% of male respondents), 312 females (55% of female respondents), nine male-to-female transgender respondents (69% of male-to-female transgendered respondents), three female-to male-transgendered respondents (27% of female-to-male respondents) and 14 'other' identifying respondents (82% of 'other' identifying respondents) said they had experienced this some form of abuse in the time frame of 2 years. These data are presented in Figure 3.3. In the last two years, respondents from the 'other' identifying category and male-to-female transgendered people were most likely to experience abuse.

Abuse Within the Last Two Years by Sexuality

As conveyed in Figure 3.4, out of the 583 respondents who reported homophobic or transphobic harassment within the past two years, respondents who identified their sexuality as 'other' were most likely to be abused. Thirty-nine 'other' identifying respondents (72% of 'other' identifying respondents) reported being abused or harassed within the last two years. Two hundred and forty-seven lesbian respondents (56% of lesbian respondents) reported being abused or harassed within the past two years. Two hundred and thirty-seven gay respondents (50% of gay

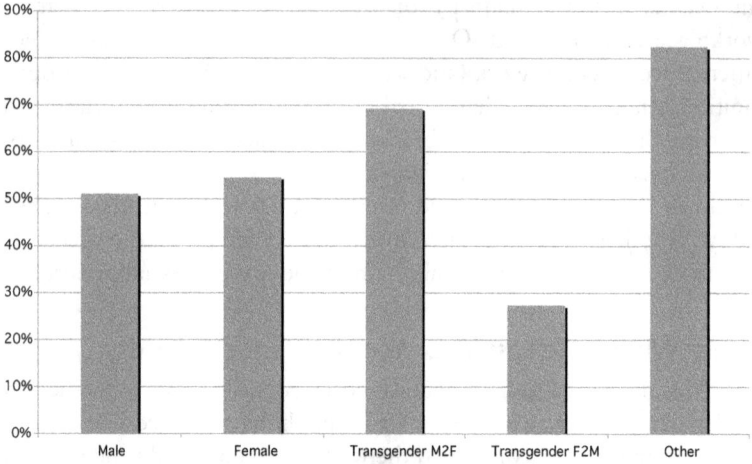

Figure 3.3
Abuse within the last two years by gender identity.

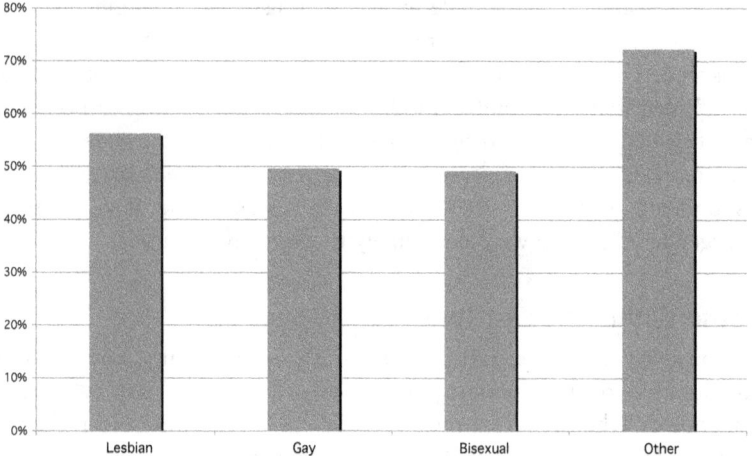

Figure 3.4
Abuse within the last two years by sexuality..

respondents) and 60 bisexual respondents (49% of bisexual respondents) reported being abused in the previous two years.

Many respondents who identified as 'other' were transgendered and the evidence presented statistically in this and the preceding chapter does reveal this community to be particularly vulnerable to harassment and violence. Tarynn M. Whitten and A. Evan Eyler have also made this point on a global level.[8]

Abuse Within the Last Two Years by Age

The average age of people who have experienced homophobic or transphobic violence or harassment in past two years is 32 (rounded to the nearest whole number). The average age of people who have not experienced homophobic or transphobic violence or harassment in past two years is 35 (rounded to the nearest whole number). These averages are calculated from the data received from the 890 respondents who specified their age. The breakdown of those respondents experiencing abuse in the last two years is divided into five age brackets. The results are presented in Table 3.1.

Based on survey responses, it seems that respondents of a younger age are more likely to be the victim of homophobic or transphobic abuse. As a result of this, recommendations made in Chapter 10 focus on initiatives that will help reduce homophobic and tranpshobic abuse towards same sex attracted youth (SSAY). The likelihood of suffering abuse reduces with age. Respondents aged between 18 and 24 were most likely to suffer abuse, with 61% of these individuals being abused in the last two years. Respondents aged between 25 and 34 were the group who were the second most likely to suffer homophobic or transphobic abuse. Anecdotal statements made during focus groups and qualitative statements made in

....

Table 3.1
Abuse Within the Last Two Years by Age

	Yes	No	Total
18–24	147 (61%)	94 (39%)	241 (27%)
25–34	151 (55%)	124 (45%)	275 (31%)
35–44	98 (48%)	108 (52%)	206 (23%)
45–54	51 (44%)	65 (56%)	116 (13%)
55+	19 (37%)	33 (63%)	52 (6%)

....

response to this survey suggest that respondents in the younger age brackets are more likely to occupy public spaces such as nightclubs and city streets at hours when attacks are more likely to occur. Furthermore, other qualitative responses also drew a link between alcohol consumption and abuse. Younger respondents indicated they were both more likely to drink alcohol than older respondents and were more likely to be in environments where alcohol was publicly consumed or individuals who had consumed excessive amounts of alcohol were present.

Abuse Within the Last Two Years by Disability

As Table 3.2 shows, respondents who have a disability are more likely to suffer abuse than respondents who do not have a disability. Sixty-one per cent of respondents who recorded that they had a disability stated that they had suffered abuse within the last two years. This compares to 52% of respondents without disabilities. It is also possible that some of those individuals might be suffering a disability as a result of a homophobic or tranpshobic attack.

Abuse Within the Last Two Years by Education

As Table 3.3 shows, respondents who are attending an educational establishment are more likely to be the subject of homophobic or transphobic abuse than respondents who are not attending an educational institution. This is probably attributable to the younger age of most individuals attending these institutions. The link between youth and vulnerability to abuse is shown in Table 3.1.

Some focus group respondents mentioned that some religious schools could be extremely homophobic or transphobic environments. The susceptibility of SSAY to bullying in schools has informed some of the recommendations in Chapter 10. Similarly, more conservative university campuses were also mentioned as a site where institutionalised homophobia and transphobia could occur.

....

Table 3.2
Abuse Within the Last Two Years by Disability

	Yes	No	Total
Disability	73 (61%)	46 (39%)	119 (11%)
No disability	486 (52%)	447 (48%)	933 (89%)

....

....

Table 3.3
Abuse Within the Last Two Years for those Attending an Educational
Institution

	Yes	No
Attending educational establishment	190 (62%)	118 (38%)
Not attending educational establishment	385 (50%)	381 (50%)

Table 3.4 shows the impact of level of education on the likelihood of becoming a victim of homophobia and transphobia. From the data, it would appear that homophobic and transphobic abuse cuts across all levels of educational attainment. Those with no formal schooling do have a higher rate of experiencing homophobic or transphobic abuse (64%) compared to individuals who have a postgraduate degree (47%).

Abuse by Association

As depicted in Figure 3.5, 186 respondents (17% of total survey respondents) felt that their family, friends or associates had been victimised as a result of their association with the LGBTIQ respondent. Four hundred and eighty-five respondents (44%) did not believe that family, friends or associates had experienced violence or harassment as a result of their association with the LGBTIQ individual. Three hundred and ninety-one people (36%) wrote that they did not know if this was the case. Thirty-two respondents to the survey (3%) did not provide a response to this question.

....

Table 3.4
Abuse within the Last Two Years by Highest Level of Education

	Yes	No
No formal schooling	7 (64%)	4 (36%)
Part secondary school	49 (53%)	43 (47%)
Completed secondary school	138 (54%)	119 (46%)
Tertiary diploma/trade certificate	138 (58%)	102 (43%)
University degree	138 (52%)	129 (48%)
Postgraduate degree	66 (47%)	73 (53%)

In the past two years have friends, family, children or associates of yours been subject to violence or harassment because of their association with you, given your sexual orientation or gender identity?

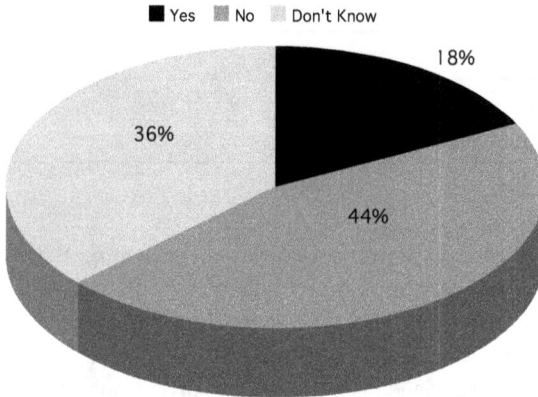

■ Yes   ■ No   ■ Don't Know

18%

36%

44%

Figure 3.5
Abuse by association.

These figures are higher than those reported in the 2008 *Coming Forward* report from Victoria. In that state, 11% of respondents felt that their family, friends or associates had been victimised as a result of their association with LGBTIQ individuals.[9]

A number of respondents outlined incidents where their family members had suffered abuse or harassment. One person noted that 'my brother has been victimised because I am gay'. Another respondent noted that their brother 'lost his girlfriend and some of his school friends when they found out he had gay siblings'.

Another reported that 'my mother has been told that she didn't bring me up right'. One male respondent described how his mother had been harassed and victimised by other family members because she chose to maintain a close relationship with him. He wrote:

My father hates me, my brother has threatened to kill me if I contact him or his kids, my mother has lost friends, and most of her friends never talk or ask about me again. My mother's relationship with her other son has been affected because she chooses to remain in a close relationship with me.

One female respondent noted that her 'stepson gets harassed and picked on at school because he has two mums'.

Some respondents described how their friends had been victimised as a result of homophobia and their association with LGBTIQ individuals.

One lesbian respondent reported that her friends had been 'harassed when with me, as people don't like the fact I am a butch dyke and look different'. A male respondent described how his group of friends defended him 'from bullying actions from a group of heterosexual men' and how this then escalated into his 'friends being verbally attacked ... for defending a gay man'.

Homophobia and Transphobia Within the LGBTIQ Community

Some respondents also pointed out that they had experienced homophobic or transphobic harassment or violence from within the LGBTIQ community. Although this falls outside the scope of this study, it is important to note these comments.

V, a participant in the Gold Coast focus group who had transitioned from male to female and identifies as a lesbian, felt that the lesbian community at times had been discriminatory towards her. She said, 'They're more discriminating than the average community, definitely'. She noted that it was particularly offensive when lesbian women were not respectful of her transition and referred to her as 'he'. S, another female who had transitioned from male, who took part in the Townsville focus group, had experienced other members of the transgender community attempting to hurt her by withdrawing recognition of her female gender.

M, a male participant in the Townsville focus group, described prejudice within the LGBTIQ community as being attributable to the fact that Townsville's crime rate 'is probably higher than the average regional town and I think a lot of the internal gay violence is probably more [to do with] that'.

It is clear that internalised homophobia and transphobia is responsible for these comments and attitudes.[10] Iain Williamson argues, 'Many individuals within the lesbian and gay community may internalise significant aspects of the prejudice experienced within a heterosexist society'.[11] As Gregory Herek, Jeanine Cogan, Roy Gillis and Eric Glunt maintain, internalised prejudices such as homophobia are:

> ... associated with lower levels of psychological wellbeing, less openness about one's sexual orientation, less sense of community involvement and a heightened sense of being stigmatised as a result of homosexual orientation.[12]

Thus, a positive set of strategies to address homophobia and transphobia in the mainstream community should also reduce these types of internalised homophobia and transphobia.

Most Recent Experience of Homophobic and Transphobic Violence and Harassment

Respondents who had experienced homophobic or transphobic violence or harassment within the last two years were also asked to describe their most recent experience of abuse. The data collated in Table 3.5 provide the quantitative information about individual cases of homophobia and transphobia in Queensland. It indicates the types of abuse respondents suffered in their most recent experience of homophobic or transphobic violence or harassment. Again, as was seen in the data relating to experiences over the course of a lifetime and within the past two years, verbal abuse (54% of most recent incidents) is the most prevalent type of abuse among respondents' most recent incident of abuse. It should be noted that 59 respondents (10%) who received some form of abuse in the past 2 years did not specify the nature of their most recent incident.

Abuse and Homophobic or Transphobic Language

Respondents were also asked if their most recent experience of homophobic or transphobic harassment was accompanied by homophobic or transphobic language. Out of the 583 respondents who experienced homophobic or transphobic harassment or violence in the past two years, 538 specified whether their most recent incident was coupled with homophobic or transphobic language. Forty-five respondents did not indicate whether homophobic language preceded or accompanied the incident. Out of the 538 respondents that did specify this, a majority of 459 respondents (79%) reported that the incident was accompanied by such language. Seventy-nine respondents (14%) wrote that it was not. The prevalence of such language accompanying homophobic or transphobic abuse indicates that it would be possible for the judicial system to legally classify the majority of these attacks as hate crimes. The mechanics of introducing such a legal change are further discussed in chapter 10.

Alone or With Others

As seen in Figure 3.6, 465 respondents out of 583 respondents who experienced a most recent incident of abuse indicated whether this abuse occurred alone or in a group. One hundred and ninety-four respondents (42%) were alone, 156 respondents (34%) were part of a same-sex couple and 115 respondents (25%) were part of a group when their most recent experience of homophobic or transphobic violence or harassment occurred.

....
Table 3.5
Types of Abuse Experienced in Most Recent Incident

Form of abuse	Total
Received written threats or abuse including emails and graffiti	6%
Verbal abuse (including hateful or obscene phone calls)	54%
Harassment such as being spat at and offensive gestures	9%
Threats of physical violence	7%
Physical attack or assault without a weapon (punched, kicked, beaten)	5%
Physical assault with a weapon (knife, bottle, stones)	1%
Sexual assault without a weapon	1%
Sexual assault with a weapon	0%
Deliberate damage to property or vandalism — House	1%
Deliberate damage to property or vandalism — Car	1%
Deliberate damage to property or vandalism — Work	0%
Theft — Money	0%
Theft — Car Theft	0%
Theft — Property	0%
Theft — House Break-in	1%
Other	3%

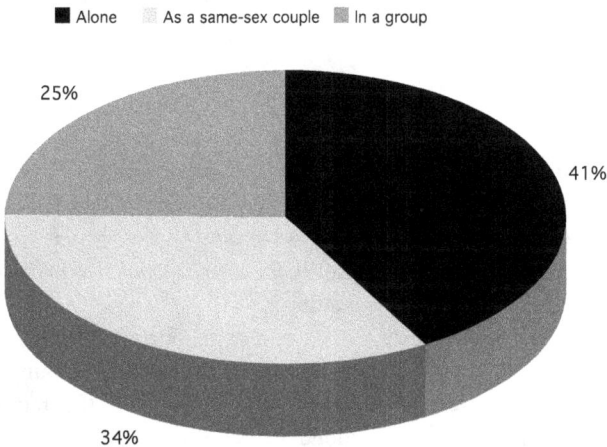

Figure 3.6
Alone or with others in most recent incident.

These data indicates that most respondents were on their own at the time of the most recent homophobic or transphobic incident. Interestingly, this finding is different to the 2003 NSW report 'You Shouldn't Have to Hide to be Safe', which found that most victims in New South Wales (45%) were with one other person (usually a same-sex partner) at the time of their reported incident.[13] The Queensland findings are similar to the 2008 Victorian report, though, which found that a majority of 60% of respondents were alone at the time of the incident, while 27% were part of same-sex couple and 12% were part of a group.[14]

Region of Most Recent Incident

As displayed in the map of Figure 3.7, the bulk of the most recently reported instances of homophobia and transphobia occurred within Brisbane. Two hundred and thirty-four incidents out of 538 reports of homophobic or transphobic harassment or violence (40% of most recent incidents), occurred in this area. The statistics are reflective of the population size of Brisbane, which holds almost a quarter of the state's residents.

Within Brisbane, 'gay identified' suburbs such as the Fortitude Valley (12% of most recent incidents), which is home to most of Brisbane's LGBTIQ nightclubs, adjourning suburb New Farm (2% of most recent incidents), and the inner-city suburb of South Brisbane (3% of most recent incidents), were the suburbs that were the frequent locations of incidents of homophobia and transphobia. The prevalence of homophobic attacks in the Fortitude Valley area was noted by Darryl Scott in his 2004 report, Everyone has the Right to be Able to Walk Safe Within Their Community.[15]

Both the 2003 NSW report, 'You Shouldn't Have to Hide to be Safe' and the 2008 Victorian report, Coming Forward, noted that the majority of cases of abuse occurred within the capital cities of Sydney and Melbourne and within suburbs that were popular with LGBTIQ individuals.[16] International studies have also shown that gay men who reside in a 'gay-defined' suburb are more likely to be physically beaten than gay men who do not live in such a suburb.[17]

Outside of Brisbane, the next greatest proportion of instances was in the remainder of South-East Queensland (excluding the Sunshine Coast and Gold Coast), with 61 incidents (11%) reported in this region. Thirty-nine respondents (7%) reported incidents on the Gold Coast. Thirty-three respondents (6%) reported incidents on the Sunshine Coast. Twenty respondents (3%) reported homophobic or transphobic abuse occurring within North Queensland. Eighteen respondents (3%) described homo-

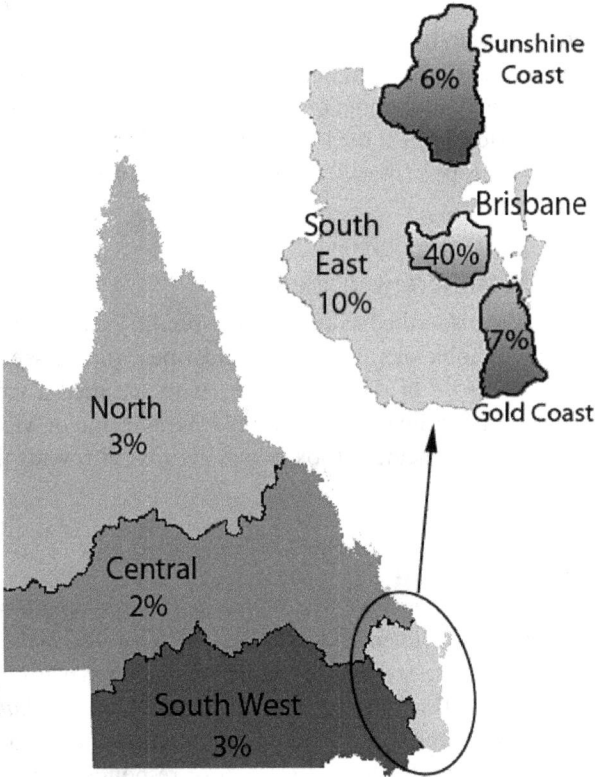

Figure 3.7
Map showing region of most recent incident.

phobic or transphobic abuse occurring within South-West Queensland. Thirteen respondents (2%) reported homophobic or transphobic abuse occurring in Central Queensland.

Further analysis of the data reveals that people living in certain parts of Queensland are more likely to experience homophobic or transphobic harassment or violence. Of the respondents who lived in Brisbane, 234 (72%) experienced a most recent incident. Members of the LGBTIQ community in the Sunshine Coast were the second most likely group to experience homophobic or transphobic harassment or violence, with 33 respondents (50%) reporting a most recent incident. This was followed by 20 North Queenslanders (40%), 39 respondents (38%) from the Gold Coast, 13 respondents (37%) from Central Queensland, 8 respondents

(25%) from South-West Queensland and 61 respondents (16%) from South-East Queensland.

One hundred and sixty-five respondents (28%) did not provide the location where the homophobic or transphobic abuse occurred. Overall, the statistics provided reflect the locations where survey respondents were based and also the percentages of people living in particular parts of Queensland.

Location of Most Recent Incident

Respondents were also asked to specify the specific location in which the incident of homophobic or transphobic harassment took place. It should be noted that 26 (4%) of the respondents who specified a most recent experience of homophobic or transphobic harassment or violence did not specify where the incident took place. Figure 3.8 reveals the trends in the data.

On the Street

Out of the 583 respondents who had experienced homophobic or trans-phobic harassment or violence within the past two years, the majority experienced this on the street. One hundred and fifty-five respondents (27%) reported this. The 2003 NSW study, 'You Shouldn't Have to Hide to be Safe, also listed the street as the most common site of homophobic harassment or violence. In that state, 29% of respondents reported that their experience took place on the street.[18]

In this Queensland study, many respondents described their experiences of being on the streets when homophobic or transphobic abuse took place. One respondent described being the target of 'abusive language' and having 'water thrown on us when we were sitting on the side of the road'. Another respondent described an incident where a 'deodorant can was thrown from a moving vehicle and I was called a faggot'.

A female respondent wrote that 'me and a mate were sitting on the side of the road and this drunk guy started yelling "fucking lesbians" as he walked by'. Another respondent described 'just being abused from the car, was in a group of guys walking along the waterfront/park area of Manly'.

Another respondent described an incident where he was on the street when:

> ... two guys came around corner towards me. They basically said 'poofter, you want a fight' and went at me with punches, which I

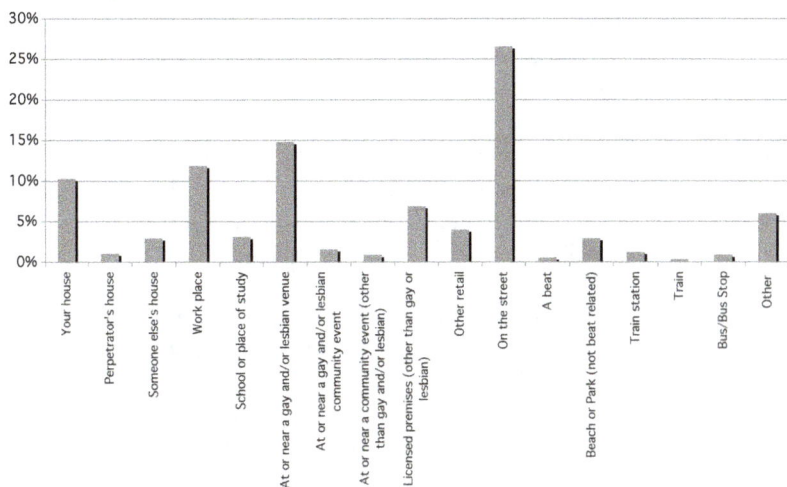

Figure 3.8
Location of most recent incident.

avoided. Then suddenly, a car pulled up and I got in, as a guy was motioning me too. I got in and as I did they were trying to punch me through the window. When we drove off, the guy said they had just done the same thing to him around the corner, so he followed them to see who was next.

The particular streets mentioned were in Fortitude Valley and Hastings Street at Noosa, and a number of respondents mentioned the streets near Brisbane's Normanby Hotel.

At or Near Gay or Lesbian Venues

The second most cited location where homophobic or transphobic harassment or violence took place was at or near LGBTIQ venues. Eighty-six respondents (15%) reported this as the location of abuse. This also matches the 2003 NSW report, 'You Shouldn't Have to Hide to be Safe', which noted that locations at or near gay or lesbian venues were the second most reported location where homophobic abuse took place. In that state, 23% of respondents listed gay or lesbian venues as the location of abuse.[19]

There were many reports from Queensland individuals describing harassment or abuse near LGBTIQ venues. One respondent described being 'hit in the face in a gay pub by a drunk straight guy'. Another respondent, who was employed in a gay bar, was abused outside that bar by a perpetrator. They described being 'called a "dyke", "faggot" outside the gay bar where I work'.

Walking between venues or being in areas known to be popular LGBTIQ areas also attracted perpetrators. One female respondent described 'having drunk people yell stuff out when you're walking down the street (when out in the Valley on the way to a gay club). Making snide or rude remarks, calling a male friend of mine names like "fag" and calling me a "dyke" etc'.

Another respondent described how he was in the Fortitude Valley, walking between two LGBTIQ venues on a Saturday night:

> ... with my straight sister and her date for the night [when I] had a bottle of water thrown on me by two intoxicated females between the MET nightclub and the Wickham. Although I was dressed in drag that night it still doesn't make it any more acceptable which I not so politely let them know.

Another respondent described walking through the Fortitude Valley's night-club district on a Saturday night and being called 'a fag, fudge packer etc'.

One respondent described an incident where 'guys drove by as we left a venue, slowed down started yelling and threw eggs and abuse'. Another person reported being at 'a local gay venue and when I left some people saw that I came from the venue and started physically assaulting me'. Another respondent wrote how he 'kissed a boy outside a venue [and was] attacked from behind by a group of assholes'.

Workplace

The workplace was the third most common location for homophobic and transphobic incidents. Sixty-nine respondents (12%) reported that their experiences of harassment or violence had taken place in that location. In focus groups, female participants were more likely to describe work places as sites of homophobic or transphobic abuse than male participants. Studies from other states have also listed homophobia and transphobia in the workplace as significant problems for LGBTIQ individuals.[20]

Written responses from a variety of individuals in this Queensland study outlined occasions of homophobia and transphobia taking place in the workplace. One respondent described 'writing on toilet walls at [my] last workplace'. Another wrote, 'In the workplace I was inappropriately addressed and asked to perform sexual acts'. Another respondent wrote that she was called a 'lesbian freak' by her boss.

S, a male participant in the Cairns focus group, described an incident that had happened to him in a Brisbane workplace.

> I used to walk down the corridor, he would actually take a wide berth. He was quite homophobic and I'd actually set up a position from scratch and the time came for it to be filled. I remember this quite clearly, at morning tea, after everyone had gone and it was just the two of us. He said 'S, are you going to apply for the job?' I said, 'I think so Mick. I've set up the whole thing for the last three years, I think I'll be applying'. He said, 'Well, you know I'm the chair of the selection panel'. I said, 'Don't you think in the interests of equity or transparency you should absent yourself from that position?' He said 'No', and he said 'As long as I am in this position, you will never get it'. And I never did.

In some instances, the abuse could come from customers, rather than other staff members. B, a female participant in the Gold Coast focus group, works in McDonalds and described how 'Once it hits about 3 am and the clubs are getting out, it's "Oh lesbian, I'll show you what a real man is like"'.

Own House

The fourth most prevalent location cited by respondents for homophobic and transphobic abuse was the house of respondents. Sixty respondents (10%) reported that they had experienced abuse in their own home. One respondent described a situation where:

> ... when my ex husband dropped off our daughter he was obviously under the influence of alcohol so I said I wasn't happy about it and then [he and his partner] both decided to abuse me and threaten to take our daughter away because they felt I was introducing the wrong way of life to her.

Licensed Premises (other than Gay or Lesbian)

The fifth most prevalent location for homophobic and transphobic abuse was licensed premises (other than gay or lesbian). Forty respondents (7%) reported that they had been abused in such a location. One female respondent outlined an incident where she:

> ... was at a pub with a girl I was seeing and some guys were obviously a bit excited seeing two women together (although we weren't all over each other) and they kept approaching us asking us to go home with them. We were polite and said no thanks they got abusive, called us dykes, and I overheard one of them say they should follow us home which therefore led me to believe they were considering sexually assaulting us. I advised a bouncer who removed them from the premises.

D, a participant in the Cairns focus group who had transitioned from male to female, was refused access to female toilets at one venue. She says 'The manager came up to me and basically said, "If you go into the ladies toilets again, I will kick you out"'. Another respondent described being 'glassed at a straight pub'.

Another participant in the Cairns focus group, outlined an incident where he was at a pub that he thought was reputed to be non-discriminatory towards LGBTIQ people. After he ordered a drink, however, he was asked to leave. He described the bouncers informing him that another patron had said, 'Okay, I want him to leave because … he touched me inappropriately'. S said, 'I got quite angry at this. I said, "This is bullshit. That didn't happen". I was actually physically removed'.

Similarly, M, a female respondent at the Sunshine Coast focus group, outlined situations she was aware of where LGBTIQ people had gone to mixed or supposedly LGBTIQ friendly venues. 'You are talking to someone's girlfriend or something like that. You are just talking. The girlfriend says, "Yeah, yeah, this is cool and I don't care" but the boyfriend does'. M said, 'These people have [then] been manhandled in an environment they had gone to thinking that they were going to be safe'.

Other Retail

Twenty-three respondents (4%) experienced homophobic or transphobic abuse in another retail location. This was the sixth most prevalent location for homophobic or transphobic abuse.

One female respondent described being called '… "dirty lesbians" while shopping with my partner and often being targeted for abuse by young males'. Another female respondent described how perpetrators abused her in a shopping complex by shouting out '… "fuckin' dyke, get a man", while … minding my [own] business after shopping and going to the car'.

School or Place of Study

Eighteen respondents (3%) experienced homophobic or transphobic harassment or violence at school or a place of study. This was the seventh most prevalent location for homophobic or transphobic harassment or violence.

One respondent described 'general derogatory terms [being] used against me whilst at the school swimming carnival'. A number of LGBTIQ individuals who were employed in a teaching capacity also mentioned their fears that their sexuality or gender identity could be used against them in homophobic or transphobic attacks from the hierarchy within the school or university system. Homophobia and transphobia in such an institutional setting has been observed in other international studies.[21]

M, a female participant in the Sunshine Coast focus group, who had been employed in schools said, 'You know, it just takes one parent to get upset and it's enough to become a big issue'. One male participant in the Sunshine Coast focus group, who used to work in two private Christian schools, was asked by senior staff if he was gay. When he answered that he was, they told him 'please don't come back Monday'.

N, another female participant from the Sunshine Coast focus group agreed that this was also an issue in the tertiary sector. She said, 'I work in a university and I know of a few staff members who go out of their way to protect their identity because there are students who will rebel against that and use that against them'.

Beach or Park (not Beat Related)

Seventeen respondents (3%) reported being harassed or abused at a beach or park (not beat related). This was the eighth most-cited location by respondents.

One respondent described 'Another incident of verbal abuse from unknown local young males in a park'. Similarly, a female respondent outlined an experience where she 'had gone to the beach with a female friend at night and been verbally harassed and threatened until we left'.

Someone Else's House

Seventeen respondents (3%) described being assaulted at someone else's house, making this the equal eighth most prevalent location for homophobic or transphobic harassment or abuse.

One respondent reported being:

... at a party, and I was being verbally abused by a group of guys, calling me fag, poof, etc. I left them alone and just spent the night with my friends, until one of them came up to me and asked me if I said anything to his girlfriend, which I didn't. I then turned away from him and he punched me in the side of the head, my head hit the wall and I blacked out, while his friend kicked me. Luckily it was broken up and they were thrown out. I didn't sustain any serious injury, just bruises and shock.

Another respondent described being the target of 'verbal abuse from a passing group while having a BBQ with friends in their home'.

At or Near a Gay and/or Lesbian Community Event

Nine respondents (2%) reported homophobic or transphobic harassment or violence occurring at or near a gay and/or lesbian community event.

One respondent described being 'verbally abused while attending a World Aids Day event'. Another wrote about being the target of fundamentalist Christian protestors while attending a same-sex marriage rally. Another respondent outlined a situation where 'eggs were thrown at Pride Parade'.

Train/Train Station

Seven respondents (1%) reported homophobic or transphobic harassment or violence that occurred at a train station. Although respondents did not outline the specifics of the incidents of homophobic or transphobic harassment at a train station, these areas have been anecdotally reported as crime 'hot spots'.

Two respondents (less than 1%) reported homophobic or transphobic harassment or violence taking place on a train. One respondent wrote that 'a guy in the train abused me and my friend. Also on a street'.

Perpetrator's House

Six respondents (1%) reported homophobic or transphobic violence or harassment occurring at the perpetrator's house. One female respondent described going to visit a female friend when 'basically, her boyfriend had to become involved and tried to beat me up'.

Bus/Bus Stop

Five respondents (1%) reported homophobic or transphobic harassment or violence taking place at a bus/bus stop. One female respondent outlined an incident where:

> I was sitting at a bus stop waiting to go home after having dinner with work mates. A group of young men walked past, who were obviously drunk. I refused to engage with them when they asked for a high five. They then became aggressive and began yelling and calling me a 'dyke'. I became scared and jumped on the next bus, even though this wasn't the right one. I became very upset and angry.

Another respondent described an incident where she was:

> ... sitting on the bus with housemate minding my own business when a group of men, mostly wearing tight white t-shirts with rat tails decided to yell things I didn't appreciate at me and my housemate, but

mostly me because my housemate doesn't look very lesbian. We got off after our stop cause we wanted to wait til they got off the bus first.

Another respondent wrote that they got off a bus when a person 'followed me [and] tried to get my attention. I walked to a service station for safety'.

At or Near a Community Event (other than Gay or Lesbian)

Five respondents (1%) reported homophobic or transphobic harassment or violence taking place at or near a community event (other than gay or lesbian). One such response mentioned the Dreaming Festival, while another mentioned an Australian Labor Party event.

Beats

Three respondents (1%) reported homophobic or transphobic harassment or violence taking place at a beat. As mentioned in the previous chapter, a number of individuals in focus groups described beats as the most dangerous of all locations for homophobic or transphobic attacks.

One respondent described an incident of homophobic violence that occurred at a beat that he believed may have also been linked to mistaken identity. He described how he was walking through a park:

... which is also a local beat ... going home after work ... a man approached me and started yelling at me that I had raped his son (it was not me. He was looking for a particular person but got the wrong one). He had a long cardboard box and out of it, he pulled a large samurai sword [and] started waving it round telling me he was going to kill me (I fully believe he was going to). He hit my bag off my back with it and kept yelling and yelling while the woman was videoing the whole incident ... I was cornered [with] nowhere to go [and this] went on for approximately seven to eight minutes and was getting out of control. [He was a] very, very angry man ... Luckily a man and lady were walking their dog in the distance and he saw them and freaked out and gave me one final punch to the eye that nearly knocked me out ... he left she left ... I was left with blood everywhere and my belongings everywhere broken and smashed (Christmas pressies for my family).

Other Responses

Thirty-five respondents selected the 'other option'. The 'other' responses showed a variety of locations. One respondent mentioned a Hungry Jacks restaurant, some described online abuse and harassment, some mentioned locations such as gyms and a doctor's surgery. Another respondent described abuse occurring 'while driving', while another wrote 'in my car'. Shopping centres, boat ramps and the creative industries sector were also cited.

Bullying

Members of the focus groups across Queensland mentioned bullying as a topic of particular concern to members of the LGBTIQ community. Same-sex attracted SSAY are particularly susceptible to school bullying, and workplace bullying can also be an issue for LGBTIQ people.

One focus group participant noted the prevalence of anti-LGBTIQ language in schools, saying that he was 'trying to get [his] nine year old to not say ["that's so gay"]'. Another participant explained: 'I've noticed amongst kids that it's awfully prevalent now. I didn't notice it before, but as a put-down, especially amongst the boys, the biggest insult you can say to another boy is, "you f...g poofter"'. A gay male participant in the Brisbane focus group observed: 'That is terrible that the worst insult you can say to another ... boy, "You're a f...g poofter ..." it's the biggest insult a little boy can cop'.

One of the young lesbian focus group participants in Toowoomba who was actively involved in the gay/straight Alliance on her university campus said she visited a grammar school in the local community for some practical experience: '... one of these prac students, some said "well all gays...should be rounded up and sent away to an island somewhere"'.

M, a lesbian participant in the Sunshine Coast focus group stated:

> ... it does depend on the workplace and I am going to use an education facility here because it's probably the worst areas. It is that even though you have got friends in that facility, when push comes to shove, you could actually get stabbed in the back. Like not physically, but if it came down to someone's job of dobbing someone in, I think nine times out of ten the people have actually lost their jobs in high schools because the hierarchy have found out of their personal choice.

A former pastor who worked in two private Christian schools was effectively dismissed after discovering his sexual orientation. He said that:

> I used to work in two private Christian schools ... when they heard the rumours they confronted me ... but if they ask I don't lie ... So I said 'Yes,' [and they said] 'Please don't come back Monday'. It happened at the other school [which] did exactly the same thing.

As bullying has been highlighted as an issue of particular concern amongst the LGBTIQ community, Chapter 10 makes recommendations that will also address this form of homophobia and transphobia.

Contributing Factors in Most Recent Incident

Out of the 583 people who wrote that they had experienced homophobic or transphobic harassment or violence in the past two years, 232 respondents (40%) stated that they believed gender was a factor in the abuse during their most recent incident. Twenty-six respondents (4%) felt that race was a factor in the incident. Fifteen people (3%) wrote that ethnicity was a factor, while nine (3%) believed disability was a contributing factor. Fifty-nine respondents (10%) selected the 'other' contributing factor option and were asked to comment on what other factors they believed the violence and harassment was related. Two hundred and thirty-three respondents did not believe there were any other contributing factors. Nine people (2%) did not select any option. These results are displayed in Figure 3.9.

Gender as a Contributing Factor

The most common factor cited by respondents as a contributing factor was gender. As explained in Chapter 2, homophobia and transphobia are often strongly correlated with sexist attitudes. This point has also been adeptly argued in a range of international studies. Gender was also the most common contributing factor selected by respondents to the 2003 NSW study, 'You Shouldn't Have to Hide to be Safe'.

A number of respondents to this Queensland study wrote that they felt their transgression of 'standard' gender roles had attracted the attention of attackers. One believed the incident was based on 'my general appearance and how easy it was to read me as a transgender person'. Another respondent reported that 'my partner has just started transitioning and is very andro. Gets a lot of stares as people try to figure out his gender'. Another wrote that 'More than likely [a contributing factor was] because I was in drag and also my sexual orientation based on what was said'.

One respondent wrote that:

> The attackers were initially confused as to what my gender was. They harassed me based on that, then decided I was female and began using sexist and sexual language. The attackers themselves had never seen me before, but personally these kinds of incidents are common and ongoing because I apparently look like a 'filthy dyke'.

One transgender respondent linked sexism and gender stereotypes in their response when they wrote that a contributing factor had been 'sexism towards transwomen [with] transwomen being seen as sex workers'.

Perhaps linked to gender were respondents who cited their appearance as a contributing factor. One such respondent believed their 'physical appearance and personal mannerisms' had been a contributing factor.

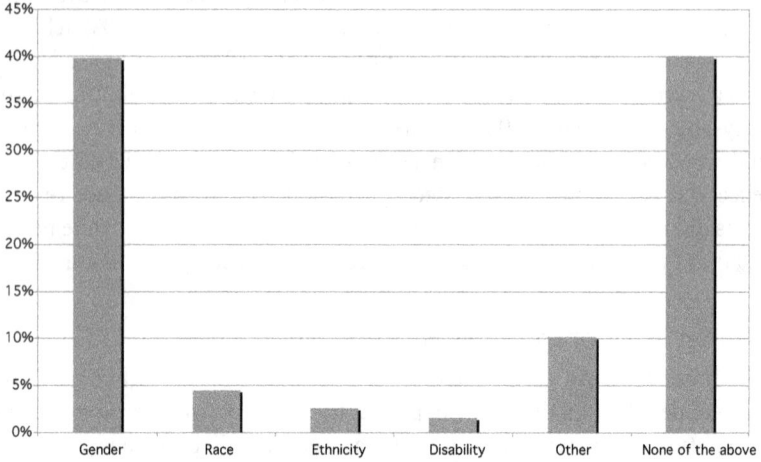

Figure 3.9
Factors respondent believed contributed to the most recent incident (besides sexual orientation and gender identity).

Race and Ethnicity as Contributing Factors

In the 2003 NSW report, 'You Shouldn't Have to Hide to be Safe', 5% of respondents cited race and ethnicity as contributing factors. Further international research has also expanded on the connections between racism and homophobia. Gail Mason has explored the interplay between racial prejudices and anti-LGBTIQ prejudices and maintains that:

> Certainly, for those lesbians and gay men who are from a white/Anglo background, racism is unlikely to be an element in the attacks. But ... we need to question the assumption that when attacks are made against lesbians and gay men who are not white or not Anglo, the only issue of importance is sexuality.

If the two categories of race and ethnicity are combined for this Queensland study, as they were in the NSW report, a total of 7% of respondents cited this as a contributing factor. The participants in the Queensland study were more ethnically diverse, so this probably accounts for this marginal statistical difference between this state and New South Wales.

Disability

Disability was not a contributing factor explored in the 2003 NSW study, 'You Shouldn't Have to Hide to be Safe'. In this Queensland study, some respondents mentioned that they had been attacked on the basis of their HIV positive status. One respondent wrote that the violence had occurred because he was 'an out HIV positive man'.

Other Contributing Factors

Another one of the major 'other' factors that was mentioned by respondents was alcohol. As D, a female participant in the Toowoomba focus group, stated, 'Some people obviously feel threatened ... and make a few sly comments and that may escalate depending on how many drinks everyone in the group has had'.

A number of other respondents were clearly able to lay the blame for the incident entirely on the psychological profiles of the perpetrators. One wrote that the incident had occurred because 'people are crazy', while another wrote that the perpetrator had been a 'wanky redneck'. Another wrote, 'He was short. Short man syndrome!'.

Single and Ongoing Most Recent Incidents

Three hundred and seventy-one respondents (64% of those who had specified recent homophobic or transphobic harassment or violence wrote that the incident had been a single one. One hundred and fifty-two respondents (26%) wrote that it had been repeated or an ongoing incident. Sixty respondents (10%) did not provide an answer. This data is presented in Figure 3.10.

Based on these figures, more Queensland respondents were suffering greater rates of ongoing abuse than NSW individuals. According to the 2003 NSW report, 'You Shouldn't Have to Hide to be Safe', 80% of respondents said the incident had been a single or one-off incident, while 19% reported the harassment or violence as being ongoing. The Queensland figures are more reflective of the 2008 Victorian study, Coming Forward, where 75% of respondents reported that their experience was a one-off incident, while 27% reported that it was one in a series of repeated offences.

Injuries and Impact of Most Recent Incident

The most frequent injury cited by respondents was psychological or emotional distress, with 251 people (43% of the 583 respondents who experienced homophobic or transphobic violence in the past two years) reporting that they had experienced this. Sixty respondents (10%)

Was the most recent incident a single incident or part of a series of ongoing incidents?

▨ Single Incident   ■ Repeated/Ongoing incident

26%

64%

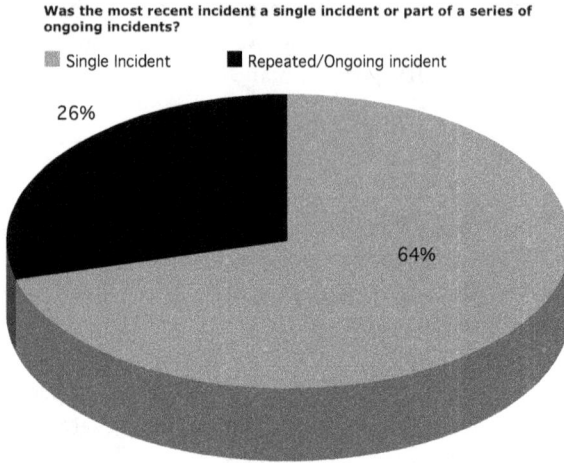

Figure 3.10
Single and ongoing most recent incidents.

reported cuts, abrasions and bruises. Eighteen respondents (3%) reported loss of consciousness. Eleven respondents (2%) reported broken bones. Thirty-eight respondents (7%) reported other physical or mental health problems. Fifty-two individuals (9%) did not provide an answer. These statistics are shown in Figure 3.11.

The psychological and emotional distress caused by homophobia and transphobia was outlined by many victims. One respondent described how they now '... felt the need to carry a gun or taser with me (which is not natural at all)'.

One respondent wrote that they now experienced 'social isolation, a fear of talking to new people, [and were] afraid to be me'. Another wrote that they had an 'anxiety attack and ongoing anxiety attacks linked to fears of being alone in public'. Another seven different respondents described depression, anxiety and post-traumatic stress disorders. One respondent wrote that the abuse had caused them to feel 'worthless, get really depressed and attempt suicide'.

The mental health consequences of harassment and violence against LGBTIQ individuals has been documented by Linda Garnets, Gregory Herek and Barrie Levy, who conclude that '... common behavioural and somatic reactions to victimisation include sleep disturbances and night-mares, headaches, diarrhoea, uncontrollable crying, agitation and restless-ness, increased use of drugs and deterioration in personal relationships'.

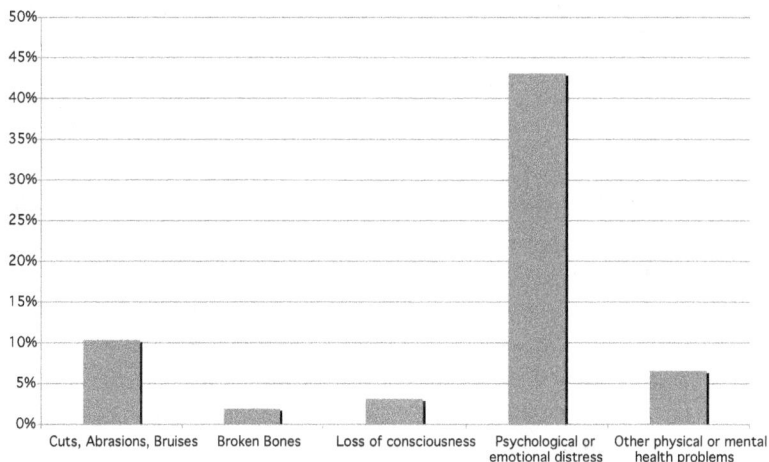

Figure 3.11
Injuries and impact of most recent incident.

E, an Indigenous participant in the Cairns focus group, outlined the toll a lifetime of transphobia took on his cousin. 'She was transgender and just a lot of the pain she's had to go through to be herself and be accepted, it's just not fair. But the way she dealt with it was through drugs, not even alcohol, just drugs, so she could get away from it for a while.'

One respondent described both psychological and physical issues. 'I developed agoraphobia for a time and became severely anxious in social situations, sometimes getting panic attacks where I was admitted to hospital for severe chest pains. [I also received] a black eye, cut eye lid and bruises to my face and shoulder.' Medical treatment such as stitches to wounds were also mentioned.

One respondent wrote that the incident they had experienced with regard to violent homophobia in their place of residence 'caused me a heart attack and another stressful fainting attack resulting in hospitalisation'. This respondent was upset that Queensland Housing, who had managed the housing situation, had not taken further action against the perpetrator.

Medical Attention Required After Most Recent Incident

Thirty-nine respondents (7% out of the 583 respondents who reported homophobic or transphobic abuse in the last two years) wrote that they had gone to see a doctor or had been an outpatient after the incident. Eighteen respondents (3%) had required hospital admission. Twenty-two respondents (4%) had required basic first aid by themselves or others. Four hundred and forty-eight respondents (77%) had not required medical attention. Fifty-six respondents (10%) did not say whether medical attention was needed. These statistics are displayed in Figure 3.12.

In the 2008 report, *Coming Forward*, 14% of respondents reported requiring some form of medical attention. This figure matches the statistics revealed during this Queensland study.

Some respondents provided further information about the treatment they had required. One wrote that he was 'hospitalised due to the beating'. One respondent described the extensive facial reconstructive surgery he had undergone. Another respondent wrote about receiving stitches in a hospital situation.

Time Off Work or Study Required after Most Recent Incident

Sixty-two respondents (11% out of the 583 respondents who reported homophobic or transphobic abuse in the last two years) wrote that they had to take time off work as a result, while 25 respondents (4%) reported taking time of study and 20 respondents (3%) took time off from 'other' commitment. Four hundred and thirty-five respondents (75%) reported that they did not take time off. Forty-one respondents (7%) did not provide an answer. These statistics are given in Figure 3.13.

These results are comparable to the 2008 Victorian study, *Coming Forward*. In that study, just over 15% of respondents took time off work as a consequence and nearly 4% reported taking time off study.

The written responses to this Queensland survey that specified 'other' illuminated the broad impact that homophobic and transphobic abuse and violence could have on its victims. One respondent described having 'to spend time out of social company due to humiliation'. Another said 'I am not currently working/studying but it has affected me socially and mentally and has caused my depression to relapse and now I am not in a position to work or study'. Another respondent stated they had not had time off from work but 'it was very embarrassing to have to go to work like that'.

A number of respondents wrote that they had resigned from their employment as a result of the homophobic or transphobic abuse and harassment. Several respondents simply wrote 'I resigned'. One summed up the continuing cost of homophobic and transphobic harassment and violence by citing a subsequent 'loss of livelihood, loss of career and employment opportunity'.

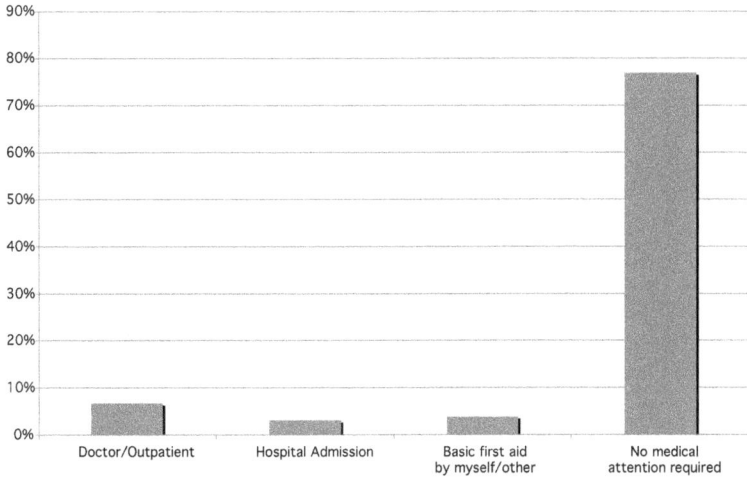

Figure 3.12
Types of medical attention required.

Conclusion

LGBTIQ respondents reported a high prevalence of homophobic and transphobic violence both over the course of a lifetime and during the last two years. This chapter has expanded on the profile of harassment and violence outlined in the preceding chapter. Fifty-three per cent of survey respondents reported experiencing homophobic or transphobic harassment or violence in the past two years. This abuse took place in a variety of circumstances and there were also differences in the way that individuals of varying gender identities experienced this prejudice.

Overall though, a number of important themes were observed in both this chapter and the preceding one. Verbal abuse was the most common form of prejudice experienced by LGBTIQ individuals, although a number of other forms of abuse were recorded. Public streets and LGBTIQ-identified areas were particularly likely to locations where homophobic and transphobic violence occurred.

The human cost of this abuse and harassment, including psychological, physical, and economic loss, was outlined by many respondents. A number of respondents noted that they did not expect to ever fully recover from some incidents of abuse. It is hoped though, that the profile of harassment and violence outlined in this and the previous chapter can

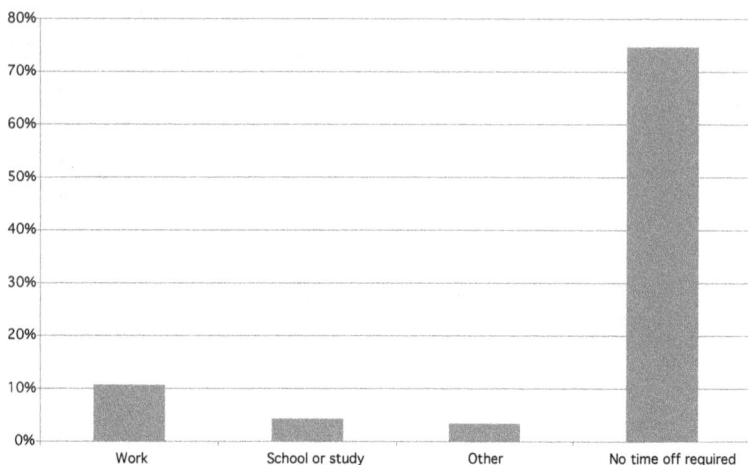

Figure 3.13
Time off work or study required.

be used to better influence police responses, victim support and improved means of targeting homophobia and transphobia in Queensland.

Endnotes

1   William Leonard and others, *Coming Forward: The Underreporting of Heterosexist and Same Sex Partner Abuse in Victoria* (Melbourne: Australian Research Centre in Sex, Health and Society, La Trobe, 2008), p.24.

2   New South Wales Attorney General's Department, '*You Shouldn't Have to Hide to be Safe': A Report on Homophobic Hostilities and Violence Against Gay Men and Lesbians in New South Wales* (Sydney: New South Wales Attorney General's Department, Crime Prevention Division, 2003), p.36; Leonard and others, *Coming Forward*, p.24.

3   See Linda Garnets, Gregory Herek and Barrie Levey, 'Violence and Victimization of Lesbians and Gay Men: Mental Health Consequences' in G. Herek and K. Berrill, eds., *Hate Crimes: Confronting Violence Against Lesbians and Gay Men* (Newbury Park, California: Sage Publications, 1992), pp. 207-226; C. Kitzinger, 'Speaking of Oppression: Psychology, Politics and the Language of Power' in E. D. Rothblum and L. A. Bond, eds., *Preventing Heterosexism and Homophobia* (Thousand Oaks, California: Sage, 1996), pp.3-19.

4   Australian Bureau of Statistics, 'Crime and Safety Australia, April 2005' <http://www.abs.gov.au/AUSSTATS/abs@.nsf/productsbyCatalogue/669C5A99 7EAED891CA2568A900139405/> (accessed 2 March 2010)

5   Martin Kantor, *Homophobia: Description, Development, and Dynamics of Gay Bashing* (London: Praeger, 1998), pp.52-62.

6   Australian Bureau of Statistics, 'Crime and Safety Australia, April 2005'
    <http://www.abs.gov.au/AUSSTATS/abs@.nsf/productsbyCatalogue/669C5A99
    7EAED891CA2568A900139405/> (accessed 2 March 2010)

7   Gail Mason, *The Spectacle of Violence: Homophobia, Gender and Knowledge*
    (London: Routledge, 2002), p.40.

8   Tarynn M. Witten and A. Evan Eyler, 'Hate Crimes and Violence Against the
    Transgendered', *Peace Review*, Vol. 11, (1999), p.461.

9   Leonard, Mitchell, Pitts and Patel, *Coming Forward*, p.25.

10 Gregory M. Herek, Jeanine C. Cogan, J. Roy Gillis and Eric R. Glunt,
    'Correlates of Internalised Homophobia in a Community Sample of Lesbians
    and Gay Men', *Journal of the Gay and Lesbian Medical Association*, Vol. 2
    (1997).

11 Iain R. Williamson, 'Internalized Homophobia and Health Issues Affecting
    Lesbians and Gay Men', *Health Education Research*, Vol. 15 (2000), p.80.

12 Herek, Cogan, Gillis and Glunt, 'Correlates of Internalised Homophobia in a
    Community Sample of Lesbians and Gay Men', p.19.

13 New South Wales Attorney General's Department, 'You Shouldn't Have to Hide
    to be Safe', p.41.

14 Leonard, Mitchell, Pitts and Patel, *Coming Forward*, p.26.

15 Darryl Scott, 'Everyone has the Right to be Able to Walk Safe in within their
    Community', Valley Walksafe Project June-November (report provided courtesy
    of author).

16 New South Wales Attorney General's Department, *'You Shouldn't Have to Hide
    to be Safe'*, p. 37; Leonard, Mitchell, Pitts and Patel, *Coming Forward*, p.30.

17 Joseph Harry, 'Conceptualising Anti-Gay Violence' in Herek and Berrill, *Hate
    Crimes*, p.118.

18 New South Wales Attorney General's Department, *'You Shouldn't Have to Hide
    to be Safe'*, p.39.

19 Ibid.

20 J. Irwin, *The Pink Ceiling is Too Low: Workplace Experiences of Lesbians, Gay
    Men and Transgender People* (Sydney: Australian Centre for Lesbian and Gay
    Research, University of Sydney, 1999).

21 Robert J. Hill, ed., *Challenging Homophobia and Heterosexism: Lesbian, Gay,
    Bisexual, Transgender, and Queer Issues in Organizational Settings* (San
    Francisco: Jossey-Bass, 2006).

22 'Assaults Increase at Queensland Train Stations', ninemsn website,
    <http://www.news.ninesmn. com.au/national/987218/assaults-increase-at-qld-
    train-stations> (accessed 17 January 2010).

23 See for example, Gregory M. Herek, 'Heterosexuals' Attitudes Towards
    Lesbians and Gay Men: Correlates and Gender Differences', *Journal of Sex
    Research*, Vol. 25, (1988), pp.451-477; M. Davies, 'Correlates of Negative
    Attitudes Towards Gay Men: Sexism, Male Role Norms and Male Sexuality',
    Journal of Sex Research, Vol. 41, (2004), pp.259-266.

24 New South Wales Attorney General's Department, *'You Shouldn't Have to Hide
    to be Safe'*, p.42.

25 Ibid., p.42.

26 Angelique C. Harris, 'Marginalization by the Marginalized: Race, Homophobia, Heterosexism and "the Problem of the 21st Century"', *Journal of Gay and Lesbian Social Services*, Vol. 21, (October 2009), pp.430-448.

27 Gail Mason, 'Heterosexed Violence: Typicality and Ambiguity' in Gail Mason and Stephen Tomsen, eds, *Homophobic Violence* (Annandale, New South Wales: Hawkins Press, 1997), p.25.

28 New South Wales Attorney General's Department, *'You Shouldn't Have to Hide to be Safe'*, p.38.

29 Leonard, Mitchell, Pitts and Patel, *Coming Forward*, p.28.

    Linda Garnetts, Gregory M. Herek and Barrie Levy, 'Violence and Victimization of Lesbians and Gay Men: Mental Health Consequences', *Journal of Interpersonal Violence*, Vol. 5 (1990), p.367.

30 Leonard, Mitchell, Pitts and Patel, *Coming Forward*, p.28.

31 Ibid, p.29.

Profiles of Perpetrators

Mel, a female in her early 20s who participated in the Sunshine Coast focus group and who has experienced various forms of homophobic harassment, observed that, in her experience, women were less likely than men to perpetuate homophobic and transphobic violence. Furthermore, she asserted that 'I guess with females, if we cop any homophobia from them, there is not going to be a violent undertone in general'.

Mel's observation is borne out by the data gathered in this survey. Women have certainly perpetuated disturbing incidents of homophobic and transphobic harassment and violence — yet male perpetrators significantly outnumber female perpetrators. The question of which individuals are most likely to perpetuate homophobic and transphobic harassment and violence is one of vital social importance. An awareness of likely perpetrators means that educational programs and policing initiatives can be better targeted towards these individuals. The information provided in response to this survey in relation to the most recent incident of homophobic or transphobic harassment or violence provides substantial information about which individuals are most likely to engage in homophobic or transphobic behaviour. It is hoped that this information can be used positively to reduce these types of harassment and violence. Strategies that can subsequently target these individuals are addressed in the concluding chapter of this book.

The 583 respondents to this survey who had experienced homophobic or transphobic violence or harassment in the last two years were asked to give details about the most recent incident. This chapter is based upon an analysis of those most recent experiences. As Figure 4.1. displays, out of the 551 people who indicated the gender of the perpetrators, 404 respondents (73%) said the perpetrator/s was male only. Eighty-eight respondents (16%) reported both male and female perpetrators. Fifty-five respondents (ten%) said the perpetrator/s was female

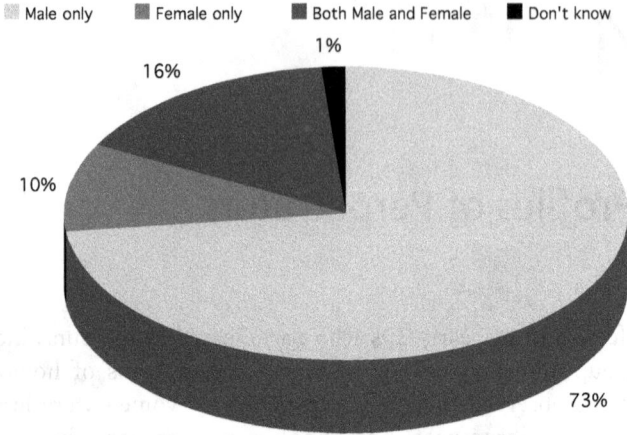

Figure 4.1
Gender of perpetrators.

only. Seven respondents (1%) did not know the gender of the perpetrator. Twenty-nine respondents (5%) did not report the perpetrator's gender.

It is worth noting that men are generally much more likely to commit violent crimes than women.[1] The data collected in this study, which indicate that males are more likely than females to perpetuate homophobic and transphobic harassment and violence, are consistent with this and with both international and national studies exploring homophobia and transphobia.[2] Gregory Herek, who has written extensively on correlations between gender roles and sexual prejudice in the United States of America, found a 'consistent tendency for heterosexual males to express more hostile attitudes than heterosexual females, especially towards gay men'.[3]

Michael Flood and Clive Hamilton, who surveyed nearly 25,000 Australians in a 2003–2004 study, found that 'men are far more likely than women to feel that homosexuality does not have moral legitimacy, and this gender gap in attitudes persists across age, socioeconomic, educational and regional divides'.[4] Gail Mason, who has written extensively about homophobic violence, has concluded that the predominant perpetuators of anti-lesbian and anti-gay violence are males.[5] Stephen Tomsen maintains that the overrepresentation of males has 'links to the masculinity of perpetrators'.[6]

The 2003 NSW study, *You Shouldn't Have to Hide to be Safe*, also found that males were significantly overrepresented as the perpetrators of homophobic and transphobic violence.[7] In that study, 77% of perpetrators were male, a figure that is remarkably close to the 73% ratio of male perpetrators revealed in this Queensland survey.[8] The 2003 NSW study also found that female-only perpetrators formed only 5% of all perpetrators, a figure very similar to the 9% of female perpetrators reported in this Queensland study.[9]

A growing body of research indicates that transphobia is deeply intertwined with homophobia, as both prejudices are driven by fears of any form of deviation from the norm of reproductive heterosexuality.[10] Heterosexual males have shown a particular resistance to any challenge to the binary division of gender upon which masculine cultural and political hegemony and privilege are based. As Jill Nagoshi, Katherine Adams, HeatherTerrell and Eric Hill have argued:

> Some men's anxieties about their masculinity are activated when these men are confronted with non-traditional gender manifestations, whether of gender identity, gender roles, or sexual preference. This anxiety, in turn, appears to promulgate both transphobia and homophobia.[11]

As a considerable number of historians have observed, Australia's national culture has rested on a number of exaggerated masculine stereotypes, including rugged pioneers of the bush, soldiers, and surf lifesavers.[12] The aggressive masculinity of early Australia has had significant implications on the development of an Australian model of homophobia and transphobia.

Y, a participant in the Sunshine Coast focus group, reported that violence 'Up here more broadly is worse than it is in other places from some of the information I have to hand. The surf culture is very hypermasculine up here, I think'. Y also said:

> Clearly if there was a heterosexual couple and you were the only people there, then you could be the focus of violence. But if the young boys had a choice between a heterosexual couple and the young boy who's just come out in drag, the young boy in drag would be the easier target and would also be the more threatening image for their sense of masculinity.

The idea of masculinity being threatened by difference was raised by a number of survey respondents and participants in focus groups. One male participant from the Sunshine Coast focus group said it's 'anybody that sticks out ... Queensland is well known for it. You have got to be the same or else'.

A substantial number of both participants in various focus groups and survey respondents recounted incidents of heterosexual men perpetrating homophobic and transphobic harassment and abuse. One female respondent recounted sitting on the side of a road with a friend when 'this drunk guy started yelling "fucking lesbians" as he walked by'. Another respondent was verbally abused by a male in a taxi, who she remembered yelling out 'fuck you dyke, why don't you go fuck a chick!'

K, a male respondent from the Cairns focus group, felt that male perpetrators were much more likely to engage in homophobic behaviour when they were with other men, rather than with females. He said, 'Often outside of the gay bar, they'll be walking past and they're looking at these guys and they realise they're poofters and they're going to say something and then the girlfriend says don't you dare. It's the acceptability. When they're with their mates they'll say it but when they're with their mum or their girlfriend they won't say it'.

Some female respondents felt that some groups of heterosexual men were likely to engage in harassment and violence when their romantic or sexual advances were spurned. Shana, a female participant in the Brisbane focus group aged in her late 20s, said that she felt a high proportion of harassment and abuse came from 'young heterosexual guys, looking at girls' who could become 'very inappropriate and very abusive' when their interest was not reciprocated. One respondent reported that 'a drunken male outside McDonalds verbally abused us, made sexual gestures, flashed his genitals and threatened to hit our car with an object he was holding' before he 'suggested we should have sex with him'.

Donna, a participant in the Toowoomba focus group, aged in her 20s, described perpetrators of homophobic harassment as 'sexist and homophobic. You're there for titillation. Then when you don't respond to things like "Kiss" and whatever, then it's like "Fucking dykes"'. As Stephen Tomsen and Gail Mason argue, many of the comments made by the male perpetrators of homophobia 'reflect a naively essentialist view that heterosexual desire could be coaxed out of any woman who identifies as lesbian'.[13]

Statistics show that male victims were particularly likely to report being attacked by other men. Eighty per cent of male respondents who had experienced homophobic or transphobic violence in their lifetime reported that the perpetrator/s had been male only. Male-to-female transgendered respondents were also much more likely to be assaulted or harassed by male perpetrators, with 75% of these respondents reporting that they had been harassed or abused by male only perpetrator/s. All female to male transgendered respondents reported that the perpetrator had been male. Table 4.1 presents these data.

Arranging the data according to the gender of the perpetrator and the sexuality of the victim also shows a very pronounced tendency for most homophobic and transphobic attacks to be conducted by men only. As shown in Table 4.2, this was particularly the case for the 181 gay respondents, who reported that 80% of cases of harassment and violence were conducted by men only, with only 4% being conducted by women only. Similarly though, lesbian, bisexual and those who identified as 'other', all reported that abuse was more likely to be perpetuated by men. Specifically, 157 lesbian respondents (68%), 36 bisexual respondents (61%) and 30 'other' respondents (77%) identified the perpetrator/s as male.

While more harassment or violence was conducted by men, many respondents outlined their experiences with female perpetuators. International studies have tended to show that women who do engage in homophobic behaviour are equally homophobic towards both gay men and lesbian women.[14] This is different to homophobic men, who tend to display greater levels of homophobia towards gay men than they do towards lesbian women.[15] Michael Flood and Clive Hamilton's extensive survey has also confirmed this to be the case within an Australian context.[16]

Table 4.1
Gender of Perpetrators and Gender of Victim

	Male	Female	Transgender M2F	Transgender F2M	Other
Male only	80%	67%	75%	100%	77%
Female only	4%	15%	13%	0%	8%
Both male and female	14%	18%	13%	0%	8%
Don't know	2%	1%	0%	0%	8%

Table 4.2
Gender of Perpetrators by Sexuality of Victim

	Lesbian	Gay	Bisexual	Other
Male only	68%	80%	61%	77%
Female only	14%	4%	15%	8%
Both male and female	17%	14%	22%	10%
Don't know	0%	2%	2%	5%

One male respondent reported that in his experience, homophobic harassment was 'fairly common' and that it 'seems to be [conducted by] single young ladies who have no men present with them'. Another male respondent reported that he had been verbally harassed by two women with children when he was walking along his street with his partner when the women and children 'started yelling "faggots" at us'. Another male from Brisbane, who had gone to the Southbank cinemas with his partner to see the film, *Milk*, about the life of Harvey Milk, the pioneering gay American politician, was confronted by a 'woman screaming to the group about gay people burning in hell'.

On occasion, female perpetrators could escalate the level of harassment and instigate and incite violence. One respondent reported that '... a girl turned around and punched me in the stomach for no apparent reason. I pushed her away and then her boyfriend punched me in the face'.

N, a female participant from the Sunshine Coast focus group in her early 20s, reported that a couple of years earlier, after some female acquaintances became aware she was attracted to women, one girl 'got it into her head that I liked her as a lesbian thing ... Then for whatever reason, she pushed me into the pool and tried to keep me there for a really long time'. N also felt that women were likely to engage in rumours and innuendo about other people's sexuality.

M, a participant at the Sunshine Coast focus group, found that older women were more likely to make homophobic comments. She said older women had told her that she '... should be ashamed of yourself ... you should be with a man, create your children ... Even though there weren't any hurtful words in that ... it is still hurtful'.

As Figure 4.2 shows, most perpetrators did not act alone. Two hundred and fifty-five out of 551 respondents (46%) to this question reported that there had been two or three perpetrators, while a further 107 respondents (19%) reported that there had been four or more perpetrators. One hundred and forty-four respondents (26%) wrote that there had been one perpetrator. Forty-five respondents (8%) were unsure as to how many perpetrators there had been. Thirty-two respondents (6% of the 583 respondents who recorded a most recent incident) did not provide a response. These statistics are similar to the New South Wales findings from the *You Shouldn't Have to Hide to be Safe* report from 2003. In that report, 65% of respondents said there had been two, three, four or more than four perpetrators involved.[17]

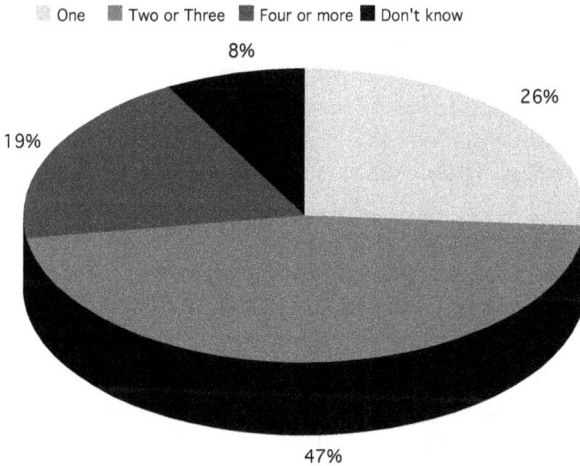

Figure 4.2
Number of perpetrators.

A number of participants found that harassment was more likely to occur when perpetrators were in groups. Mel, a participant in the Sunshine Coast focus group described being with a group of other lesbians when a ute full of men drove past and threw eggs at them. G, a male participant from the Townsville focus group, had people yelling abuse at him from cars as he walked towards the Sovereign Hotel, a popular gay venue in that city.

M, a female participant from the Sunshine Coast, described being out wearing a rainbow-coloured t-shirt while stopping at an ATM machine in the main street of Nambour at around 6:30 pm. She said, 'A car of young men went past yelling out "Fucking weirdo"'. Although she yelled back at them, she then realised '... there were six of them in the car ... I didn't know if they would do a u-turn or what'. J, a middle-aged member of the Gold Coast focus group, said that harassment was 'always in groups. Pack mentality. These young guys. Never one by themselves'.

S, a participant of the Townsville focus group, was threatened with attack by a group of three males after he left the West End Hotel. He was with his partner when three men, two who appeared to be in their 30s and one who appeared to be in his 20s, came towards them acting aggressively. S and his partner managed to run back to the Hotel where they were able to avoid their attackers.

A, a male participant at the Gold Coast focus group, was attacked by a group of men at the Palm Beach beat at around 1.00 am on a Friday morning. He recalls maybe 'half a dozen' people coming out from the darkness behind the toilet block and 'hurling broken pieces of pipe' at him. He said '... they hurled them at me, they smashed every piece of glass in my car. There wasn't one single piece of glass that wasn't broken. They hurled it with such force'.

One transgender woman reported that 'I went to the convenience store at night as I wanted milk for my coffee the next morning. As I got out of my car, a group of about seven male persons began to harass me regarding my appearance as a trans woman at that particular time'.

While the perpetrators were more likely to be in groups, the victims were not. As Chapters 2 and 3 outlined, they were more likely to be alone. Out of the 465 respondents who indicated who they were with when their most recent incident of harassment or violence took place, most respondents (42%) indicated they were alone. A further 34% indicated that they were with a same-sex partner.

Table 4.3
Number of Perpetrators by Gender

	Male	Female	Transgender M2F	Transgender F2M	Other
One	26%	26%	38%	0%	15%
Two or three	48%	46%	25%	100%	31%
Four or more	17%	20%	38%	0%	38%
Don't know	9%	8%	0%	0%	15%

Table 4.4
Number of Perpetrators by Sexuality

	Lesbian	Gay	Bisexual	Other
One	27%	25%	24%	31%
Two or three	48%	50%	38%	28%
Four or more	20%	16%	21%	33%
Don't know	5%	9%	17%	78%

Table 4.3 and Table 4.4. show further information about the relationship between the number of perpetrators and the sexuality and gender identity of the victims. All female-to-male transgender respondents indicated that they were attacked in groups of two or three. A majority of male and female respondents also reported that they were attacked in groups of two or three. Male-to-female transgender respondents were equally likely to be attacked by either one person or four or more people.

As Table 4.3 shows, an overwhelming majority of respondents had no previous relationship with the perpetrator. Three hundred and ninety-five respondents (69%) out of 547 reported that the perpetrator was a stranger or someone with whom they did not share a prior relationship. Forty-seven respondents (9%) said that the perpetrator was a work colleague. Thirty-four respondents (6%) reported that it was a casual acquaintance. Fifteen respondents (3%) reported that the perpetrator was a neighbour. Eight respondents (1%) named a student or client as perpetrators. Two respondents listed housemates as the perpetrators. This is consistent with international research.[18]

Table 4.5 and Table 4.6 provide further information about the relationship between the victim and perpetrator/s. The evidence suggests that most homophobic and transphobic violence and harassment is conducted by per-

....

Table 4.5
Relationship to Perpetrator by Gender of Victim

	Male	Female	Transgender M2F	Transgender F2M	Other
Stranger/ no prior relationship	76%	70%	44%	100%	62%
Casual acquaintance	8%	5%	11%	0%	8%
Parent	0%	1%	11%	0%	0%
Sibling	0%	1%	0%	0%	0%
Other relative	0%	1%	0%	0%	0%
Housemate	1%	0%	0%	0%	0%
Neighbour	3%	2%	0%	0%	15%
Work colleague	5%	11%	33%	0%	8%
Teacher	0%	0%	0%	0%	0%
Student client	1%	2%	0%	0%	0%
Other	6%	7%	0%	0%	8%

....

Table 4.6

Relationship to Perpetrator by Sexuality of Victim

	Lesbian	Gay	Bisexual	Other
Stranger/no prior relationship	69%	79%	57%	74%
Casual acquaintance	4%	6%	17%	5%
Parent	1%	0%	0%	0%
Sibling	1%	0%	0%	0%
Other relative	1%	0%	2%	0%
Housemate	0%	0%	2%	0%
Neighbour	2%	3%	2%	8%
Work colleague	11%	6%	9%	8%
Teacher	0%	0%	0%	0%
Student client	3%	1%	0%	0%
Other	7%	4%	12%	5%

sons unknown to the victim. This supports previous research that indicates homophobic and transphobic attitudes are less severe when heterosexual individuals know homosexual or transgendered individuals.[19] This also reflects the findings of surveys undertaken in Victoria and New South Wales.

Most perpetrators who were known to respondents were known through the workplace. Institutional settings have been identified as a major problem for LBGTIQ individuals.[20] Workplace homophobia was identified as a major issue for LGBTIQ individuals in the 1999 Sydney report, *The Pink Ceiling is Too Low*.[21] The 2008 Victorian study, *Coming Forward*, found that 8% (rounded to the nearest percentage for consistency) of perpetrators in that state were drawn from the workplace. This closely mirrors the findings of this Queensland study, which found 9% of perpetrators were drawn from the workplace.

These findings indicate that homophobia and transphobia in the workplace is an issue of ongoing concern for LGBTIQ individuals. This was a point that was reiterated in responses to the survey and in all focus groups, by both male and female participants and by participants of a variety of sexual orientations and gender identities. In some instances, a culture of workplace prejudice made respondents reluctant to discuss their sexuality. J, a female participant from the Gold Coast focus group, reported that in the 1980s and 1990s, she had worked for 16 years as a customer service shift supervisor. She said, 'I couldn't tell any one of those [people I worked with] for 16 years that I was gay because they were narrow minded'.

One female respondent aged in her mid-20s from Brisbane noted that 'I am out at my workplace [as a lesbian] and people do make jokes at my expense'. Another female respondent, also from Brisbane aged in her late 20s, said that she felt she was making herself vulnerable towards harassment if she was to bring her female partner to work functions.

G, a middle-aged man from the Brisbane focus group, said that:

> You'd think there would be more tolerance in the Queensland public service because of standards and all that, but for my recent experiences in the last 12 months [in the Department of Primary Industries and Fisheries I] was on a short-term contract and they had an anti-discrimination seminar and I raised the issues of homosexuality and I may have been a bit more passionate about homosexuality than other issues ... and a few days later lewd comments were appearing in the men's toilets and there was an investigation and all that. You know, G sucks c...k, and all that. Right down from the field worker to senior management, their relationship to me changed overnight and I could no longer operate professionally in that sector of the workforce because of my homosexuality, and I was surprised that level of homophobia existed within a mainstream government department ... and they got away with it. No one was punished.

Another respondent wrote that he was 'vilified by work colleagues, conversation centred around my sexuality and how I performed sex and whether I was a top or bottom. The same colleagues submitted unjustified complaints about me to management'. Another respondent wrote that they had experienced 'derogatory comments, invasion of personal space, sexual harassment, [and had been] denied paid sick leave'. They also cited bullying, 'harassment, unfair treatment', were denied promotion and were transferred to workplaces where they 'would be isolated when attacked'. They were also abused in front of customers.

S, a transgender woman who participated in the Townsville focus group, also experienced harassment in the workplace on the grounds of her gender identity. She worked in agriculture and recalls that she 'got fired for being transsexual'. She said:

> We were in the middle of winter planting and I was fired because they didn't have enough work. I found out two days later by the bush telegraph that [the boss's] friends at the local community centre ... had been taking the piss out of him ... for employing a transsexual. So he fired me.

Some perpetrators occupied positions of social authority. One respondent noted that the 'medical doctor of my female partner refuses to acknowledge our relationship because she is married to a male person and constantly encourages my partner to leave the relationship stating to my partner that things won't get better for her unless she leaves the relationship'. Y, a male participant in the Sunshine Coast focus group aged in his early 30s, outlined an experience that had occurred at a medical centre when he was in his 20s. Y said he had glandular fever and had 'broken out in lumps'; however, the '... doctor just looked me up and down and said, it's probably AIDS. That's the first thing he said to me'.

Family relationships provided another terrain where homophobia and transphobia were expressed. Three respondents recorded a parent as being the perpetrator of homophobic or transphobic harassment or violence, a further three recorded a sibling as the perpetrator and a further five respondents described another relative as the perpetrator. In total, this meant that 2% of overall respondents to this question experienced homophobia or transphobia from a family member.

A number of participants provided accounts of homophobia and transphobia experienced from within the family system. G, a male participant in the Brisbane focus group said that:

> I think there's a high degree of unspoken violence in families if you're going through the process of identifying your sexuality. From my own experiences, and those of others I know, their understanding of accepting their sexuality, primarily based on their fears of rejection from one's family, is enormous and high rates of teenage suicide are a direct correlation between families' inability to accept their child's sexuality.

Another male participant in the Brisbane focus group noted that some members of his family were 'incredibly homophobic'. He said that 'my brother's threatened to kill me if I ever set foot near him or the kids'.

Some respondents described family members threatening to challenge their custody of their children as a result of their sexuality. One female respondent from Brisbane reported that 'My husband and his family have threatened quite a lot about taking the children and stuff if I do sort of come out'.

A Brisbane respondent described a number of older male acquaintances, who had 'come out' later in life and have 'found themselves excluded' from the family's estate because 'their elderly parents have discriminated against them in terms of denying them a fair share'. Other respondents described more subtle forms of homophobia. One female respondent from Brisbane talked about family members practising 'exclusion and avoidance'.

In the survey, 35 respondents (6%) selected the 'other' option when asked to describe the relationship to the perpetrator/s and 32 respondents wrote in a response detailing the reelationship. There was some overlap with members of family groups as perpetrators. Three respondents described the perpetrator of harassment or violence as an ex-husband and a fourth female respondent reported the perpetuator as her 'ex-male partner'. Other respondents noted that the homophobia or transphobia had occurred within the context of an educational institution. One listed 'school peers' as perpetrators, while another described 'people I went to school with'. Another respondent experienced homophobia from a 'principal/mentor teacher for a university prac experience'.

Some respondents described abuse that had come from within their social, religious or community networks. A male participant from the Sunshine Coast focus group, who had previously been a pastor, received verbal harassment from members of his former church. He said, 'It's like they'll see me down the beach and they will yell and scream at me. I have been thrown over the coals here in the plaza just walking through the main eating area and people are yelling at me, saying that I am going to hell and all that kind of stuff'.

Influence of Drugs and Alcohol

A considerable number of participants at various focus groups mentioned that alcohol was a factor in homophobic and transphobic violence and harassment. Again, this is a factor that has been noted in other Australian studies.[22] K, a male participant from the Gold Coast focus group, asserted that:

> I would definitely say when there's alcohol involved … it either lowers people's inhibitions but also [with] some other groups, it brings them to a fighting capacity. They just want to have a go at someone … But if you try to confront them, you could probably get flattened out. That's alcohol because they're just coming out of the clubs … It gives them that extra boost, they think they can take on the whole world. So alcohol is one of the biggest dangers I can think of.

B, a female participant at the Gold Coast focus group also agreed. She declared, 'Once it hits about three o'clock and the clubs are getting out [you hear] "Oh, lesbian! I'll show you what a real man is like"'. S, a female respondent from the Brisbane focus group, aged in her mid-20s, said that in rural areas '… sometimes you get scared of how much alcohol some guy has had … because you know if you say, oh fuck off, you're afraid of what's going to come next'.

E, a transsexual participant in the Townsville focus group, said that 'Flinders Street East, for arguments sake, at five o'clock in the morning, is not a good place to walk because of the fact ... that there's so many drunks at that stage that ... you're liable to get attacked. Your safety would be compromised by stupidity and alcohol'.

K, a participant in the Cairns focus group, said that 'I feel quite safe being gay during the day. I can go anywhere being gay, being out. But once it gets to night, the alcohol, the homophobia comes out in men'.

Women who engaged in homophobic or transphobic harassment or violence were also often identified as affected by alcohol. One male participant in the Brisbane focus group said that, in his experience, harassment tended to come from '... the young women, the young unattractive, larger women in groups that are drunk'. This would suggest that insecurities fuelled by alcohol were serving as a motivating factor in such cases.

Conclusion

Quantitative and qualitative information gathered during the course of this research provided a relatively consistent picture of those who are most likely to engage in homophobic or transphobic harassment or violence. Data revealed about the characteristics of perpetrators of homophobic and transphobic violence and harassment mirrors closely findings in other Australian states and also international research. The average perpetrator in Queensland is remarkably similar to the perpetrator characterised in a 1990 American study by Joseph Harry. He described the perpetrators of this violence as 'very largely male, in their late teens or 20s, strangers to the victim(s) in groups, and not engaging in violence for profit'.[23]

While this information provides a solid indication of groups who need to be provided with anti-homophobic and anti-transphobic education and information, strategies should not be solely targeted towards the overrepresented demographics. It is evident that respondents experienced anti-gay, anti-lesbian and anti-transgender prejudice in different forums and by a variety of perpetrators. Family members, work colleagues and casual acquaintances were all mentioned in the course of this survey and its associated focus groups.

Endnotes

1   Australian Institute of Criminology, 'Selected Offender Profiles' <http://www.aic.gov.au/publications/current%20series/facts/120/2008/4%20 selected%20 offender %20profiles.aspx#alleged (accessed 3 March 2010)

2   See, for example, Joseph Harry, 'Conceptualizing Anti-Gay Violence', *Journal of Interpersonal Violence*, Vol. 5 (1990), pp.350-358; Gregory M. Herek, 'Gender

Gaps in Public Opinion About Lesbians and Gay Men', *Public Opinion Quarterly*, Vol. 66 (1992), pp.40-66; David Plummer, *One of the Boys: Masculinity, Homophobia and Modern Manhood* (New York: Harrington Park Press, 1994).

3   Gregory M. Herek, 'Heterosexuals' Attitudes Towards Lesbians and Gay Men: Correlates and Gender Differences', *Journal of Sex Research*, Vol. 25, (November 1988), p.451.

4   Michael Flood and Clive Hamilton, 'Mapping Homophobia in Australia' in Shirleene Robinson, ed., *Homophobia: An Australian History* (Annandale, New South Wales: Federation Press, 2008), p.16.

5   Gail Mason, 'Violence Against Lesbians and Gay Men', *Crime Prevention Today*, No. 2 (Canberra: Australian Institute of Criminology, 1993), p.3.

6   Stephen Tomsen, 'Hate Crimes and Masculine Offending', *Gay and Lesbian Law Journal*, Vol. 10 (2001), p.34.

7   New South Wales Attorney General's Department, *You Shouldn't Have to Hide to be Safe: A Report on Homophobic Hostilities and Violence Against Gay Men and Lesbians in New South Wales* (Sydney: New South Wales Attorney General's Department, Crime Prevention Division, 2003), p.43.

8   Ibid.

9   Ibid.

10 Jill. L. Nagoshi, Katherine A. Adams, Heather K. Terrell and Eric D. Hill, 'Gender Differences in Correlates of Homophobia and Transphobia', *Sex Roles*, Vol. 59 (October 2008), p. 527.

11 Ibid., p.527.

12 Shirleene Robinson, 'Introduction' in Robinson, ed., *Homophobia: An Australian History*, p.5.

13 Stephen Tomsen and Gail Mason, 'Engendering Homophobia: Violence, Sexuality and Gender Conformity', *Journal of Sociology*, Vol. 37, (2001), p.262.

14 Mary E. Kite and B. E. Whitley Jr., 'Do heterosexual women and men differ in their attitudes towards homosexuality? A conceptual and methodological analysis' in G. M. Herek, ed., *Psychological Perspectives on Lesbians and Gay Issues, Vol. 4, Stigma and Sexual Orientation: Understanding Prejudice Against Lesbians, Gay Men, and Bisexuals* (Thousand Oaks, California: Sage, 1998), pp.39-61.

15 Mary E. Kite, 'Individual Differences in Males' Reactions to Gay Males and Lesbians', *Journal of Applied Social Psychology*, Vol. 22 (1992).

16 Flood and Hamilton, *Mapping Homophobia in Australia*, p.27.

17 New South Wales Attorney General's Department, *You Shouldn't Have to Hide to be Safe*, p.43.

18 Gregory M. Herek and J. P. Capitanio, '"Some of My Best Friends": Intergroup Contact, Concealable Stigma and Heterosexuals' Attitudes Toward Gay Men and Lesbians', *Personality and Social Psychology Bulletin*, Vol. 22 (1996).

19 Sheela Raja and Joseph P. Stokes, 'Assessing Attitudes Towards Lesbians and Gay Men: The Homophobia Scale', *International Journal of Sexuality and Gender Studies*, Vol. 3 (April 1998); Gregory M. Herek, 'The Psychology of Sexual Prejudice', *Current Directions in Psychological Sciences*, Vol. 9 (February 2000), pp.19-22.

20 Robert J. Hill, *Challenging Homophobia and Heterosexism: Lesbian, Gay, Bisexual, Transgender, and Queer Issues in Organizational Settings* (San Francisco: Praeger, 2006)

21 J. Irwin, *The Pink Ceiling is Too Low: Workplace Experiences of Lesbians, Gay Men and Transgender People* (Sydney: Australian Centre for Lesbian and Gay Research, University of Sydney, 1999)

22 New South Wales Attorney General's Department, *You Shouldn't Have to Hide to be Safe*, p.44.

23 Harry, *Conceptualising Anti-Gay Violence*, p.350.

CHAPTER 5

Seeking Help

This chapter explores the types of assistance sought by those who were victims of homophobic or transphobic abuse, harassment or violence. Only 143 respondents (25%) of the 583 who experienced homophobic or transphobic harassment or violence in the previous two years sought help While Chapter 6 explains the reasons why most victims of homophobic and transphobic harassment and violence currently do not seek assistance, it is important to recognise the avenues that individuals did seek help through, so that these channels can be better supported and promoted. It is also important to map the quality of assistance received. Thus, this chapter focuses on the help sought after the most recent incident of homophobic or transphobic harassment or violence. It makes observations about the organisations that individuals are most likely to seek help from. It also finds that individuals who report incidents to the police are also likely to seek assistance from other sources.

Types of Professional Assistance Sought

The data in Table 5.1 show the different organisations from whom individuals sought assistance following their most recent incident of homophobic or transphobic harassment or violence.[1] Seventy-two respondents (16%) reported the incident to the police or a liaison officer; 12 respondents (2%) sought assistance from the Gay and Lesbian Welfare Association Telephone Support; 17 respondents (3%) from the Queensland Anti-Discrimination Commission (ADCQ); seven respondents (1%) from the Queensland Association of Healthy Communities (QAHC); 14 respondents (2%) sought help from the LGBTIQ community or a LGBTIQ support group; seven respondents (1%) sought assistance from a sexual assault service; five respondents (1%) sought assistance from a community health service; and nine respondents (2%) sought assistance from Work Cover. Forty-eight respondents (8%) sought assistance from a counsellor, psychologist or social worker. This is significant as 43% of relevant respondents indicated the most recent incident caused them psychological or emotional distress. This accords with national studies.[2] As documented in Chapters 2 and 3, one of the lingering effects of homophobic or transphobic abuse, harassment or violence is its emotional and psychological damage.[3]

Three respondents (1%) sought assistance from a faith-based organisation and six respondents (1%) from the Victims of Crime Helpline, while 36 respondents (6%) sought assistance from other sources. These included reporting to a variety of organisations and individuals, such as lawyers, politicians, university queer support organisations and so forth.[4]

Quality of Assistance

Table 5.2 shows the experiences of respondents with the organisations to whom they reported their most recent incident. Although the numbers are too low to draw any inferences as to how supportive each of the organisations contacted was in providing assistance, most found the professional assistance they sought to be reasonably or very supportive. For example, of those who reported the incident to members of the police

....

Table 5.1
Source of Professional Assistance

The police	12%
Police lesbian, gay, bisexual, transgender, intersex (LGBTI) liaison officers	4%
Gay & Lesbian Welfare Association Telephone Support	2%
Queensland Anti-Discrimination Commission	3%
Queensland Association of Healthy Communities (formerly QuAC)	1%
Other gay, lesbian, bisexual, transgender community or support group	2%
Sexual assault service	1%
Community health service	1%
Work Cover	2%
Counsellor, psychologist or social worker	8%
Faith-based organisation	1%
Victims of Crime Helpline	1%
State government violence services	0%
Other	6%
Did not seek professional assistance	75%

....

Table 5.2
Support Levels of Professional Services

Quality of response	Not supportive	Reasonably supportive	Very supportive	No response
The police	25	23	19	5
Police lesbian, gay, bisexual, transgender, intersex (LGBTI) liaison officers	4	5	11	2
Gay & Lesbian Welfare Association Telephone Support	1	5	6	0
Queensland Anti-Discrimination Commission	4	3	9	1
Queensland Association of Healthy Communities (formerly QuAC)	2	1	4	0
Other gay, lesbian, bisexual, transgender community or support group	1	2	8	3
Sexual assault service	1	3	2	1
Community healthservice	0	2	3	0
Work Cover	4	2	2	1
Counsellor, psychologist or social worker	0	0	0	48
Faith-based organisation	0	0	3	0
Victims of Crime Helpline	0	4	2	0
State government violence services	1	0	0	0
Other	3	10	13	10

service, the majority found them to be reasonably (23 respondents, 32%) or very supportive (19 respondents, 26%) as opposed to those who found them not supportive (25 respondents, 35%). There was no response from five individuals (7%). The GLBTI liaison officers contacted were found to be reasonably (five respondents) or very supportive (11 respondents) in the majority of cases but not supportive (four respondents), with no responses from two respondents.

Almost all respondents who used the Gay and Lesbian Welfare Association Telephone Support found them to be reasonably (five respondents) or very supportive (six respondents) with one respondent finding them not supportive. The majority of individuals who sought assistance from ADCQ found them to be reasonably supportive (three respondents) or very supportive (nine respondents) with four respondents who found them not supportive and no response from one individual. The few individuals who approached QAHC found them reasonably (one respondent) or very supportive (four respondents) with only two respondents finding this organisation not supportive. Other LGBTIQ community or support groups were found to be very supportive in eight cases and reasonably supportive in two instances while just one respondent found them to be not supportive and three respondents did not provide an answer. The Sexual Assault Service was found to be reasonably supportive in three instances or very supportive in two cases while just one respondent found them not supportive and one respondent failed to respond to this follow up question. All respondents who approached community health services found them to be reasonably supportive (two respondents) or very supportive (three respondents). Those who sought workers' compensation for their injuries found them to be not supportive in four cases, reasonably supportive in two and very supportive in two other cases with no response from one respondent who sought assistance from this organisation.

There were no responses received from the 48 respondents who sought support from a counsellor, psychologist or social worker. This is extremely surprising but it is not possible to draw inferences from this. The three individuals who approached a faith-based organisation found them to be very supportive. The Victims of Crime Helpline was found to be reasonably (four respondents) or very (two respondents) supportive by those individuals who contacted them. One respondent contacting a state government violence service found it not to be supportive. Of those who sought assistance in other ways, the assistance they received was reasonably supportive in 10 instances, very supportive in another 13 and not supportive on three occasions. Ten respondents failed to respond to this question.

Respondents were given the opportunity to tell us about their experiences of professional services, if they wished. Fifty-three survey respondents took the opportunity to do so. While personal experiences with members of the Police Service and liaison officers are discussed in Chapters 6 and 7, respondents reported positive experiences with counsellors and psychologists which they described as reasonably or very supportive. One respondent indicated they sought support from a psychologist some months after the incident and found the 'services helpful as I was able to build more acceptance and confidence in my sexuality'. QAHC in Cairns was reported as having a very friendly and supportive staff, while one respondent indicated there was 'really nothing' QAHC could do in the circumstances of abuse they outlined.

One respondent reported that the:

Surf Club Manager and his committee were most concerned and totally regretted this happening and apologised to me in writing after giving the abusive member several warnings to stop or have his membership terminated which is ultimately what happened.

Another respondent expressed high satisfaction with a local Youth Centre, stating:

> The Cooloola Youth Centre was fantastic and thoroughly assisted me in many ways, including helping me to find a new place to live and connect me with support services in my new home. They even ensured the perpetrators were evicted from the property.

One respondent expressed dissatisfaction with a university counselling service as non-responsive to staff phone calls. They took one week to respond after a request for help was made. One respondent expressed positive experiences with LifeLine: 'LifeLine on a number of occasions has been a godsend. They have helped me through near suicide thoughts and gave me some sort of hope. As too did my therapist'. One respondentl found the Toowong private hospital post-traumatic stress disorder course very helpful. One respondent expressed their positive experiences with the ADCQ: 'Going through the Anti-Discrimination Commission is a good way to seek justice for this sort of discrimination' while another respondent acknowledged that there was 'nothing that ADCQ could really do' in the circumstances.

Respondents were also given an opportunity to explain how they determined to which organisation their complaint should be directed.[5] Some respondents indicated that they were referred to various other agencies by their physician, solicitor or another source of 'legal' advice. One individual replied: 'Unbelievable. I paid a lawyer $300 an hour; he was too scared to shake my hand once he found out I had HIV'. One respondent indicated they sought support from their union, the gay press, advice from friends, and a psychologist to help with 'all the angst'. Another respondent confirmed they sought assistance from multiple sources: 'Tried to search a range of support to meet complex needs caused by assault. Different agencies offered different services'. One respondent stated: 'No brainer. Discrimination. Go to the Commission'. Several respondents indicated they had prior knowledge of organisations through QAHC, or through having had contact with the Anti-Discrimination Commission at a Pride Rally. In one instance, mediation was suggested in an instance of homophobic or transphobic harassment or violence in a workplace situation. One individual indicated they were referred from a university to QAHC Rainbow Service.

In a rural focus group, one young lesbian participant stated she would also seek assistance from a local community support group. She felt, however, that there was little support from the local LGBTIQ community. As a consequence, she and her partner eventually formed their own organisation. She stated:

> After the whole you can't be my friend on Facebook, we don't want to work with you, I'm not even going to warrant your message with a response, you know, one of the members went down there to see what it was like with a couple of friends and stuff on Friday night because they were at another party ... So they turned up and we were like ... you're from the [local gay group] aren't you, you're here too ... I hear you only get eight people ... grilling her and harassing her and making her feel uncomfortable and excluded. She just went 'what the f...k is going on ... I thought this was a safe place to be but I might just go somewhere else' and that's an issue, like, 'so you didn't run it by me first, I'm the boss of every gay [here] ...'

Her partner added:

> They're obviously not going to listen to reason or be mature about anything and that's another problem I think is the level of maturity and levels of experience in community relationships ... They've been so closeted for so long and it's ... why would you want to be loud about it now, like ssshhh ... instead of saying 'it's great, we've been silent too long, this is great, we've got a safe place to go ...' We eventually organised a lesbian club to be out in the open because if someone hears about it, they see the sign on the chalkboard ... The good thing about it is it's marketed purely towards lesbians because there was a gap there and we needed to make sure that a safe place where even couples could go ... we've had a lot of people come to the events that haven't gone out in ten years but they've come out as a couple and had a good time and they keep coming back ... And gay guys came too.

A lesbian in the Sunshine Coast focus group said there is not a large group of community support organisations:

> It is an issue that on the Sunshine Coast, there is not a big known base of organisations, whether it's medical or whatever, that people can go. There are still a lot of homophobic doctors on the Sunshine Coast who as soon as you identify and my experience it is more with gay men. As soon as they identify that they have a same sex partner, the doctor changes his attitude bang and doesn't really — still sees a client, but doesn't seem to give two rats.

The homophobia and transphobia that many members of the LGBTIQ community experienced from the medical profession made some individuals reluctant to seek help from this avenue. A lesbian participant in the Sunshine Coast focus group noted that some doctors would not support or work with LGBTIQ patients. She said 'Yeah, [there are] doctors, dentists, massage therapists [etc.] on the Coast that will not go anywhere near someone who is LGBT[IQ]'.

It seems there is less support to assist LGBTIQ individuals in remote and regional areas, even among some tertiary educational institutions when individuals are subject to homophobic or transphobic harassment and violence. For example, in one regional focus group, a participant stated:

> We had a girl here — well she was here, she was in the university here … and she was doing nursing training. She's been hounded out, she's now doing off campus studies … She was transsexual. She was hounded out by the rest of the students and the faculty did not do anything to help her …

Another participant in that focus group indicated another university was fantastic 'with the services to the GLBT[IQ] community'.

Funding was an issue that impacted on the formation of some community-based support services. There was no funding to support the Anti-Violence Committee in Townsville that was set up after the bombing of the AIDS Council offices, nor was there any funding for a local support group for transsexuals, known as Transbridge. In these regional and rural areas, individuals have had to be imaginative and creative in forming groups without funding to serve as a support mechanism for the LGBTIQ community.

Many sought informal assistance from their partner, friend, family and relatives, etcetera, but a majority of 60% did not even seek any informal assistance, as shown in Table 5.3.

Conclusion

It is clear that the overwhelming majority of respondents did not report the incidents of abuse, harassment and/or violence to law enforcement or seek assistance from a community or other support mechanism, including

Table 5.3
Sources of Informal Assistance

Partner	14%
Friend	21%
Family, Relatives	7%
Passer-by	3%
Other	12%
Did not seek help	60%

family, partners and friends. As Chapter 6 explains, many respondents indicated they would be more likely to report an incident (and presumably seek other assistance) if they considered the incident to be more severe. This considered, the quantitative data provided throughout this book indicates that some respondents who had experienced serious forms of abuse did not seek assistance. Yet those who did seek assistance from any of these support based organisations, found them to be reasonably or very supportive with the exception of some legal and medical professionals. The wide array of individuals and organisations contacted after their most recent experience of homophobic or transphobic abuse or harassment is a testament to the fact that individuals have been subjected to such incidents in a variety of contexts, each of which required assistance from a diverse assortment of professional organisations and support groups as well as seeking legal advice and help from psychologists and counsellors.[6]

It is clear there are fewer such support systems outside the metropolitan Brisbane and Gold Coast areas. The rural and regional communities find it difficult to form support groups to assist LGBTIQ individuals, particularly after incidents of homophobic or transphobic verbal abuse, harassment and violence. Nonetheless, even within these communities, there have been sufficient informal networks established that have proven amazingly resilient in the face of ongoing abuse, harassment and widespread violence. The information in this chapter played an important role in shaping recommendations in Chapter 10 as to the availability of resources and development of awareness of the need for further support mechanisms (both formal and informal) in rural and regional communities.

Notes

1 The respondents to the survey were able to indicate they sought assistance from more than one organisation.

2 New South Wales Attorney General's Department, 'You Shouldn't Have to Hide to be Safe': A Report on Homophobic Hostilities and Violence Against Gay Men and Lesbians in New South Wales (Sydney: New South Wales Attorney General's Department, Crime Prevention Division, 2003), p.67.

3 See also Martin Kantor, Homophobia: Descriptions, Development, and Dynamics of Gay Bashing (London: Praeger, 1998); New South Wales Attorney General's Department, 'You Shouldn't Have to Hide to be Safe'; and William Leonard and others, Coming Forward: The Underreporting of Heterosexist Violence and Same Sex Partner Abuse in Victoria (Melbourne: The Australian Research Centre in Sex, Health and Society, La Trobe University, 2008).

4 There were 32 written responses (though 38 ticked the box 'Other') as to a variety of other individuals and organisations from which support or assistance was

sought, including, but not limited to, reporting the incident to Facebook, mother of the perpetrator, Residential Tenancies Authority, Small Claims Court, security guard, surf club manager, sex worker organisation, politicians (Department of Housing), Lifeline tele-counsellor was cited by two respondents, physician was cited by three people, Family Court, youth centre, higher level management in the workplace was cited by two individuals and one individual sought assistance from a work colleague. Five cited counsellors or mental health professionals, such as psychologists or social workers (in some instances at their schools or university), lawyer, gay websites where the thief had a profile, university queer support from colleagues, Club security, union, ATASQ, and a community member. One individual stated: 'Given ... the police were the perpetrators of harassment, I would not turn to them for help'.

5 Responses regarding complaints directed to the police and liaison officers have been excluded from this analysis as they are dealt with separately in Chapter 7.

6 Leonard and others, *Coming Forward*.

CHAPTER 6

The Unreported Incidents of Homophobic and Transphobic Violence and Harassment

Seventy-five per cent of respondents to this survey did not report their most recent experience of homophobic or transphobic abuse, harassment or violence to police or seek professional assistance. This rate of non-response matches a range of national and international studies, which have found that LGBTIQ individuals are significantly less likely than other victims of crimes to report harassment or violence.[1] This is particularly disturbing, given the deep damage that can be caused by homophobic and transphobic attacks.[2]

The main reasons that LGBTIQ individuals are less likely to report abuse are that a significant proportion of LGBTIQ victims believe that the incident will not be taken seriously or that they will not be treated fairly. Many respondents to this survey spoke of a feeling that justice would not occur as a result if they reported incidents of abuse. Furthermore, some members of the LGBTIQ community are concerned about the consequences of reporting the harassment or abuse. Kevin Berrill and Gregory Herek have pointed out that, in the aftermath of hate crimes, members of the LGBTIQ community face secondary victimisation. 'As crime victims, they are likely to experience indifference, rejection or stigmatisation from family, friends, community agencies and society in general.'[3] This chapter explores the barriers that have resulted in LGBTIQ individuals being much less likely to report instances of harassment and violence. It also considers the factors that are likely to increase the rate of reporting from this marginalised community. These factors inform the recommendations in Chapter 10.

Out of the 440 respondents who did not report homophobic or transphobic harassment or violence, 258 respondents (59%) recorded that they did not do so because they considered it a minor incident. Seventy respondents (16%) did not believe their report would be dealt with fairly.

Fifty-three respondents (12%) had previous negative experiences of reporting. Forty-five respondents (10%) did not know where to go for assistance. Forty (9%) feared further violence or discrimination. Thirty-four respondents (8%) feared being 'outed' about their sexuality or gender identity. Thirty-one respondents (7%) feared the homophobia of the institution to which they would report. Seven respondents (2%) feared the transphobia of the institution to which they would report. Twenty-five respondents (6%) selected the 'other' option. As some respondents selected more than one option, the total number of responses to this question exceeds the total number of respondents.

Aside from the quantitative information provided in Figure 6.1, respondents were given an opportunity to provide written responses as to their barriers to seeking help. Many of the barriers were similar to the ones stated in the quantitative data of Figure 6.1. However, of the 340 people who provided written responses, 167 (49%) listed the police themselves as being a barrier to reporting. The remainder of responses were clustered around several other factors. They included: (a) 39 or 12% who believed the incident was not serious or would not be able to be proven; (b) 37 or 11% who provided reasons that were not able to be classified; (c) 31 or 9% who feared being 'outed'; (d) 26 or 8% who feared it would exacerbate abuse; (e) 21 or 6% who believed it would be a waste of time; (f) 17 or 5% did not know who to contact; (g) 14 or 4% who feared workplace problems; and (h) 35 or 10% who felt there were no barriers.

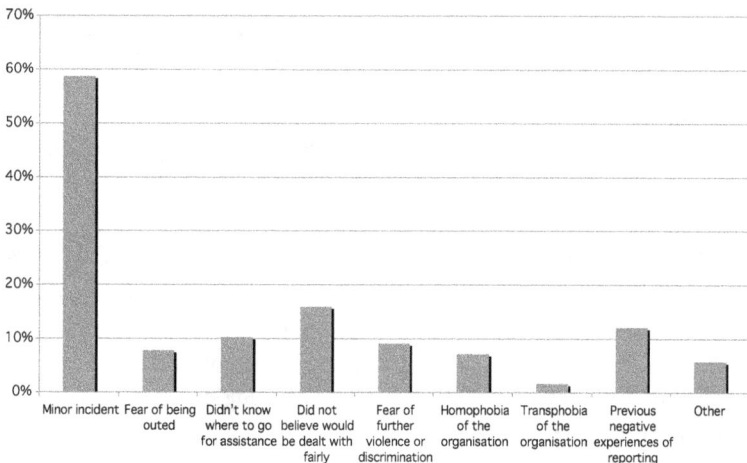

Figure 6.1
Barriers to seeking help.

Minor Incident

The majority of respondents who did not report their experience of homophobia or transphobiastated that they had not done so because they considered the incident to be a minor one. This finding matches the results of the 2008 Victorian study, *Coming Forward*.[4]

Some respondents attempted to minimise their experience and stated they did not believe verbal abuse required reporting. One respondent wrote that they '... didn't see the point [of reporting the incident], as no physical harm actually occurred. I didn't want to be seen as a whinger or a nuisance'. Another respondent reported that they had not reported the incident as it 'was relatively mild compared to what it could have been'.

Some respondents did not report abuse because of overlapping factors. One respondent wrote that 'I didn't report it because it was a minor incident, but had it been more serious I wouldn't be sure where to go'.

Concerns Regarding Fair Treatment

The fear that the abuse would not be taken seriously was frequently cited by many who took this survey. One respondent wrote they did not report the incident because 'generally homophobic violence is not taken seriously when reported'. This links up with the fears of secondary victimisation that have been observed in international studies.[5]

One respondent wrote that even if they had reported the incident, they 'suspected nothing would be done anyway'. One female respondent reported that:

> Too many organisations are not run by, or do not have, LGBTQ friendly staff. Often if you approach these types of places, they too can look at you oddly (because I appear very lesbian like), or they snub you off saying, 'Are you sure that's what happened? Are you sure it wasn't just your impression?' Very rarely do they actually listen objectively to the situation or take it seriously.

Previous Negative Experience of Reporting

One respondent stated that he had not reported his most recent incident and had 'just ignored it' because he saw 'no point' in reporting it. The '... Valley cops already said it's not a hate crime. I got beaten up for being gay once they told me there was no point pressing charges cause it's not a hate crime and it's a minor offence'.

Another respondent described a previous experience trying to report a situation of domestic violence and the way this negative experience impacted on the likelihood of reporting future incidents.

I sought assistance from the police years ago when my partner was hitting me and I ran over to the police and asked for help and they said for me to go away before they arrested me. It was clear to me then and there [what] my worth [was] and where I stood in their eyes.

Did Not Know Where to Go for Assistance

Many respondents wrote that they had not reported abuse because they were not sure where they could go for assistance. One respondent wrote that 'there are not appropriate services in my community that fit my needs'. Another respondent wrote a similar response, writing that, for them, reporting abuse would be '... embarrassing. I don't know who to speak to. I live in a hick town where homophobia is everywhere'. Another respondent wrote that they had not reported the incident of abuse because they 'really don't know where' to start.

For some respondents who were harassed or abused within the workplace, there were concerns about the place to seek assistance and the potential ramifications this may have on careers. One respondent wrote, 'No support at work is one barrier to me reporting it. It can also feel embarrassing to tell people about the abuse and what people have said'.

Another respondent wrote that 'I suppose it didn't occur to me there was much anyone could do'. This, and a variety of other statements made during the course of the survey, indicates that a proportion of survey respondents were unaware of avenues of assistance that might be available to them. This is information that needs to be very clearly conveyed to the LGBTIQ community.

Fear of Further Violence or Discrimination

A number of respondents from different circumstances wrote that fears of further violence and discrimination from perpetrators and other institutions served as barriers to reporting abuse. As Gregory Herek has argued:

> Despite their achievement of greater visibility and acceptance in recent years, lesbians and gay men continue to be targets of widespread institutional prejudice. Although racial, ethnic, and religious minorities also suffer from such prejudice, gay people are unique in that overt discrimination and intolerance against them often are officially condoned by governmental, religious, and social institutions.[6]

One respondent wrote of the difficulties they feared experiencing within court, based on past experience. 'I have had bad experiences with reporting abuse to the legal system and was treated like a retard by the judge because I have a physical disability and the judge refused to acknowledge any existence of same-sex legislation.'

Several respondents wrote that they feared losing their job if they reported the incident. One individual wrote, 'When you report it, you usually do lose your job. Being a casual worker, all they need to say is I don't need you tomorrow, and that means you're fired. Sometimes it is worse and they say they do not want you anymore'. As Chapter 3 outlined, homophobia and transphobia in the workplace are issues of ongoing concern for many respondents.[7]

As Chapter 4 explains, not all perpetrators are unknown to their victims and some forms of homophobia and transphobia are ongoing. A number of other respondents wrote they were fearful of the future actions of perpetrators. One respondent wrote they were 'scared of repercussions from [the] perpetrator and scared of the effect on my children since I am not out'.

One respondent described their motivation for not reporting the incident by writing that 'I was directly threatened and felt best to leave situation before it became violent'. Another respondent wrote that the main barrier to them reporting the abuse was 'the perpetrators knowing and the issue escalating'.

Another respondent spoke of their fears of further discrimination within the legal system:

> I am used to it. I have had to put up with it for 15 years and there doesn't seem to be much that can be done about this. I do feel it would make the harassment worse. I am afraid of worse repercussions from it and having to go through court proceedings and maybe have to face more homophobia from legal professionals. I would feel like I am on trial and being judged more than offenders. It seems very hard to fight this type of behaviour when it is still condoned so much in general community attitudes and sex roles

Fear of Being 'Outed'

As Gregory Herek has argued:

> ... along with the problems faced by other crime victims, lesbians and gay survivors often are blamed by others for their assault and accused of inviting or deserving the attack. In addition, if their sexual orientation becomes public knowledge as a result of an attack, they subsequently may experience heightened discrimination in employment, housing, or services.[8]

One respondent explained how some reasons for not reporting the incident overlapped. 'At the time, I didn't believe that it was "serious enough" to "bother" the authorities, and I was unwilling to divulge my sexual identity to others (given what had happened in this situation).' Another respondent stated that they were not 'openly out because of community perceptions', and that reporting the incident would change this.

Another respondent wrote that 'it is my problem and I do not wish to be outed'. Along similar lines, another respondent stated a barrier that had prevented them reporting the incident was their 'parents not knowing/approving of the same sex relationship, fear of judgmental remarks, not wanting to talk about it'. Another respondent wrote that their 'local paper reports everything' and to lodge a complaint 'would have outed me and my family'. Another respondent wrote that they had not reported abuse due to 'concern that it won't be taken seriously and that 'outing' my partner's transition might be more detrimental to him'.

Fear of the Homophobia of the Organisation

Many members of the LGBTIQ community are fearful that they may encounter further homophobia upon reporting incidents. Gregory Herek has argued that law enforcement agencies must work together with the LGBTIQ community if reporting rates are to be increased. Herek states that 'law enforcement agencies ... must obtain the trust and cooperation of local gay and lesbian communities, and they must establish uniform reporting procedures across jurisdictions'.[9] International studies have shown that the LGBTIQ community in other nations such as the United States and Great Britain still shows a reluctance to engage with institutions of policing. This is a legacy of the historic homophobia and transphobia associated with policing.[10]

The Queensland Police Service is still remembered by some older respondents as an institution which would deliberately entrap men in sexual situations and subsequently arrest them for indecent exposure. Male-to-male sexual acts were not decriminalised in this state until 1990. Consequently, it is not surprising that there is still a high degree of mistrust towards the Queensland Police Service by some older respondents. One respondent obviously still remembered this, when he wrote in his response, 'I just don't have much confidence in the police. I was bashed 20 years ago and they weren't all that interested. And let's face it. Police are police'.

One younger respondent outlined his belief that the Queensland Police Service would be homophobic if he reported his incident:

What's the point? Nothing would be done about it. I've gone to a police officer in the past after being verbally and physically assaulted for no reason at all while walking home from the Beat nightclub to my residence above the Brunswick Street Mall and was ignored. Ninety-nine per cent of my experiences with the police have had as much homophobic language or references used as I receive on a usual weekend. They don't give a shit.

Another respondent wrote, 'What's the point? The police are also homophobic unless the officer is female'. Another respondent stated they did not report their incident because they harboured '... concerns that I will be subject to further homophobia as a result of reporting the incident'. Another respondent wrote, 'I didn't think it was worth it ... and I am quite embarrassed to report gay abuse as I feel I may be discriminated against or looked down upon by the authorities as a weak person'.

Fear of the Transphobia of the Organisation

Transgendered respondents also raised transphobia within the police service as a barrier to reporting abuse. One respondent wrote that 'I have had police harassment before with incorrect name/gender'.

Another respondent described the way transphobia has permeated many levels of society. They wrote:

A lack of gender awareness still permeates our culture regardless of the cultural leaps society has made in the past few decades. Also, many of the abuses towards transgender people have historically been at the hands of health care professionals, police and other people in positions of power. Being transgender is still classified as a mental disorder in the DSM health manual, so that, for starters, is a grave injustice and bias/hurdle to face for any transgender person.

Other Concerns

A variety of other responses were also listed. One respondent wrote that they did not report the incident as 'I thought I could deal with it myself. I was in the police force'. Another respondent wrote, 'Being a lesbian means dealing with this alone'.

Another respondent believed the time and effort required to punish the perpetrators was not worthwhile. They wrote a barrier to reporting the incident is '... getting involved in a drawn-out process that'll have no impact or outcome for the random idiots, but will consume lots of our time'.

Similarly, another respondent wrote that 'I didn't feel like it would change anything. When you deal with it on a day to day basis, it takes a lot out of you. You're already thinking about yourself and your lovers, friends, partners and community. You don't have much more energy to be bothering with reporting it or involving anyone else in the matter'.

One respondent wrote that they had not reported the incident because of 'feeling like an idiot for letting it upset me [suffering from] embarrassment'. Another respondent described feeling 'fear, hopelessness of fight, repercussions, judgement'.

Out of the 583 respondents who had experienced homophobic or transphobic abuse or harassment within the past 2 years, 329 provided written responses indicating the factors that would increase their willingness to report this abuse. Fifty-two respondents (16%) stated they would report the incident if they expected more results and understood it would be taken seriously. Forty-eight respondents (15%) stated they would report the incident if it was more serious/more violent. Forty-three respondents (13%) stated they would report the incident if more sensitive, non-homophobic/non-transphobic support was provided. Thirty-nine respondents (12%) stated they would report the incident if there was increased availability of LGBTIQ police officers. Twenty-seven respondents (8%) of respondents said they would report if there was a greater accessibility of services. Twenty-three respondents (7%) stated they would report the incident if there were more anti-homophobia and anti-transphobic campaigns/education. Nine respondents (3%) stated they

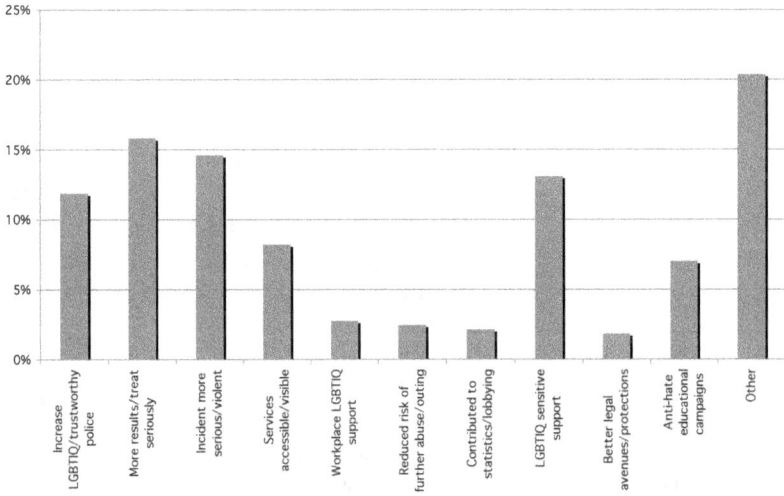

Figure 6.2
Factors which would lead to greater reporting of homophobic and transphobic harassment and violence.

would report it if there was better support in the workplace. Eight respondents (2%) wrote that they would report it if they felt it would not exacerbate the situation. Seven respondents (2%) said they would report it if it contributed to statistics or an inquiry. Six respondents (2%) said they would report it if legal avenues provided better protection. Sixty-seven respondents (20%) selected the 'other' option.

If Results Were Expected and It Was Taken Seriously

One respondent wrote that the strongest contributing factor to reporting the incident would be 'the thought that my complaint would actually be taken seriously and that I would be treated with respect'.

Another respondent echoed this sentiment, writing that they would have reported the incident if they believed the report would be taken seriously and would 'actually have consequences for the offenders, otherwise you are just wasting everyone's time'.

One male respondent felt that their status as gay meant that he would be perceived as a 'dizzy queen, making a mountain out of a molehill'. This respondent felt that if his complaint would be treated as serious, he would report abuse.

The researchers involved in the *Coming Forward* report from Victoria also found respondents cited these concerns. They noted that a number of individuals expressed '... frustration and disappointment at the ways in which heterosexist abuse and its effects are ignored or trivialised'.[11]

If It Was More Serious/More Violent

Many respondents reported that they would be more likely to report an incident that they considered to be more serious or violent. One respondent wrote that 'If it was physical, I would report it'. Similarly, another respondent wrote that 'If I experienced more serious harassment then I would consider following it up'.

Y, a male participant in the Sunshine Coast focus group said that the extent of the abuse would determine whether he reported it to police. He stated:

> It would depend on the severity. If perhaps someone just pushed me up against a wall, clearly that's common assault. I couldn't be bothered reporting common assault. I would just continue to walk on. If someone king hit me and broke my nose in four places and fractured my jaw, then I probably would. So it would also be contingent on what it was.

This result matches the findings of the 2003 'You Shouldn't Have to Hide to be Safe' report from New South Wales, where most respondents stated they were more likely to report more extreme violent crimes.[12]

If More Sensitive, Non-Homophobic/Transphobic Support Was Provided

One respondent wrote that they would report their incident of abuse if police had 'better LGBTQ understanding'. Another respondent expressed very similar sentiments, writing that 'a better understanding from professionals, particularly the police' was required before incidents could be reported.

Another respondent wrote he would have reported the incident if 'there were more services or contacts trained in this type of thing'. Similarly, another respondent wrote that reporting rates would increase if there was more:

> ... open-mindedness and staff were employed and trained to always be sensitive (which includes body language) to clients needs, regardless of stereotypical physical appearance and sexual orientation and/or gender.

Increased Availability of LGBTIQ Police Officers

Many respondents stressed that they would be more likely to report homophobic and transphobic abuse if LGBTIQ police officers were available. The need for LGBTIQ police officers to be more prominent was emphasised by a number of respondents. One wrote that:

> I wish I knew where the LGBTI police were. I hear about them, but have never met one. Even at Pride day I am too scared to go and talk to the police and ask them about the LGBTI cops. Maybe cause I don't believe it or know really who or what they are. But I would really like to know who they are and how to contact them.

Another respondent stressed the need for transgender representation and contacts within the police service.

> Having transgender people employed in a police team or in an anti-discrimination office could help. Transgender people have historically been so disadvantaged that many accept a low social bias as normal. Also, having some of the extreme past injustices faced by transgender people dealt with, instead of just being swept under the carpet, would also send a clear message to the community.

Several respondents suggested that LGBTI police liaison officers wear identifying badges so that they were more visible to LGBTIQ people. One respondent wrote, 'I think if police that were gay-friendly (I know they are all supposed to be) [I would report]. But maybe a small team of them, could have a rainbow iron-on label put on their shirt. Or a badge'.

Greater Accessibility of Services

One respondent wrote that he had been prevented from reporting a previous incident because 'I could not locate a police officer and then went home as soon as I could'. Another respondent believed that there should be an increased police presence near LGBTIQ venues, where a high proportion of homophobic and transphobic attacks take place. They wrote that a factor that would make them more likely to report abuse would be '... a more supportive and proactive approach from Queensland Police in areas such as the Valley around gay and lesbian establishments'.

Respondents in non-urban locations also outlined difficulties in accessing services. One respondent outlined a situation where an incident had unfolded over two hours but there were not sufficient police officers to investigate the situation. They wrote that:

> The police at the time didn't have a person on the island [where the incident occurred] and it can take several hours for them to come out and the last time I got them to come anyway, it was all over before they arrived, even though I rang them straight away and [the incident] lasted for almost two hours.

One respondent from the Sunshine Coast also wrote that it was the inaccessibility of support services in this location that had prevented him from reporting harassment. Increased police presence and accessibility of services would certainly seem to be something that would increase reporting.

More Anti-Homophobia and Anti-Transphobia Campaigns/Education

One respondent felt so strongly about increasing awareness and understanding through public campaigns that they wrote that, rather than funding be spent pursuing the perpetrator of the abuse against them, they 'would prefer the funding went towards educating the public about discrimination and violence towards same-sex couples and transgender people'.

Another respondent wrote of the need for 'a positive, comprehensive education on LGBTIQ people and sexual identity'. Another respondent pointed out that 'there are no ads on TV (like anti-smoking campaigns) and not many education programs that are focusing on stopping homophobia, homophobic violence and heterosexism'. The need for such campaigns and initiatives was mentioned by a many respondents.

Better Support in the Workplace

As has been mentioned in this study and in national and international studies, workplaces can often be sites where homophobia and transphobia occurs.[13] They can also be locations where a lack of support is given to those who are subjected to homophobic or transphobic abuse. Providing better support structures that would enable victims to report abuse would certainly increase reporting rates. One respondent expressed this by writing that that they would be more likely to report abuse if there was:

> More support at work and a more gay-friendly atmosphere would help me report abuse at work. I would be more willing to report if I was more aware of people and organisations I could report abuse to.

Another respondent stressed the need for anti-homophobia and anti-transphobia campaigns within the workplace. The need for 'less tolerance of such attitudes and expressing them at work' was also mentioned by one individual.

If It Would Not Exacerbate the Situation

The fear of exacerbating the situation was a fear expressed by a number of respondents. This was such a concern to one respondent that they wrote that they feared 'advising the police will only increase my fear or chance of retribution. I would only report or take action if I was allowed to carry a Taser afterwards at all times. Seriously'.

If It Contributed to Statistics or an Inquiry

Seven respondents wrote that they would have reported the incident if the information had been used for broader statistical purposes or for an inquiry into homophobia or transphobia. One respondent wrote that they would have reported the incident 'if I thought it would make a difference, that is, was recorded for statistics'.

Another respondent wrote that they would have reported their incident if 'I knew that reports were really needed for some lobbying or inquiry or something'. Another respondent wrote that they would report the abuse if 'LGBTQ assaults were separated out of the overall general assault statistics and made separate — to identify just how fucking bad the situation is'.

If Legal Avenues Provided Better Protection

A number of respondents felt they were already legally disadvantaged within the judicial and legal system and that this made them reluctant to engage with official institutions. One respondent wrote that they would have felt more comfortable reporting homophobia if they had legal 'equality/same legal rights as married couples'. Similarly, another respondent noted that they would be more inclined to report abuse if there were:

> ... anti-vilification laws in Queensland, which would include religious institutions. [We would also like] a court of law to settle these domestic problems and for Queensland Health and Queensland Housing to step in and stop harassment of their clients. Access to proper legal assistance. Equality before the law.

Another respondent wrote that they would 'like there to be a formal channel to report incidents of harassment — so these incidents can be recorded and thus give a victim an avenue to be supported by the legal system if the matter becomes worse'.

Other Factors

A male Indigenous respondent outlined the need for cultural sensitivity, as well as sensitivity towards LBGTIQ people on the part of the police service. He wrote that he would feel more confident reporting abuse if there was 'an Aboriginal Liaison Officer in all Police stations and Gay and Lesbian Liaison Officer in all Police stations' as this person would be of the right sex for 'Men's business to be discussed'.

A number of other respondents stressed the need for anonymity and wrote that they would be much more likely to report the abuse if their identity was protected. One wrote they would report if they were assured 'anonymity, protection from retribution'.

Some respondents emphasised that they would find it very awkward discussing their sexuality or gender identity with officials not trained to respect this. One respondent suggested more reporting would occur if they could make contact with:

> A department that dealt specifically with this area [as this] would make me less anxious about talking to authorities about my personal situation ... I wouldn't experience any awkwardness from them, or an unwillingness to listen in full to what occurred.

Many respondents stated that they would be more likely to report instances of abuse and harassment if there were more advertising campaigns and dedicated telephone numbers that victims could call. One respondent wrote that he believed people would report abuse if there was:

> A phone number that is easy to remember, that you can call to report any kind of discrimination ... also knowing that even small incidents will be acted upon. Posters at the venues that display this number and encourage people to report even small incidents.

Conclusion

Elizabeth Peel, who has studied the low rates of crime reporting by LGBTIQ individuals in Britain, has argued that 'respondents grounded their experiences within a much broader social and political context'.[14] This is certainly clear for the victims of homophobic and transphobic crime who responded to this survey. Many respondents felt that their reports would not be taken seriously or treated fairly. Furthermore, it is important to recognise that those who are members of the LGBTIQ community are marginalised within a society and reporting a homophobic or transphobic crime can involve victims exposing themselves to secondary homophobia or transphobia.

Respondents to this survey outlined some of the reasons why they did not report crimes and also set forward some changes that would make them more likely to report homophobic or transphobic harassment or violence. These factors have informed some of the recommendations for legal reform, educational and governmental initiatives and policing responses that are outlined in chapter 10.

Notes

1 New South Wales Attorney General's Department, 'You Shouldn't Have to Hide to be Safe': A Report on Homophobic Hostilities and Violence Against Gay Men and Lesbians in New South Wales (Sydney: New South Wales Attorney General's Department, Crime Prevention Division, 2003), p.50.

2 Martin Kantor, Homophobia: Description, Development, and Dynamics of Gay Bashing (London: Praeger, 1998), pp.67-74.

3 Kevin T. Berill and Gregory M. Herek, 'Primary and Secondary Victimization in Anti-Gay Hate Crimes: Official Response and Public Policy' in Gregory M. Herek and Kevin T. Berill, eds, Hate Crimes: Confronting Violence Against Lesbians and Gay Men (Newbury Park, California: Sage Publications, 1992), p.289.

4 William Leonard and others, Coming Forward: The Underreporting of Heterosexist and Same Sex Partner Abuse in Victoria (Melbourne: Australian Research Centre in Sex, Health and Society, La Trobe, 2008), p.38.

5 Berill and Herek, 'Primary and Secondary Victimization in Anti-Gay Hate Crimes, p.289.

6 Gregory M. Herek, 'Hate Crimes Against Lesbians and Gay Men: Issues for Research and Policy', *American Psychologist*, Vol. 44, No. 6 (June 1989), p.949.

7 Robert J. Hill, ed., *Challenging Homophobia and Heterosexism: Lesbian, Gay, Bisexual, Transgender, and Queer Issues in Organizational Settings* (San Francisco: Jossey-Bass, 1996), pp.29–40.

8 Herek, *Hate Crimes Against Lesbians and Gay Men*, p.953.

9 Ibid., p.951.

10 Krishten Kuehnle and Anne Sullivan, 'Patterns of Anti-Gay Violence: An Analysis of Incident Characteristics and Victim Reporting', *Journal of Interpersonal Violence*, Vol. 16 (2001), p.929.

11 Leonard and others, *Coming Forward*, p.39.

12 New South Wales Attorney General's Department, '*You Shouldn't Have to Hide to be Safe*', p.50.

13 See for example, J. M. Croteau, 'Research on the Work Experiences of Lesbian, Gay, and Bisexual People: An Integrative Review of Methodology and Findings', *Journal of Vocational Behaviour*, Vol. 46 (1996).

14 Elizabeth Peel, 'Violence Against Lesbians and Gay Men: Decision Making in Reporting and Not Reporting Crime', *Feminism Psychology*, Vol. 9 (1999), p.165.

CHAPTER 7

The Police and Police Liaison Officers

The three jurisdictions that have conducted surveys similar to the one that is the subject of this book include New South Wales (NSW), Victoria (VIC) and Queensland (QLD). Police in New South Wales regard themselves as 'pioneers' in the way in which they have engaged with the gay, lesbian, and transgender communities in Australia. This chapter explores both broader experiences with the Queensland Police Service and the operation of the LGBTI liaison program in Queensland. It provides detailed data pertaining to the way members of the Queensland Police Service record and treat homophobic and transphobic harassment and violence. It also considers barriers that prevent LGBTIQ individuals from reporting homophobic and transphobic harassment and violence to the Queensland Police Service.

Background to Australian Gay and Lesbian Liaison Programs

In 1990, the first Gay and Lesbian Liaison Officers (GLLOs) served in four locations in Sydney. There are currently over a hundred GLLOs working throughout the State. The police force in this jurisdiction is committed to the LGBTIQ communities by fostering:

> Greater reporting and [and a reduction of] the incidence of violence, crime and harassment and fear within these communities; ensuring the provision of high quality, professional policing services, building and maintaining effective partnerships, ensuring a supportive workplace for gay, lesbian and transgender employees and those performing gay and lesbian liaison duties.[1]

The GLLO Program is considered a fundamental component of the NSW Police Force effort to counter violence, harassment and domestic violence within the gay and lesbian community, and to boost trust in the Police Force so as to advance the goal of reporting homophobic violence and crimes.[2] The Senior Programs Officer (Gay, Lesbian and Transgender Issues), a civilian employee, manages the GLLO program and takes a leading role in providing executive advice and formulating policies to enhance safety, reduce crime against gay, lesbian and transgender individuals and foster community outreach as well as developing the curriculum for new cadets and specialist training of GLLOs. The NSW police have provided advice, assistance and training on issues of liaising with the gay and lesbian community to police in other jurisdictions within Australia and globally.[3]

In Victoria, a part-time position was created to deal with gay and lesbian liaison issues in 1990. In 2000, Victoria created a full-time position for a GLLO. The position was brought about by members of the LGBTIQ community, through a Police/Equal Opportunity Commission working group. A mission statement was issued by this working group which states:

> The Gay and Lesbian Liaison mission is to contribute to the creation of mutual trust between police, lesbians, gay men, bisexuals, transgender and intersex persons so that they have increasing confidence in police through the provision of a fair and equitable policing service.[4]

There are now GLLOs throughout the state who are provided with specialised training in LGBTIQ issues. The GLLOs in Victoria do not actually investigate a crime motivated in part by prejudice (bias or hatred) toward the actual or perceived sexual orientation or gender identity of a victim. Their function is to provide 'discreet, non-judgmental advice and assistance in the reporting of crimes ... and expert advice and assistance to police investigators'.[5]

The GLLO brochure explicitly states: 'Victoria Police recognises that for victims of prejudice motivated crimes, such as homophobia, it can be one of the most traumatic experiences of the victim's life, and the crime can be felt throughout the entire homosexual community'. The Victorian Police also expressly recognise that 'prejudice motivated crimes not only harm the victim, they harm the victim's group and society as a whole'.[6] Victoria records prejudice motivated crimes which allows GLLOs to provide assistance to victims and ascertain 'crime trends within and against the GLBTI community'.[7] The Victorian Police recognise there is an issue with underreporting of crimes motivated by prejudice toward homosexuality or transexuality and the array of factors that contribute to such underreporting, including 'mistrust of police, fear of reprisals, fear of having to "out" themselves through a court process and the perception that the incident is not serious enough to report to police'.[8]

The Queensland Liaison Program

In Queensland, a GLBT liaison program commenced operation in 1997. According to Queensland Police Commissioner Robert Atkinson: 'The purpose of the Queensland liaison program is to provide a professional, non-discriminatory, accessible policing service to members of the LGBTI Communities ... by:

- developing an awareness and understanding of LGBTI communities
- developing partnerships with LGBTI communities
- ensuring equality, accountability and professionalism in our contact with LGBTI communities
- improving service delivery to LGBTI communities'.[9]

There is a state-wide GLBTI liaison officer who is a member of the Queensland Police Service (QPS). There are also liaison officers located throughout the state of Queensland who are intended to advance the goals enunciated by the Queensland Police Commissioner. It is not possible to discern whether the state-wide liaison officer undergoes specialised training and/or if any of the liaison officers throughout the state receive specific training at the present time. The authors have also not been able to discern if the state-wide liaison officer is a full-time position. The rank of the state-wide liaison officer within the QPS has varied over time. The liaison officers located throughout the state are not full-time positions and there is no correlation between rank within the QPS and serving in the role of a liaison officer. The liaison officers serve as members of the QPS and may serve in other roles, such as liaison officer for domestic violence. They may also be detective inspectors as well as a liaison officer. There has been a relatively high turnover in the role of state-wide liaison officers in the last several years, as well as the liaison officers located throughout the state. The information gathered from the focus groups suggests professionals, such as psychiatrists, members of community support groups and others, were involved in the training program of either or both cadets and liaison officers when the liaison program was initially established in 1997. In the last several years, the authors understand these professionals are no longer involved in the training of cadets or liaison officers. The authors understand a system known as QPrime has been set up by the QPS since June 2007 to collect statistical data relating to criminal activity which can allow the police to track crimes committed on the basis of animus toward LGBTIQ individuals. [10]

The differences in the models of each state and the quantitative data and qualitative information gleaned from the written responses to survey questions as well as focus groups has served as a basis for the Recommendations in chapter 10 on ways in which the liaison program in Queensland can be resharpened so as to achieve the purposes enunciated by the Queensland Police Commissioner. A review of the liaison program may also lead to an increased emphasis on some of the objectives of the GLLO's in NSW and Victoria, such as:

1. creating more trust and confidence in the QPS so as to create greater partnerships in crime prevention
2. increasing the reporting of prejudice motivated violence
3. reducing the incidence of crime, harassment and fear within these communities
4. ensuring a supportive workplace for LGBTQ individuals employed by the QPS and as liaison officers.[11]

Quantitative Analysis Based on Statistical Data
Reporting to and Experiences with Police
As canvassed in Chapter 3, 53% of the respondents to this survey experienced some form of homophobic or transphobic harassment or violence in the past two years. Just 12%, or 72 respondents, sought assistance from the police following their most recent incident of homophobic or transphobic harassment or violence to the police.[12] As seen in Table 7.1, while 58% found the police to be reasonably or very supportive, 26% found them not supportive in the assistance they provided. This indicates a low willingness to engage with law enforcement. Seven per cent provided no response.

Table 7.2 reveals police attended the incident in 28% or 20 of the reported cases. Twenty-nine per cent or 21 of the cases were reported in person at a police station. Fourteen per cent or 10 individuals reported the incident over the telephone. Eight per cent or 6 respondents specified 'other' and 15 respondents or 21% of individuals did not respond to this question. Five of the six persons who specified 'other' provided written responses that could have been subsumed under previous categories. Four of the five responses indicated the police either attended the incident (two); the victim visited the police station (one) and reported over the telephone (one). One particular response discussed below is rather disturbing. As indicated in Table 7.3 and Table 7.4, while members of the QPS took written reports of the incident in 39% of cases, only 17% of the victims were provided with copies of the reports. The police investigated the matter further in 21% of the cases, and failed to do so, or the victim was unaware if they had done so, in 60% of the cases. This data is highlighted in Table 7.5. The manner in which officers handled the ten matters that proceeded to court are dealt with in Chapter 8.

....
Table 7.1
Responses to the Question 'How valuable was the service provided by the police?' (For those who specified that they sought assistance from the police)

Response	Number	Percentage
Not supportive	25	35%
Reasonably supportive	23	32%
Very supportive	19	26%
No response	5	7%
Total	72	

....
Table 7.2
Responses to the Question 'How did you report the incident to the police?' (for those who specified that they sought assistance from the police)

Response	Number	Percentage
Police attended this incident	20	28%
Phoned a police station	10	14%
Reported in person at a police station	21	29%
Other	6	8%
No response	15	21%
Total	72	

....
Table 7.3
Responses to the Question 'Did the police take a written report of the incident?' (for those who specified that they sought assistance from the police)

Response	Number	Percentage
Yes	28	39%
No	19	26%
Don't know	12	17%
No response	13	18%
Total	72	

Table 7.4
Responses to the Question 'Did the police provide you with a written report of the incident?' (for those who specified that they sought assistance from the police)

Response	Number	Percentage
Yes	12	17%
No	41	57%
Don't know	4	6%
No response	15	21%
Total	72	

Table 7.5
Responses to the Question 'Did the police investigate the incident further?' (for those who specified that they sought assistance from the police)

Response	Number	Percentage
Yes	15	21%
No	27	38%
Don't know	16	22%
No response	14	19%
Total	72	

The number of responses to many of these questions renders them statistically insignificant. In other words, it is difficult to draw any inferences given the low numbers of individuals who sought professional assistance from the police service and, in particular, liaison officers.

Awareness of and Experiences with the LGBTI Liaison Officers

Five hundred and sixty-four respondents or 52% of survey respondents, when answering the question shown in Figure 7.1, indicated that they were aware of the existence of liaison officers. This is in sharp contrast to the Victorian *Coming Forward* report in 2008 which found almost 83% of respondents had heard of GLLOs.[13] Figure 7.1 also shows that 32% of survey respondents had not heard of the liaison officers and 16% did not provide an answer to the question.

For the majority of survey respondents who were aware of the existence of the liaison officers (564 respondents), this awareness came from a variety of sources. The sources are summarised in Figure 7.2 and Table 7.6, with the four predominant ones being community newspapers and

Magazines (35%), Gay Media (33%), Gay Publication (33%) and GLBT Community Organisation (27%).

Of the 9% or 50 respondents who answered *Other*, a variety of other sources were provided. These included personal knowledge from having served as a police officer or having had a partner/friend who served as a police officer. One respondent had become aware of the officers because they had wished to take up this type of employment. Another was involved in the committee that established the liaison program, while one individual had previously undertaken some training for the program several years ago (which still predominantly employs heterosexuals). Other respondents specified the type of media that had mentioned the liaison officers, including the television news or the Koori Mail. Community events, such as the Brisbane Pride Fair and Gay and Lesbian Mardi Gras, were also mentioned. Other respondents reported becoming aware of liaison officers through visual cues, including posters or signs or business cards at LGBTIQ venues as well as at the Fortitude Valley police station. Others cited the public visibility of liaison officers on the street. Others became aware of the officers through their work in sexual health, through the Queensland Ambulance Service, Queensland Association of Healthy Communities (QAHC) or through the welfare industry. LGBTIQ support groups and a workshop on homophobia had also promoted the officers. The Gold Coast Transgender Yahoo Group had introduced one respondent to the program. Research at a university had also exposed respondents to the officers. Some respondents noted they had first become aware of the liaison officer program as a result of undertaking the

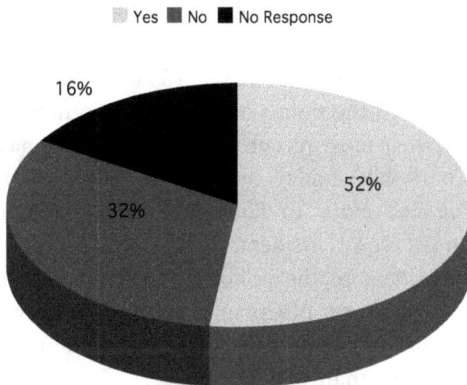

Figure 7.1
Responses to the question 'Have you heard of the Queensland Gay, Lesbian, Bisexual, Transgender, Intersex Liaison Officers?' (For all survey respondents)

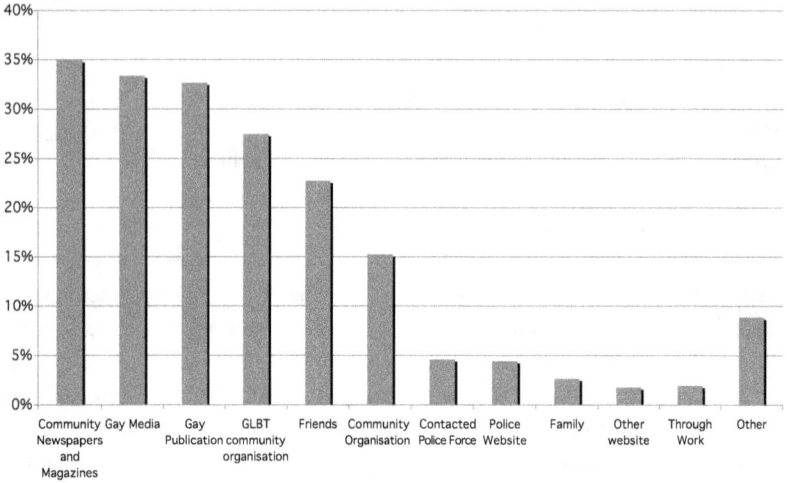

Figure 7.2
Responses to the question 'How did you become aware of these officers?' (for those who specified that they had heard of the LGBTI Liaison Officers).

survey that forms the basis for this book. Two respondents stated they had become aware of the program via word of mouth.

Merely 4%, or 22 respondents, sought assistance from a liaison officer following their most recent incident of homophobic or transphobic harassment or violence. As summarised in Table 7.7, 11 individuals found them very supportive, five reasonably supportive and four non-supportive with no response from two individuals. In total, following their most recent experience in the past two years, 16% of respondents had either reported the incident to the police or to a liaison officer. The percentage of those reporting their most recent incident within the past two years to the police is remarkably similar to the data found in the 2003 NSW report *'You Shouldn't Have to Hide to be Safe'* in which 13% had reported their most recent incident of homophobic abuse or violence within the previous year to the police.[14] Again, as with the police, the numbers reporting to liaison officers are too low to draw any statistical inferences from them except that the LGBTIQ community engages even less with liaison officers than with the police.

As seen in Figure 7.3, only 96 or 9% of survey respondents have contacted a police LGBTI liaison officer. An overwhelming majority of 799, or 73% of survey respondents, had never contacted a LGBTI liaison officer.

Table 7.6
Responses to the Question 'How did you become aware of these Officers?'
(for those who specified that they had heard of the LGBTI Liaison Officers)

Response	Number	Percentage
Community newspapers and magazines	197	35%
Gay media	188	33%
Gay publication	184	33%
GLBT community organisation	155	27%
Friends	128	23%
Community organisation	86	15%
Contacted police force	26	5%
Police website	25	4%
Family	15	3%
Other website	10	2%
Through work	11	2%
Other	50	9%

Table 7.7
Responses to the Question 'How valuable was the service provided by the
LGBTI Liaison Officers?' (for those who specified that they sought assistance
from the LGBTI Liaison Officers)

Response	Number	Percentage
Not supportive	4	18%
Reasonably supportive	5	23%
Very supportive	11	50%
No response	2	9%
Total	22	

One hundred and ninety-nine or 18% provided no response to this question.

Significantly, 634 out of the 835 respondents, or 76%, indicated the existence of liaison officers increased the likelihood that they would report an incident of homophobic or transphobic harassment or violence to the Police Service. This closely parallels the 2008 Victorian *Coming Forward* survey, in which 79% responded in the affirmative to such question.[14]

Of the 96 individuals who had contacted a liaison officer in the past, a majority of 56 individuals or 58% contacted a liaison officer by telephone

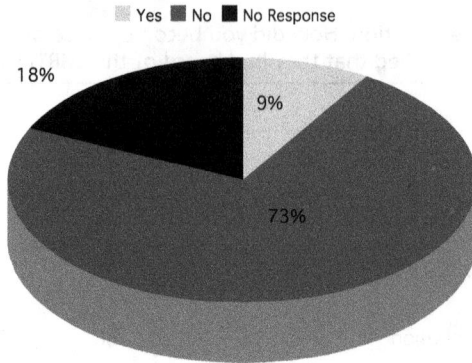

Figure 7.3
Responses to the question 'Have you ever contacted a Police LGBTI Liaison Officer?' (for all survey respondents).

as a first means of contact. Seventeen individuals or 18% first contacted a liaison officer at a community event. Ten respondents or 10% first contacted them in person at a police station. Seven respondents or 7% first contacted them via email. Five respondents first contacted a liaison officer via other means, such as through a mutual friend, as a result of this survey, and as a professional contact through work as a Health Promotion Officer. One person had made contact with a liaison officer using the telephone and in person in New South Wales, and one person had worked with such officers in the past. No response was received from one individual. This data is summarised in Figure 7.4.

When survey respondents were asked how they would prefer to contact a liaison officer, the preferred method was the phone. This was followed by face to face, email, website form, and police station, in descending order of preference.

The qualitative data from the written responses to some of the survey questions as well as the statements made in the focus groups provides a telling insight into the low rates of reporting, particularly with regard to the liaison officers. Although it is difficult to draw any firm inferences from the written responses to some of the survey questions about general trends, they help shed some light on why some members of the LGBTIQ community are reluctant to report incidents to the police. The opinions of individuals in the focus groups about their perceptions of the police and their personal experiences with reporting incidents of homophobic abuse,

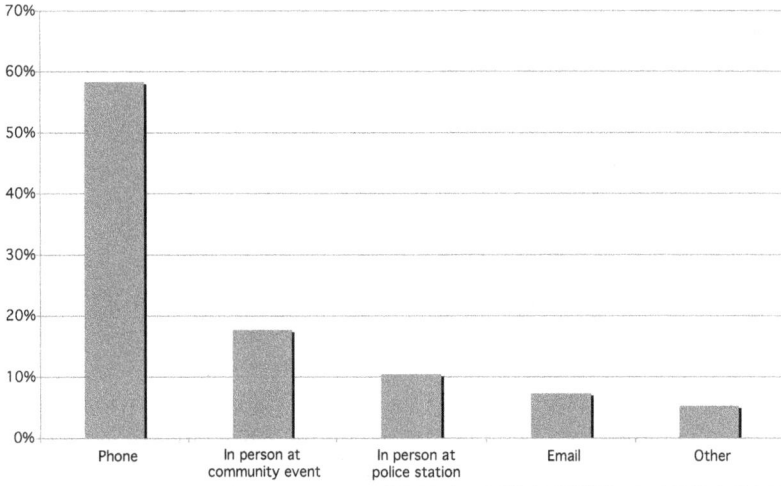

Figure 7.4
Responses to the question 'When you first contacted a police LGBTI Liaison Officer, how did you contact them?' (for those who specified that they sought assistance from the LGBTI Liaison Officers).

harassment and physical threats to law enforcement varied considerably. Some expressed positive experiences with the police and generally positive changing perceptions of how the LGBTIQ community is viewed and treated by the police and liaison officers (such as the Gold Coast focus group). Others expressed the view that homophobia is more prevalent in the QPS than in any other governmental department in Queensland. Some also indicated their reporting of homophobic or transphobic abuse, harassment or violence was greeted by officers with homophobic or transphobic attitudes. The overwhelming majority of complaints were directed towards the liaison program, especially in the regional, remote and rural areas of Queensland.

Analysis of Written Survey Responses

Of the 27 respondents who answered *No* to the question, 'Did the police investigate the matter further?', 19 reported the explanation that the police provided for this. Various reasons were provided by the police, including the right of persons to their own opinions, lack of evidence (three cases, including an instance where there were no cameras in a particular place in the Fortitude Valley), unwillingness of the attending officer to discuss the matter aside from providing a 'report number', being advised to change numbers and move, individuals should be aware 'hanging out in places like this', inability of officers to act in the absence of actual physical violence (three cases) with one such situation involving a stalker, the officer going on leave a week after reporting the incident with an assurance of getting in contact upon return which never occurred, and inability to locate the perpetrator. One respondent replied *None* to this question.

These responses suggest the police are unaware the victims might have had remedies that could have been pursued through ADCQ. Section 124A of *Queensland Anti-Discrimination Act* provides for civil remedies for sexual or gender identity vilification.[16] Police cadets should be informed of these potential remedies and refer the individuals who are the subject of non-violent homophobic or transphobic abuse and harassment to ADCQ rather than dismissing them as matters over which they have no control. Police are understandably reluctant to act even in instances involving physical threats (which could amount to common assault) because of difficulties with problems of proof. However, there are theoretically potential remedies available under Section 131A of the *Queensland Anti-Discrimination Act* that provide for potential civil and criminal penalties for severe sexual or gender identity vilification involving physical threats.[17] (See chapter 10 for Recommendations on Amendments to the Law.)

Some of the above responses also suggest a lack of resources to assist in law enforcement and failure to follow up on reported incidents. Five written responses were received from the six participants who answered 'other' to the question, 'How did you report the incident to the Police?' One of the respondents stated: 'Visited police station, sent registered mail to officer in charge at West End police to resolve the matter. Did not hear from police for months until I complained to Premier Anna Bligh'. Information obtained in the focus groups indicates a possible trend rather than a rare occurrence of failing to respond to incidents in a timely manner. This perception garnered widespread agreement from many participants in virtually all the focus groups where this arose as an issue.

A few of the respondents indicated the police did follow up to an extent but the perpetrator might be difficult to track down because the victim could not provide a clear description as the incident occurred in the evening. Two others did not wish to pursue the matter further because of concern over their own safety or the safety of their children or involving the police in issues from work.

One written response provided was troubling in that the officer allegedly did not act in an instance involving actual physical violence: 'We were at a non-gay/lesbian venue where my partner was assaulted by a male with verbal and physical abuse. Went to police who replied with: "There are gay clubs here". Blatant discrimination'.

Without drawing any inferences because the sampling is so small, some of the above statements could be construed as reflections of externalised homophobia and exacerbate pre-existing internalised homophobia. This might help explain one of the many factors some members of the public do not report incidents of homophobic or transphobic abuse or violence to the Queensland Police Service (QPS).

Of those whose incidents that were not taken further by police, 15 (56%) of these respondents provided responses to the question: 'What are the barriers to your reporting or seeking professional assistance following an incident of homophobic or transphobic harassment or abuse in the future?' Many of the reasons provided were similar to the above question, including an inability of police to act in the absence of actual physical violence; forcing the respondent to move house because of a stalker and lack of police action; a perception of wasted of time and effort; homophobic police and the legal system; a concern the police would not believe them; fear of being 'outed'; general lack of public understanding; and because the respondent was a member of the LGBTIQ community. One response was particularly notable: 'That no matter how many times the police were called, they always took the side of the "poor incent [sic — innocent] grandmother", just desperate to see her daughter and granddaughter. Regardless of the fact that she had bashed her daughter while she was eight months pregnant for wanting to live with her girlfriend'.

Some of the respondents indicated the police will always provide assistance even if they 'experience negative or awkward attitudes' from the police.

Seventy-eight responses were received to the question: 'How did you decide on the agency or agencies you reported or sought professional assistance?' Sixteen responses related to the police. Four of the 16 responses imply dissatisfaction with having sought professional assistance from the police and relate to inability and unwillingness of police to act (three cases) because the incident did not involve physical violence and failure of police to follow up on the incident reported over the phone. Some of the remaining 12 responses indicated the individuals knew the police or officer in the area (two cases), fear of imminent danger, and because the situation involved criminal vandalism. Some expressed positive impressions of the police service, including the following: 'The police are always the first and best people to turn to in situations'.

Fifty-three written responses were received to the remark: 'Tell us about your experiences of any of these services if you wish'. There were 17 responses that related to the police, including 11 negative references about experiences with the QPS. The majority of these have been previously addressed, including lack of timely response, inability to act until the stalker actually committed physical violence, insufficient evidence to take the matter further 'even though it was caught on a council camera', and unwillingness to act in a domestic situation. One respondent stated: 'We went immediately to the Fortitude Valley police to report while my arm was dislocated. They were too busy to help and simply said I needed to get a taxi straight to the hospital which was only five minutes away so we did'. The remaining responses related to the QPS were positive and included the following: 'Police are awesome, gave me the courage to make and implement some really hard decisions; The police were reasonably supportive but as I did not want to press charges as I would lose my job and I lost my job anyway; Police tried and recorded a conviction against the person responsible which included an 18-month suspended sentence $1,000 fine and $500 compensation; very supportive but they couldn't catch the perpetrator] as they had left the area and may have been on holidays; Police in most cases do their jobs well; and the local police were very understanding and took the details for report and insurance purposes, but admitted there was little chance of anything eventuating (charges being laid)'.

Barriers to Reporting or Seeking Professional Assistance from the Police Service

Of the 340 individuals who wrote responses to the question regarding barriers to reporting or seeking professional assistance (see Chapter 6), 167 (49%) were related to the police service.

- Twenty-six (8%) of respondents were concerned that reporting the incident would lead to further homophobia and exacerbate the abuse. Interestingly, amongst this cluster of respondents, some expressed concern that if they complained to the police service, the accused could get access to the paperwork they filled in so the offender can find out where they live. Concerns were also expressed for the safety of their children and partners if the offender has access to this information.

- Sixty-one (18%) expressed that they were treated without any sensitivity and that the police are homophobic. The prevailing perception from this cluster of individuals suggested (implicitly if not explicitly) that the police are more homophobic than the individuals who attack them.

- Fifty-nine (17%) perceived that reporting to the police would prove ineffective. Some of those in this cluster explained they have been told by the police there is nothing they can do about verbal abuse. It must be physical violence.

- Twenty-one (6%) viewed reporting as a waste of time and effort. Those in this cluster said the process takes too long and they do not have the time or energy to cope with the stress.

Factors Increasing Willingness to Report or Seek Professional Assistance

Of the 329 individuals who wrote responses to factors that would increase their willingness to report or seek professional assistance (see Chapter 6), 99 (30%) of the responses were directly related to the police service. Factors cited included increased availability of officers or liaison officers who are LGBTIQ or at least officers who are not homophobic as well as fostering greater police understanding of the distinction between homophobic abuse and violence as opposed to ordinary abuse and harassment and greater anonymity in reporting so as to minimise the potential for exacerbating physical violence.

Thirty-nine respondents or 12% cited increased availability of GLBTI police officers and police that are more trustworthy. This group of individuals want LGBTIQ individuals who are police or liaison officers or at least police that are not homophobic.

Fifty-two respondents (16%), indicated if they witnessed positive outcomes more often and knew homophobic or transphobic abuse and violence was taken more seriously, they would be more likely to report them. Respondents from this group reported that the police need to understand the distinction between homophobic abuse and violence from other abuse unrelated to homophobia. Greater confidence in the police would be inspired if the police actually acted on the reports victims make.

Eight respondents (2%) indicated they would be more willing to report if it did not exacerbate the violence. This group of individuals wanted greater anonymity in reporting.

The qualitative data above gleaned from this research reported by members of the LGBTIQ community could be construed as problematic if the Queensland Police Service (QPS) wishes to fulfil the purposes for which the Queensland liaison program was set up in 1997 not to mention help achieve some of the other objectives mentioned in the introduction to this chapter.

Focus Groups

The qualitative data reflected in the focus groups dealt mostly with the liaison officers. However, statements were made about dealings with the police (both positive and negative) as well as many negative experiences and perceptions about the liaison program.

The main problems identified with the liaison program in most of the focus groups included, but were not limited to, the following:

1. High turnover of liaison officers, including state-wide liaison officers, through their positions far too often, thereby undermining the ability to develop meaningful relationships with the community and gain their trust and confidence. There have been approximately four or five state-wide liaison officers in the past couple of years.

2. Lack of availability to get timely responses from liaison officers to enquiries from the LGBTIQ community, particularly in rural, regional and remote areas of Queensland. Police officers are in most instances the ones who respond to incidents and the cadets currently have extraordinarily limited training in LGBTIQ issues.

3. Some liaison officers are covering territory far too wide to perform their functions effectively (even those who have garnered the respect of the LGBTIQ community). They are thus unable to respond to calls on a timely basis.

4. There is a perception among some in the LGBTIQ community that members of the police force express a willingness to take on this added responsibility with no real interest in advancing the purposes of the program as evidenced in their failure not only to respond to phone calls but also to attend LGBTIQ functions to which they are invited as well as in their failure to respond to enquiries relating to their role as liaison officers on a timely basis. In the Townsville focus group (reiterated to the facilitator in other focus groups), one of the members said: 'That is why they do it actually, it's another step up. In the police, like the army, the more functions you perform, the more bickie points you get'.

5. Lack of effective training of cadets and liaison officers.

6. A state-wide liaison officer who is lower in rank (e.g., Sergeant) giving orders to the precincts to implement new procedures, such as QPrime or asking a liaison officer to attend a Pride event, to officers of higher rank in the precinct, such as Inspector. Such orders are less likely to be obeyed coming from a state-wide liaison officer of lower rank.

7. Some liaison officers are too high in rank (e.g., Inspector) and, even if well intentioned, their other responsibilities overwhelm their ability to perform their functions as liaison officers.

8. There has developed a degree of cynicism amongst those who have had longstanding dealings with the liaison program and liaison officers about the real motives for establishing the program in the first instance. The sceptics feel the program was established by the QPS when LGBTIQ outreach was viewed as a progressive move. These same cynics view the liaison program as ineffective to achieve the purposes for which the program was originally established in 1997.

The following extracts from the Gold Coast focus group suggest frustration with locating a liaison officer after an incident of serious homophobic violence, but also a positive and supportive experience with the liaison officer once he was located one month later. Several other participants in the group also had positive impressions of improvements in law enforcement and experiences with the police over time on the Gold Coast.

Example 1: A, a mature-age gay male was walking towards his car near a beat when a group of individuals smashed all the windows in his car and tried to bash him. He was frustrated in his attempts to reach a liaison officer:

A: 'So I reported this attack to the police liaison officer and I have to tell you, I had to be bloody determined to unearth who this person was and where they were ... Eventually after being fobbed off to about four different police stations ... You had to be determined'.

Facilitator: 'So what eventually transpired?'

A: 'Eventually I got in touch with this guy and I have to say that ... eventually the police responded very positively and were very supportive'.

Example 2: S, a middle-aged woman who identifies as a lesbian, feels law enforcement attitudes have changed considerably on the Gold Coast since she has been living on the Gold Coast for many years:

If anything, I feel more protected now. Mainly on the law side because the police before, in the past, would be hassling me. Now I've got the power to do something if certain policeman or someone hassles me, I can come back at them. So I've got protection there ...

Example 3: N, a young gay male, said he felt protection by the police and by his employer:

N: 'I used to work at Hungry Jack's in Surfers, doing the graveyards and if someone did come in and go, "You're a poofter" or "You're gay" or "You're this" — I'd be just like, "Well thanks and you're a heterosexual. I'm not going to serve you now because you just want to act like that and get out of the store". I had that right because I guess the managers knew they were fine with it ...'

Facilitator: 'So what happened with the customers?

N: 'Well, I'd tell them to get out — 'Go to Macca's' ... There were a few that would retaliate but then, in saying that, the police station is right next door.

Facilitator: Right — retaliate in what sense?

N: 'Throw verbal abuse; throw anything that they could get their hands on, like rubbish that was on tables, chair's.

B (a young lesbian woman employed at McDonald's): 'Large coke, back of the head'.

N: 'Yeah, all those things, But I'd go get the police and the police knew me as well, so they would treat that person as maybe a little more than they should have'.

B: 'Yeah, I definitely find the police are definitely on our side now ... from my point of view, yeah'.

Example 4: M, a mature-aged gay male stated:

The ones that aren't on your side, which you still do have them, a small majority of them, you can actually have their knuckles rapped and you feel confident about it. If you start getting hassled by the police, just threaten them ...

Example 5: K, a mature-aged gay male added the following observation:

The perception of the police has not been helpful. I think that's an age thing also because being a child of the '50s, I was terrified of the police and you never trusted the police ... The last person you would ever go to would be the authorities, if you needed help you dealt with it yourself. Nowadays, you've got the police liaison officers in most major cities. Our age group are still a bit reserved to rely on the police ... I think the breakdown between the police barrier and yourself has experienced has really changed in the last 10 years, dramatically. They [are] accessible and they have to be accountable too. You always get your rogue ones; they'll always try something on ... But I think that has changed a lot, that perception that you can't go for help. There's always help there, it's just a matter of asking for it and being prepared to front up to ask for it.

Example 6: There was consensus amongst members of the focus groups that violence generally — not just violence directed at the LGBTIQ community — has increased over the years with glassings and 'yobbos' harassing people generally, particularly when they are intoxicated or on drugs. Nonetheless, several mentioned that measures were undertaken by law enforcement to protect the LGBTIQ community several years ago and it continues to this day:

S: 'I actually grew up in Surfers and from the time I was about seven or eight years old ... I used to walk the streets when I was 10 years old at night and it was safe then. Today there's no way in the world I'd have my 10-year-old out there walking through the streets at 7 o'clock at night, no way.'

J: 'They are changing Surfers ... Wherever you go, they've got cameras everywhere ... and they want to make it family friendly safe ... Palm Beach is very feral and in Burleigh Heads they started up and they're trying to clean that up. A lot more police presence there. That's why they've put Palm Beach police station down there because [of yobbos], yahooies ... just going past throwing bottles out and doing stuff like that. It's that 20-year-old age group ...'

N: 'Can I just say the police do have cameras outside [the gay bar] now and all security guards at all night clubs in Surfers have a radio through to the police, so they come out quicker. But if the security guards care for the gay people at all, is a different question like because I know friends that dress up in drag, and we're like, 'Come on let's go to another club'. They'll be like, no, they won't let me in and I think that's pretty disgusting. Come on, I'm sure we can get you in. And they're like; no they won't let me in. They're right. Bouncers will not let them in to the night club because of the way they look ...'

Some of the participants in the Brisbane focus group expressed positive impressions of the police in Brisbane but did not concur with some of the sentiments expressed by participants in the Gold Coast focus group about the police. Others had positive impressions of some of the police in Brisbane:

Negative impressions of Gold Coast police and positive impressions of Brisbane police.

> S (a lesbian in the Brisbane focus group): 'Coppers are straight to it too; they're really quick in response, whereas down the Gold Coast it's up to two hours'.

> G (gay male): 'The Gold Coast is hideous. It's the worst place.'

> S: 'My brother's roomie is a bouncer and he got knocked out ...'

> G: 'Yeah, and [my partner's] been punched because he was dancing with the girls because the straight guys didn't want to be with them and he's dancing with them and the next 45 minutes when we went to McDonald's he gets punched in the back of the head just because he danced with them. Like as if he wants to be with them ... But the police, you know you can tell by the police in the Valley. If they're walking around in twos, it's normal. If they're walking around in threes, they don't know. They never walk in fours; they walk in sixes. When walking in groups of six, you use a cab everywhere ...'

....

One of the participants in the Brisbane focus group stated: 'I think [places such as NSW and Victoria] are further down the road in terms of normalising gay rights stuff [than] Queensland ... because a lot of people are coming up here and saying, what are you putting up with this b...s... for, this is crap.'

However, even in metropolitan Brisbane, some of the focus group participants were very sceptical about reporting incidents to the police and about the liaison program while others said it depended upon the particular police officer with whom one was dealing:

> A lesbian in the Brisbane focus group stated: 'No, no way, not even in the Valley because they don't care. They won't even give you the paperwork for it ... Unless you've got witnesses and it's on camera and all that sort of stuff, you might as well [forget about it].'

> A gay male participant was even more blunt: 'The police are the enemy. ... I don't trust them ... The police are antagonistic towards gays in Queensland. I don't care what anyone says'.

....

A different gay male stated: 'The confidence of all the police officers is hideous, like the city police are hideous … but the Valley coppers in a general rule are fabulous, and whether they're straight, gay or bi or whatever it is, in a sense, and the way they carry about their duty and give confidence from what they do is really good.'

A lesbian stated: 'I think it might be easier to be gay in the police force if you're a girl than if you're a guy.'

....

The extracts below from one of the focus groups held in a regional community in Queensland reflect good working relationships with the police. They also exhibit frustrations with lack of timely police response to calls because of overly burdensome workloads, lack of training of police in LGBTIQ issues, and some of the problems associated with high turnover of liaison officers so often that it is difficult to determine who to contact. An instance of outright hostility directed at a transsexual is an example of the transphobia of a senior police officer and the general lack of interest in liaison issues by such officers because their motives for serving in these capacities is to get promoted rather than to advance the purposes of the program.

In this regional focus group, the members were asked: 'How confident would you feel about reporting homophobic abuse or violence to the police if you felt the matter was serious enough?'

T (middle-aged gay male employed in a gay venue): 'Can we all say together — it doesn't work.'

S (mature-aged gay male proprietor of another gay venue): 'The police will help but the police are under such strain with their workload, they have to prioritise things. We do have a good working relationship with the police. If we call them, it's their job, and they will come, but yes, they're slow — like T said, they're slow at chasing things up. If they can let the case get buried and never be looked at again — I've had to call in and call in and call in to make sure this guy that did this to me [broken arm] is going to be arrested over it.'

T: 'It's not that they dislike gay people. I think they're not trained to be like that anymore.'

Facilitator: 'Does everyone here know about the liaison officers?'

Group: 'Yes'.

S: 'The police couldn't tell me who they were. They've both got the same sign that we've got in our venue with the names of them. I said,

"Are those names there still the liaison officers in this town?" And they didn't know ... The police are here this week and gone the next, you never strike the same one a year down the track, they'd be at another station or Cairns.'

....

Example: E, a mature aged transsexual, stated:

E: 'I had cause to ring the police one night and there were no liaison officers on call, not one, out of [many] officers ... We have a young girl who is in the same position. She's had an organectomy, so therefore two stone lighter if you want to put it bluntly. So she has no sexual ability, castrating, call it what you want.

'She was assaulted, her jaw was broken, the police were called, and they said you'll have to come in to make a statement. She went into the [suburban] police station [located in this regional community] and she was explaining to the officer why and how she was assaulted.

'He said: "How come this person attacked you?" She said: "I'm trans-sexual". He said, "What do you mean?" She said: "I was dressed female". He said: "What do you expect?" We don't deal with people like you and pulled his service revolver out, put it on the table and said: "Why don't you ping off?" So she did.'

Facilitator: 'That wasn't the liaison officer over the counter.'

E: 'No, just an ordinary officer over the counter.'

Facilitator: 'Do you know his name?'

E: 'No I don't unfortunately; otherwise I'd try and have his tail.'

J, another mature aged transgendered individual, stated: 'We have actually brought this up with the liaison officers.'

J: 'There is supposed to be three liaison officers here in town most of the time.'

E: 'It's pretty hit and miss ... I know a high-ranking police official in [this regional community] who is — shall we say homophobic. He, in actual fact, says, if you asked him, he is not prejudiced against gay or transsexual people. He in no way discriminates against them, he just doesn't care who shoots them. That's the way he feels about people.'

....

Issue: Availability and training of liaison officers.

P (mature-aged gay male owner of a gay establishment): 'I think every policeman should be a liaison officer, as part of the job.'

....

B (middle-aged gay male): 'They all should be trained.'

M (middle-aged gay male): 'If the excuse for not training them sufficiently — I still think three days is insufficient for the LGBTIQ community ...'

S: 'It is like that now, because if you ask the police where they are, they can't tell you. If you ask them: Is that a list of names still current? They can't tell you ... We have [a] gay venue in town and they never walk through our door. We never get a phone call from them. So they're not there. In actual fact, they're not there and we deal with the general rank and file police. As we said before, T and I, they will help you. They'll put you on the backburner if you let them and deal with other things ...'

P (raising the problem of reaching a police officer): 'Another problem we have here in [this regional community of Queensland] is when you ring the police station, how often does the phone ring out? This is the main police station.'

E: 'I have rung communications and had to wait for about 5 minutes before I got an answer.'

P: 'I've had to ring the police station at night time when we've had a drama at the hotel or in front of the hotel or something and the phone has rung out many a time, and you think: God, this is the main police station in [one of the larger cities in Queensland], there's nobody to answer the phone.'

S: 'If you ring 000 it tells you if it's not life threatening or an emergency, ring the other number. But you ring the other number and it says, only if it's life threatening or an emergency, ring 000, so the two recordings refer you the opposite way.'

P: 'Or a crime in progress.'

S: 'That's it, life threatening or a crime in progress. Unless it's that, don't ring 000.'

P: 'I'm standing here getting my head bashed in, is that a crime in progress?'

....

The extracts below from the Cairns focus group question the motives for initially establishing the liaison program, raise the problems associated with having a lower ranked state-wide liaison officer giving orders to a higher ranking official, as well as the difficulty of having high-ranking officers serving as liaison officers. In addition, several of the participants suggested homophobia and racism were not uncommon in the police force.

K (middle-aged gay male): '[The GLBT liaison program was] like the flavour of the month, too, because when I first came up here they had those liaison officers for cultural awareness, those people were in town. There was a Japanese liaison officer and they were just pushing big time, the police. They were advertising the position, they were doing lots and lots of things and now you don't see the people. It was like the flavour of the month. When that gay thing first came out in Queensland, the gay liaison officer, because I was in Brisbane then, it was the flavour of the month. They did the training, seven years later there's nothing.'

....

Discussion in the focus group turned to a lesbian who had previously served as a state-wide liaison officer and was perceived by many as trying to do her job effectively but her junior rank precluded her ability to do so.

K: 'We asked for the police to be involved in our Gay Pride [day] the first year and we couldn't understand why they couldn't be there because we felt it was a big enough community for them to be there. But when we contacted our liaison coordinator here they said they'd do something about it and nothing happened and we were asking and asking and they were saying yes, yes, yes. So in the end we contacted, [the state-wide liaison officer] ... She was really good and ... she said "Leave it with me, it will happen". She sent out the thing and said you will be there and no one was there because it was that thing where she was a sergeant and she's telling a detective inspector what to do. He's not going to listen to her. They just came back and said there's no one available on that shift unfortunately ...

'This year was different because we did the same thing again this year and the state-wide liaison officer sent an email, because she has a higher rank as [Senior Sergeant]. I think they just got sick of us. They got sick of us going on and on and asking and asking and in the end they got a friendly ... LGBT officer ... [whom I did not recognise and had never seen previously].

'They shouldn't call themselves liaison officers because they're not that. They're not doing an extra good position, like they're not liaison, liaising with the community at all.'

....

A discussion ensued about what type of training program exists for the liaison officers:

> N (middle-aged gay male): 'We keep on being told that [community support groups are going] to be invited at some stage to go and do some training with the recruits in the Townsville Academy and I went to Mr J ... the other day ... our local inspector, "What's happening, we've been waiting for a year saying when's this training program going to be happening". We were told [the state-wide liaison officer is] organising it. Now, the [liaison officer whose territory includes Mt. Isa and Townsville], in Townsville keeps on saying to me she keeps on pestering the Brisbane office to say we want this training put in place. There are two sets of training that needs doing ... The LGBTIQ liaison officers need training because the turnover and the new people keep coming to the positions that have no training and then the recruits need training as well.'

> K: 'Well they have in the past ... Half to full day training.'

> N: 'How long ago did that stop?'

> K: 'It stopped ... [maybe in] 2004.'

> N: 'But we keep on being told it's in the pipeline, it's in the pipeline and it never comes through the pipeline.'

....

The discussion also dealt with the issue of the difficulty of a high ranking official serving as a liaison officer.

> K: 'It's part of the role. Like up here the detective inspector in charge of crime in Cairns, his position, one of his positions is LGBTIQ liaison coordinator. That's just been the theme. Now he is the major person in charge of crime. He's on the TV every night talking about all the crime in town. That's a very small, very, very small part of his job. [Whenever he is invited to community discussions] ... he sends apologies but you can understand for someone of that stature to have that role is inappropriate.'

> Facilitator: 'I think that they have so many things on their plates that they're exhausted ...'

> K: 'I don't agree at all with that ... I wouldn't use that as a reason. I would see that it's not facing up to the realities of living in a world that we live in today. I think the resources of the police force should, in the world that we live in now in Australia, the community expects these standards of all their other workers, in ... all other government areas ...'

The conversation then turned to the issue of homophobia in the Police Service as well as the experiences of Indigenous individuals who are part of LGBTIQ community.

K: 'There's not acceptance of obvious homophobia [in other government departments] like there would be in the police force. But there's no expectation of the police force on these things happening ...'

D (transgender woman in her late thirties): 'You hear police on a round, the terrible things they say to everybody, the way they treat people generally. I mean they have poor communication skills ...'

K: 'Compared to other police forces ... their values and the way they're expected to treat people. No one says it's an easy job.'

E (Aboriginal gay male in his mid-30s): 'I've experienced similar police like Queensland in the Northern Territory and the way that they treat people and violently as well. Apart from the lesbian and gay and bisexual and transgender thing, the way they treat Indigenous people and the deaths in custody that they still won't look at. If they had to actually try and treat lesbian and gay people better, they'd have to go back and look through all those deaths and stuff ... And personally, my family has actually been affected by a death in custody ... I think bigotry is so institutionalised in the police force that there is no way of changing ...'

K: 'Like everything, corruption, everything. It sucks. There's a bad smell.'

N: 'I think the racism stands out more than anything. I've seen it so blatantly on the street ...'

K: 'We have to ask ourselves why open lesbians can't be open about their sexuality in their workplace as a police woman. What does that say about your environment? That you're open in the community, you can't be open about your sexuality at work and you're a policewoman.'

D: 'Let's be honest here. We've been saying now about homophobia and all this sort of stuff. We've already been labelled by the police ... [and] put us in a box already before ...'

D: 'Before they can address the fact that [there is discrimination], they've got to understand they've already started. Before the slate's even been drawn they've already started discriminating themselves. If they can't see that as being endemic already within the system, it's already set up.'

E: 'Can I just mention, recently two Indigenous, one gay and one transgender, were recently thrown into the lockup at the courthouse, and they're ... 20 years of age, and they were both thrown into the lockup and most other young people are drunk in Cairns and if you can't see any drunk teenagers than you are blind. They're all over the bloody place. But they managed to single out two gay or transgender Aboriginal kids and threw them in the watch house and we didn't find out about it until after the weekend when they actually felt that they needed to come and see someone. They didn't even feel that they could go to Legal Aid or anybody.'

Facilitator: 'Why?'

E: 'Because they're black and they're gay and no one can help them ... Bigotry in Australia is institutionalised. It's in every pocket of society now and if you don't, if you're not a bigot you don't fit in. It goes across communities, like tourists and immigrants who come to Australia, they learn very quickly to put people down if they want to fit in and if they don't put people down then they're going to be one of the ones put down as well ... coming to Australia you see what racism's like here. It slaps you right in the face ... Then it's your Asian. It's always minority ...'

....

The notion of less tolerant attitudes towards LGBTIQ people and different gender identities in rural and remote areas, discrimination in the workplace, and a sense of feeling less safe because of being different were also raised:

S (middle-aged gay male): 'I think it's in these regional communities that homophobia is even more intense. Then they actively shut you down ... at times, to be honest with you, because we were a same sex couple that went up [at the Atherton Tablelands], I honestly thought for a while there, you hear trucks or utes coming up the drive and stuff like that that, we were isolated and we were on this acreage, and I honestly thought ... one day we're going to look out there and there's going to be a truck load of blokes with bloody sheets on their faces you know? That's what it was like. Then it extended into my workplace. I had members of my staff who would make all these comments and they would be getting their children as well to make these comments. If I went into the supermarket I was virtually abused by not only adults, but their children as well. It resulted in a member of my staff holding a [BBQ] on a weekend and inviting all of these people to attend, and this was her undoing actually, to get a petition signed to get rid of the openly gay person because we don't have that sort of thing in our community ...'

....

The notion of institutionalised bigotry was also implicitly raised in the Sunshine Coast focus groups:

E (gay male): 'The way I see it is I am just as subject to d…kheads as I would be if I was black or fat or I don't know anything. People will pick on you. My theory is if you are not a man, white and religious, you are going to be attacked somehow.'

M (lesbian woman): 'I totally agree with E … that it doesn't matter so much whether we are gay … if we were black, we would cop it.'

E: 'If you had a shaved head. It depends where you are — they will get you for something.'

Another gay male stated: 'I used to have a mohawk before it was in fashion, before a lot of people started to do it and I lived in a town of 8000 people. Well hell did I get a hard time … Anybody that sticks out. I wore braces at school … A totally normal haircut and all that sort of stuff and man was I harassed because [I was] different. Queensland is very well known for it. You have got to be the same or else.'

....

General violence and less tolerant attitudes in areas of the Sunshine Coast was also a theme touched upon which has had a chilling effect on the willingness of some individuals to attend gay events or frequent gay venues:

D (gay male): 'Certainly … we are safer in places like Brisbane and Sydney and Melbourne where there is a very clear demarcated gay population and gay venue area … The problem with the coast in terms of comparing it to sort of more urbanised centres there isn't that kind of distinctive, I will use the word "ghetto" for lack of a better word. But if you go to Brisbane, you go to the Valley even though there are some problems there, they are very clearly marked areas. We have been here for two years and I have never been out once because there is nowhere to go and I am sure as hell not going to the club that has the gay night because the first thing my partner [who is a crown prosecutor] said is "No way. I have had three cases come through this week from people being glassed in the face. So we are not going there" … [in this instance it wasn't because of sexuality] but just the violence in general. I am not going to put myself in violent situations regardless of sexuality.'

Another gay male in the Sunshine Coast focus group expressed these same concerns about [places such as Mooloolaba and Maroochydore]:

....

Crush [a gay venue] used to be run by a bloke called J. There was a once a month gay deal ... I had only been going out there for the last couple of years and even then there would be still guys jeering and stuff like that. But before that, guys used [to tell me] that there was quite a lot of violence. A lot of young guys would hang out outside and bash up whatever gays they could find ... They would be there and wait, just to pick them ... off ... if you want to go out on a Saturday night, you don't.'

M (lesbian woman): 'They go to Brisbane ... I am sure that you could go and approach venues and find out whether they are [a gay friendly venue] and they will say "Yeah, yeah, yeah". As soon as you say to them "Hey will you put a poster up on your wall to identify as a gay friendly venue?" No, they don't want to do business ... [They do not even want to be identified as a safe place] because there is that fear there that [they will] lose business if [they] display [themselves] as being a gay friendly venue.'

....

The issue of non-reporting of homophobic violence, including rape was also raised as an issue:

C (gay male in the Sunshine Coast focus group): 'A very, very good friend of mine works in a gay and lesbian counselling service in Melbourne and he was actually telling me that a surprising number of attacks against single males at night also have the potential to turn into sexual based attacks and men don't report it.'

Y: 'Of course they don't. There was one recently in Townsville and actually they used the word rape which obviously is very broad under the current legislation ... [I asked my partner the Crown Prosecutor what is this all about] That's very interesting, you don't see that all that often. He said that will be a single sexual assault. It would have been violent. Somebody would have attacked somebody and then they have either inserted into an orifice or made some kind of attack. But of course the shame and the stigma that goes along with that in a crisis of masculinity, men will just not report it. That's exactly right, there is that potential to be violent.'

C: 'Exactly and it doesn't restrict itself to women. In extreme violent situations that risk is even higher, because once someone who is attacking someone loses control, they will lose control completely and it does have the catastrophic potential regardless of whether you are male or female.'

M, a lesbian respondent from the Sunshine Coast described how some members of the LGBTIQ community were reluctant to seek help after being assaulted in mixed venues. 'It is unfortunate that when they have gone to take it to the authorities it's been pushed under the carpet because unfortunately our authoritative base, there would only be one or two people that would actually file that complaint properly in the Sunshine Coast region.'

A gay male stated, 'I don't know what it's called, but the police have a program where you can contact ... the gay/lesbian cop'.

....

The issue of difficulty in contacting LGBTIQ liaison officers who are in senior positions and will respond on a timely basis was also raised in the Sunshine Coast focus group.

M: 'The LGBT liaison officer and that is what I'm talking about. There is not a specific person on the Sunshine Coast who will advocate and support the LGBT community. Mark is about the only person ... but because he is the senior officer in the whole crime prevention unit, it is very rare to be able to talk to him ... He is one of the designated officers but because he is the head of the crime prevention unit, it is very hard to contact him. So people will then come to [a community support group] or myself at the university ... and then I will call him and say "hey, look, what the hell?" Then he will try and talk to that person. But with all that to-ing and fro-ing the victims are like forget it. I don't want it brought up again ... 80% of the people I know would let it go because they know there is no support there ...'

C: 'From a personal point of view and from experiencing it and witnessing it amongst my friends and things like that, that goes a long way towards preventing homophobia because if people don't speak up about it, it doesn't get made public, it doesn't get addressed ... The most significant homophobia and transphobia and violence ... comes as a result of being outed.'

Policing in Context

Members of any governmental organisation reflect prevailing social norms in any community. As outlined in preceding chapters, Michael Flood and Clive Hamilton's 2005 report found attitudes with regard to homosexuality less progressive in some regional, rural and remote areas of Queensland. Two of the three most homophobic regions in the country were respondents from Central/South-West Queensland and the Moreton area (not including the Sunshine or Gold Coast). Half of the respondents from these two regions of Queensland viewed homosexuality as immoral.[18] The sentiments expressed in the focus groups conducted in Toowoomba, Rockhampton, Townsville, Cairns, and the Sunshine Coast seems consistent with these findings.

The qualitative data in this research survey suggests that the police service reflects wider social norms in the general community with officers who perform their duties effectively and with whom some of the respondents in this survey have had good experiences. Some of the data also suggest there is a perception among the respondents that homophobia exists among members of the police service that is in some ways even more prevalent than in other government departments. K, a gay male in one focus group stated: 'There's still that mentality amongst the ground force that it's okay [to be homophobic] because I believe they're training officers to be strong, to go out, to combat and part of that combat, that thing is to make them, is allowing them to be macho'. This sentiment was echoed in other focus groups. Another gay male in the Brisbane focus group expressed cynicism about the GLBTI liaison officers, stating:

> No guy as far as I know, and I'm pretty well informed, there are no gay officers amongst any of those heterosexual officers and they're more heterosexual in the police service, there is a culture of a man's man. Heterosexual, heterosexual, and there is no room for that sexuality to be ambiguous because they need to be tough and butch to enforce the law and I feel very strongly about this. There's a homophobic culture in the Police Department. And the Samoans, the Aboriginals and other minority groups have dedicated liaison employed police officers who have separate uniforms. The gay liaison is a farce. Their consultation process is a joke. Very few gays go to their consultation process because they cannot get any satisfaction from the gay community as far as I know ... I know two gay police officers who are loathe being out in the Police Department. That says it all to me. Employed police officers are even petrified themselves to be open about their [homosexuality].

As Flood and Hamilton explain, not all homophobes engage in discriminatory behaviour. However, their approach, outlook, and manner can be affected by their beliefs about sexual identity: 'They are more likely to contribute to a general attitude of intolerance that is interpreted by those who are actively homophobic to condone their vilification of gay and lesbian people. It is for this reason that derogatory and insulting remarks ... contribute to and reinforce the intolerance of those already homophobic ... [and] it is likely that the small minority who are prone to commit acts of violence against [GLBTI individuals] are encouraged to act aggressively because they feel that their homophobia is sanctioned by influential voices in the community.'[19]

A focus group participant in Cairns stated:

We have become such second-class citizens in this society ... that's been created for our community. That's not something we've chosen to do because we've been marginalised and forced into creating these little communities because we haven't been accepted in a wider community.So we've been forced out and living in a country run by a Liberal government for so long that we don't have the same laws ... Queensland still has unequal laws.

This quotation is particularly telling from a member of the general public who is unfamiliar with the law. His perceptions are accurate. Many of the recommendations in Chapter 10 are designed to make Queensland more progressive to bring it in line with other jurisdictions in Australia and globally in many disciplines.

The above qualitative data provided suggestions on different options for liaison officers, such as having officers identify themselves by wearing a badge, representation of actual LGBTIQ individuals serving in the role of liaison officers or (as with the Victorian model) a GLLO unit within the police who do not have to be or identify as LGBTIQ provided they are sensitive to issues affecting the LGBTIQ community. As far as the authors are aware, according to information gleaned from the various focus groups, there are few, if any, gay men who are 'out' in the QPS. The authors are aware of at least one lesbian who is 'out' and served in the role of state-wide liaison officer for a period of time. Given the information provided in focus groups, the authors believe it is unrealistic to expect liaison officers to be or identify as members of the LGBTIQ community. The culture in the QPS at the present time is not conducive to such an expectation and the sheer numbers of liaison officers located throughout the state make this an unrealistic expectation. The authors have suggested in Chapter 10 that the QPS try to recruit more members of the LGBTIQ community as cadets through community events, such as Brisbane Pride, Sunshine Coast Pride and Cairns Pride as well as in the queer and mainstream press. As social norms change over time, it might be realistic to expect greater representation of members of the community to serve as members of the QPS and/or as liaison officers. At the present time, the authors believe it is more important for the cadets to receive training on issues affecting the LGBTIQ community since the police are usually the first to respond to a complaint. They should also be trained to refer the complainant to the appropriate liaison officer and/or unit within the QPS and provide their contact details to members of the community at the time a report is made and/or to the appropriate agency, such as ADCQ, in the event they are unable to act, such as in situations involving non-violent homophobic or transphobic abuse and harassment.

In Chapter 10, a number of recommendations have been made in connection with the training of cadets, greater collaboration between the state-wide liaison officer with those in New South Wales, Victoria Tasmania and specialised training programs for liaison officers modelled on the NSW (GLLO) training program in an attempt to reinvigorate and resharpen the liaison program. Thirty-two per cent of the respondents to this survey were unaware of liaison officers. This is in sharp contrast to the approximately 17% who were unaware of such liaison officers in the recent 2008 study in Victoria. An encouraging sign is that 76% of respondents indicated the existence of liaison officers increased the likelihood that they would report an incident of homophobic or transphobic harassment or violence to the Police Service. This is similar to the 79% who responded to the same question in the Victorian survey.

The authors are under the impression that fewer LGBTIQ individuals are willing to accept the status quo and are speaking out about their experiences in a variety of fora (including studies such as this one) and taking concrete positive steps to change social norms which will ultimately filter into attitudes in the wider community as well as the QPS. The importance of role models who are out and proud can also help in this regard. As one focus group participant stated: 'I celebrate that we have emerging heroes [such as Matthew Mitcham, a Queenslander who won a gold medal in the last Olympics and came out in a courageous way in the Sydney Morning Herald] that are breaking the stereotypes. We need more leaders, and especially young people who are prepared to stand up and say, I'm out and I'm queer; too bad if you don't like it.'

Conclusion

In conclusion, the levels of reporting of incidents of homophobic abuse, harassment and violence to the police and liaison officers is just 16%. This low level of reporting is consistent with both the data from NSW and more recent study in Victoria in 2008. The quantitative data suggests those who reported to the police or liaison officers generally found them reasonably or very supportive. However, the number of individuals who sought assistance from the police (72 respondents) and the liaison officers (22 respondents) in relation to the number of individuals who experienced an incident of homophobic or transphobic harassment or violence in the past two years

(583 respondents or 53% of survey respondents) are so low that it is not possible to draw any statistical inferences other than that the LGBTIQ community's engagement with the police service is low, and even lower with liaison officers.

The findings from the qualitative data in this chapter are consistent with the writings of some commentators who have suggested that lesbians and gay men generally hold negative images of law enforcement and are thus reluctant to invoke the apparatus of state law enforcement in response to hate crimes. As the above statements and data reflect, harassment and violent hate crimes committed against LGBTIQ individuals that are tolerated by society propagate intolerance against these sexual minorities and provoke fear in this community.[20] Some of the written responses in the survey canvassed above, as well as responses obtained in the focus groups, support these observations. These experiences have left indelible imprints in the memories of mature-age LGBTIQ individuals. Additionally, the negative attitudes toward reporting incidents to the police can also be explained by real life personal experiences of respondents to this survey as well as participants in the focus groups.

The recommendations in chapter 10 are designed to help empower the LGBTIQ community. Aside from recommended changes in policing responses, governmental initiatives are also suggested to help shape social attitudes in Queensland so that the principles of sexual diversity, inclusiveness, personal dignity, autonomy and privacy are celebrated as values which will serve to further the goals of all societies for greater social cohesion. The authors sincerely believe training of cadets as suggested in the recommendations section, along with a resharpened LGBTIQ liaison program, would garner the support of the LGBTIQ community groups so as to create greater partnerships in crime prevention, increase the reporting of prejudice-motivated violence, reduce the incidence of crime, harassment and fear within these communities and create a supportive workplace for LGBTIQ individuals employed by the QPS and as liaison officers.

Notes

1 New South Wales Police Service, <www.police.nsw.gov.au> <GLLO> (accessed 24 February 2010).

2 Ibid.

3 Ibid.

4 Victorian Police Service, <www.police.vic.gov.au> <GLLO> (accessed 24 February 2010).

5 Ibid.

6 Victorian Police, 'Preventing Homophobic Crimes' (25 June 2007), available at

<http://www.police.vic.gov.au/content.asp?Document ID=308> (accessed 25 February 2010)

7   Ibid.

8   Ibid.

9   See Queensland Police Service, Robert Atkinson, Commissioner, 'Working in Partnership' (2009), available at <http://www.police.qld.gov.au/programs/ community/lgbti/equality.htm> (accessed on 14 January 2010).

10 'Gay men targets of violence', *Brisbane Times*, 2 November 2008 available at <http://www.brisbanetimes.com.au/news/queensland/gay-men-targets-of-violence/200811/02/1225560616212.html> (accessed 30 January 2010).

11 See notes 1, 4.

12 The respondents could tick one or more of the boxes under the questions relating to homophobic and transphobic harassment or violent incidents experienced within the past two years, including written threats and abuse (including emails and graffiti); verbal abuse (including hateful or obscene phone calls); harassment (such as being spat at and offensive gestures); threats of physical violence; physical attack or assault without a weapon (punched, kicked, beaten); physical attack with a weapon (punched, kicked, beaten); sexual assault without weapon, deliberate damage to property or vandalism — House; Deliberate damage to property — Car; Deliberate damage to property or Vandalism — Work; Theft — Money; Theft — Property; House — Break In. Amongst the 20 who ticked the box 'other', 9 responses were given including some of the following: sexually explicit verbal comments and gestures; eggs thrown, discrimination in the work place (2), Queer Business Broken into and threat to discredit through disclosure of personal information from a hostile ex partner.

13 William Leonard and others, *Coming Forward: The Underreporting of Heterosexist Violence and Same Sex Partner Abuse in Victoria* (Melbourne: The Australian Research Centre in Sex, Health and Society, La Trobe University, 2008), p. 53.

14 New South Wales Attorney General's Department, *'You Shouldn't Have to Hide to be Safe': A Report on Homophobic Hostilities and Violence Against Gay Men and Lesbians in New South Wales* (Sydney, New South Wales Attorney General's Department, December 2003), Executive Summary, p.3.

15 Ibid , p.54.

16 See *Anti-Discrimination Act 1991* (QLD) s 124A, providing 'Vilification on grounds of race, religion, sexuality or gender is unlawful' and stating that:

(1) A person must not, by a public act, incite hatred towards, serious contempt for, or severe ridicule of, a person or group of persons on the ground of the race, religion, sexuality or gender identity of the person or members of the group.

(2) Subsection (1) does not make unlawful-

(a) the publication of a fair report of a public act mentioned in subsection (1); or

(b) the publication of material in circumstances in which the publication would be subject to a defence of absolute privilege in proceedings for defamation; or

(c) a public act, done reasonably and in good faith, for academic, artistic,

> scientific or research purposes or for other purposes in the public interest, including public discussion or debate about, and expositions of, any act or matter.

17 See *Anti-Discrimination Act 1991* (QLD) s 131A, providing an 'Offence of serious racial, religious, sexuality or gender identity vilification' and stating that:

(1) A person must not, by a public act, knowingly or recklessly incite hatred towards, serious contempt for, or severe ridicule of, a person or group of persons on the ground of the race, religion, sexuality or gender identity of the person or members of the group in a way that includes—

(a) threatening physical harm towards, or towards any property of, the person or group of persons; or

(b) inciting others to threaten physical harm towards, or towards any property of, the person or group of persons.

Maximum penalty—

(a) for an individual—70 penalty units or 6 months imprisonment;

(b) for a corporation—350 penalty units.

(2) A Crown Law Officer's written consent must be obtained before a proceeding is started by complaint under the Justices Act 1886 in relation to an offence under subsection (1).

(3) An offence under subsection (1) is not an offence for section 155(2) or 226.

(4) In this section— Crown Law Officer means the Attorney-General or Director of Public Prosecutions.'

18 Michael Flood and Clive Hamilton, 'Mapping Homophobia in Australia' in Shirleene Robinson, ed., *Homophobia: An Australian History* (Annandale, New South Wales: Federation Press, 2008), pp 20-26.

19 Ibid.

20 Alan Berman, 'The Experiences of Denying Constitutional Protection to Sodomy Laws in the United States, Australia, and Malaysia: You've Come a Long Way Baby and You Still Have a Long Way to Go!', Oxford University Comparative Law Forum Article 2 (2008) fn 147 and accompanying text, citing Andrew Fitzgerald, 'Australia's Criminal Justice System Fails Lesbians and Gay Men', *Murdoch University Electronic Journal of Law* Vol 3 (1996), p.1-3, available at <http://www.murdoch.edu.au/elaw/issues/v3n2/fitzgera.html> (accessed 31 December 2009).

CHAPTER 8

Experiences With the Judicial Process

As outlined in Table 8.1, of the 583 respondents (53%) who experienced an incident of homophobic or transphobic harassment or violence in the past two years, 10 (2%) indicated their cases proceeded to court. This low percentage is due to a number of factors. First, the level of reporting is low, with only 72 respondents (12%) reporting incidents to the police and 22 respondents (4%) reporting incidents to liaison officers. Furthermore, police officers are unable to act in cases of verbal abuse and harassment and, as Chapter 7 outlines, are often reluctant to act even in instances of threats of physical violence.[1] Consequently, it is not surprising that the number of cases actually proceeding to court was so low. The low number of cases proceeding to court and the lower number of respondents to the survey questions makes it difficult to draw any inferences about the extent to which homophobia or transphobia was perceived to play a role in the way individuals were treated in the judicial process. The limited data available does provide some degree of insight into the experiences of LGBTIQ individuals in the judicial process and is thus explored in this chapter.

Table 8.2 reveals three cases proceeded to the Magistrates Court, three to the District Court and two proceeded to the Supreme Court. One respondent was unsure of where the case proceeded. No response was received from the tenth individual who reported the case proceeded to court. Five of the ten, or half of the individuals who proceeded to court, indicated they would go through the process again, while one stated 'No' and two were unsure. Two individuals did not respond to this question. Amongst those who were unsure or indicated they would not go through the process again (three respondents), no written responses were received to explain their reasons. This is shown in Table 8.3.

As summarised in Table 8.4, there was no consensus among the respondents as to whether court staff were sensitive or insensitive to their situation as a LGBTIQ person and whether they were treated in an unprofessional manner because of their sexual orientation and gender identity.

Similarly, there was also a split of opinion about whether the prosecutor kept them informed about the court process and was sensitive to their situation as a LGBTIQ person.

Three respondents agreed the magistrate or judge kept them informed of the judicial process, one disagreed, two did not know and no response was received from the remaining four. Four agreed the magistrate or pre-

Table 8.1
Responses to the Question 'Did the incident go to court?'

Response	Number	Percentage
Yes	10	2%
No	384	66%
Don't know	13	2%
No response	176	30%
Total	583	

Table 8.2
Responses to the Question 'Which court did the case go to?' (For those who specified that the incident went to court)

Response	Number	Percentage
Magistrates	3	30%
District	3	30%
Supreme	2	20%
Not sure	1	10%
No response	1	10%
Total	10	

Table 8.3
Responses to the Question 'Would you go through this process again?' (For those who specified that the incident went to court)

Response	Number	Percentage
Yes	5	50%
No	1	10%
Unsure	2	20%
No response	2	20%
Total	10	

siding judge was sensitive to their situation as an LGBTIQ person while one disagreed and two indicated they did not know. Similarly, just one found the magistrate or judge was insensitive to their situation as a LGBTIQ person while three disagreed and two did not know. No responses were received from four individuals.

Although the number of LGBTIQ respondents to this survey were over two and a half times greater than the number of respondents to the *Coming Forward* survey conducted in Victoria in 2008 (even though Queensland has a lower population demographic), few respondents noted that their cases proceeded to court. This is indicative of several factors.[2] Current laws are arguably ineffective in providing adequate remedies to LGBTIQ individuals who experience the type of low-level homophobic abuse, harassment and physical threats that continue to afflict LGBTIQ people's lives. There are potential civil remedies available through the complaint mechanism procedures of the Anti-Discrimination Commission for sexual and gender identity vilification.[3]

In 2008, a gay couple in Brisbane, one of whom was a high school history teacher, were successful in bringing an action for civil damages for sexual vilification under presumably Section 124 A of the Queensland Anti-Discrimination Act after being 'stalked and harassed' by some neighbours over a period of 9 months, although the dispute began 3 years earlier when the gay couple complained about the neighbours' barking dogs to the RSPCA. The police suggested the couple change residences. Their neighbours told them gay people should not be living in the suburbs [Woodbridge] and should instead move back to New Farm, a suburb popularly known to have a high LGBTIQ population. McCollum, a high school teacher, emphasised it was important for gay people to use the legal procedures available if they are experiencing harassment and vilification: 'I guess the message here is that as gay people the law will protect us, but we need to be more resilient than we are and the law is very slow.'[4]

Many in the LGBTIQ community may not be aware of these potential civil remedies because they do not possess the legal knowledge that such avenues for legal redress exist, or have the resources and energy to pursue such remedies. As canvassed in Chapter 7, the qualitative data indicate many are not referred to the ADCQ upon reporting such incidents to the police service. This information has informed some of the recommendations in Chapter 10 to improve knowledge about legal remedies and thereby improve access to justice so members of the LGBTIQ community are aware of these potential remedies.

Table 8.4

Responses to the Question 'How were you treated by the police officers, court staff, prosecutor, magistrate/judge handling the matter?'

Treatment by justice system staff	Agree	Disagree	Don't know	No response
Police officer				
Kept you informed of court process	8	0	0	2
Was sensitive to your situation as a LGBTIQ person	6	3	0	1
Was insensitive to your situation as a LGBTIQ person	4	3	0	3
Acknowledged that the incident was prejudice motivated	7	1	0	2
Treated you in an unprofessional manner because of your sexual orientation or gender identity	3	4	0	3
Court staff				
Kept you informed of court process	6	2	1	1
Was sensitive to your situation as a LGBTIQ person	3	4	1	2
Was insensitive to your situation as a LGBTIQ person	3	3	2	2
Acknowledged that the incident was prejudice motivated	4	3	1	2
Treated you in an unprofessional manner because of your sexual orientation or gender identity	2	4	1	3
Prosecutor				
Kept you informed of court process	4	2	2	2
Was sensitive to your situation as a LGBTIQ person	3	2	2	3
Was insensitive to your situation as a LGBTIQ person	1	3	2	4
Acknowledged that the incident was prejudice motivated	4	2	1	3
Treated you in an unprofessional manner because of your sexual orientation or gender identity	1	4	1	4

continued over

Table 8.4 (continued)
Responses to the Question 'How were you treated by the police officers, court staff, prosecutor, magistrate/judge handling the matter?'

Treatment by justice system staff	Agree	Disagree	Don't know	No response
Magistrate or Judge				
Kept you informed of court process	3	1	2	4
Was sensitive to your situation as a LGBTIQ person	4	1	2	3
Was insensitive to your situation as a LGBTIQ person	1	3	2	4
Acknowledged that the incident was prejudice motivated	4	2	2	2
Treated you in an unprofessional manner because of your sexual orientation or gender identity	2	2	2	4

Second, as previously canvassed, there are perceived difficulties in proving cases involving only physical threats as a criminal assault so many law enforcement officers will not act in instances of abuse limited to physical threats. There are potential civil and criminal remedies available through the current *Anti-Discrimination Act* for severe sexual and gender identity vilification that includes physical threats.[5] Some commentators have criticised similar anti-discrimination legislation in jurisdictions throughout Australia because of the complicated process for bringing prosecutions. The police service are not involved in the process and a request must be made for approval to commence proceedings (that carry potential criminal penalties) by the Anti-Discrimination Commissioner to the Attorney General (AG) or Director of Public Prosecutions (DPP).[6] The authors understand in many jurisdictions in which this has occurred, the AG or the DPP has failed to approve the commencement of such proceedings even in the face of substantial evidence. As Gail Mason has pointed out, there have been no prosecutions or convictions in any jurisdiction in Australia under similar provisions.[7] Thus, this provision of the legislation has proven ineffective in providing redress in instances involving severe sexual and gender identity vilification that includes physical threats. For this reason, the authors have made certain recommendations for legislative reform in Chapter 10 to address this deficiency in the legislation so that offenders can he held accountable.

Furthermore, there is a general reluctance of individuals to report such incidents in the first instance because of the barriers to reporting an incident or seeking professional assistance, as canvassed in Chapters 6 and 7 on the police service. The qualitative data gleaned from the written responses regarding barriers on reporting an incident or seeking professional assistance, factors that would increase willingness to report an incident as well as the information provided in the seven focus groups have informed many of the recommendations in Chapter 10 for strategies to help encourage victims of homophobic and transphobic abuse, harassment and actual violence to engage more actively with law enforcement, ADCQ and the court system.

Finally, there can be a disinclination to insist on prosecuting even in cases involving actual severe physical violence. As one of the participants in the Sunshine Coast focus group stated:

> I was just going to say ... I think you would find across the board regardless of whether it was a homophobic assault, assault in general, or child sex abuse, domestic violence, there is a reticence amongst the community in general to report a crime. The very kind of knowledge that you know most crime is never reported because people know that there's a lot of — you know, that's the nature of the system, but there is a lot of to-ing and fro-ing and you do have to go to court and you are going to be cross examined on the witness stand etcetera ...

Valerie Jenness, a sociologist and criminologist in the United States has aptly acknowledged that bias-inspired violence against particular minorities has previously been perpetrated by the 'state rather than addressed by the state'.[8] This was certainly the case in Queensland during Sir Joh Bjelke-Peterson's reign in power.[9]

In one of the rural focus groups, a mature-age gay male indicated he was caught in a Brisbane bathhouse during the days of the Bjelke-Peterson government. Unbeknown to him, following this incident he had been placed under surveillance by the QPS. He was subsequently interrogated by the QPS for four hours on the Gold Coast. He was told by officers at the time, 'Now you need to leave and don't come back to Queensland'. He left Queensland at the time and returned to a rural community at a later time. In 1990, the same year male-to-male sexual activity was decriminalised in Queensland, this gay male was lured by a group of strangers to his car where they tried to bash him to death. He reported the incident to a senior detective who cautioned him against pressing charges because the perpetrators would know where to find him, implying his life would once again be in danger. He decided not to press charges.

In other jurisdictions, such as Victoria, homosexuality was decriminalised in 1981. The Victorian GLLO brochure explicitly mentions that prior to this time, 'Police were actively involved in the arrest of members of the GLBTI community which ... led to these communities feeling isolated and reluctant to trust police'.[10] For this reason, many crimes were not reported to the police. The brochure explicitly acknowledges that 'whilst homosexuality was decriminalised over 20 years ago, changes in attitudes have come about slowly'.[11]

Things have changed since those dark days of special operations squads harassing sexual minorities in Queensland. As stated in Chapter 7, in 1997 the Queensland Police Service set up an LGBTI liaison program throughout the state. Yet, when the facilitator pointed out to the focus group participant referred to above that his experience of reporting severe physical violence to the police occurred two decades ago, the victim felt the social norms operating at that time might have changed incrementally over time in this rural community but not tremendously. A gender queer transsexual participating in the same focus stated:

> As for the man sitting next to me who was told to leave Queensland and later almost bashed to death ... I must say his story scared the shit out of me, and not only for what he said but how short amount of time that was in the past. I worry if we had government that suppressed emotions and sexuality again, those days may be back on our door steps but I hope that history will not repeat itself again and the GLBTI support members will never let it happen.

A gay male from the Sunshine Coast focus group who did press charges against individuals in a case in Victoria more recently involving grievous bodily harm with intent to kill recounted:

> It was actually grievous bodily harm with intent to kill. Because I actually had a bus driver get off his bus, physically drag me away from these boys and drag me onto the bus and he turned around to everyone on the bus and he said I am taking this kid to the hospital. If anyone doesn't want to go with me get off my bus right now and drove me to the hospital.

> But they were going to kill me and they said as much in court. They said their intention was and if they ever saw me again they would follow through with it. So they got lifelong — each and every one of them got lifelong [unclear] and they are not allowed to come within I think 50 km of me. Things like that. I am on a first call basis when they actually get out.

He also explained the difficulty of prosecuting a case through the court system:

> Maybe because of my background in seeing it. I just know how difficult this is and how much long everything drags on. People think these things are going to be expedited quickly. They never are. You are going to have to [report to the] police, then it's going to have to go committal, and then that could take months. Then from committal to trial, it could take another year. These things can take years to get expedited ...

Social norms have certainly changed in the past two decades and the laws, community support groups and institutions, such as the Anti-Discrimination Commission and liaison program in the QPS providing avenues for redress, reflect these changing social norms. Nonetheless, LGBTIQ awareness, perceptions and experiences of how the typical low-level abuse and harassment, not to mention cases of severe physical violence, will be handled by the judicial process is important. As the Victorian Police Service has explicitly acknowledged, a shift in attitudes has been lethargic even though homosexuality was decriminalised in 1981, almost a decade before male-to-male sexual activity was decriminalised in Queensland.

The qualitative data and the anecdotal experiences of those who have invoked legal remedies through the judicial process suggests the need to be vigilant, persistent and exceptionally resilient to overcome the actual and perceived barriers to accessing justice. It also suggests a need for ongoing legislative and social reforms advocated in Chapter 10. One of the purposes of this book is to strengthen LGBTIQ agency and resilience by presenting not only the quantitative data but also the real life experiences and stories of members of our community who continue to feel impacted upon by the legacy of an era in which bias inspired harassment and violence against our community was perpetrated by the state rather than prohibited by the institutions of government. Hopefully, the last chapter of this book will contribute to promoting sexual diversity and social equality and justice as well as reduce homophobic and transphobic harassment and violence.

Endnotes

1 See William Leonard and others, *Coming Forward: The Underreporting of Heterosexist Violence and Same Sex Partner Abuse in Victoria* (Melbourne: The Australian Research Centre in Sex, Health and Society, La Trobe University, 2008).

2 Ibid.

3 See *Anti-Discrimination Act 1991* (QLD) s 124A.

4 'Gay Couple Wins Landmark Hate Case': The Brisbane gay couple who won a landmark $23,000 anti-vilification case against their former neighbours have told of the ordeal that forced them to flee their Woodbridge home', *Queensland Pride*, 17 November 2008 available at <http://qlp.e-p.net.au/news/gay-couple-wins-landmark-hate-case-2318.html >(accessed 15 January 2010).

5 See *Anti-Discrimination Act 1991* (QLD) s 131A

6 Ibid.

7 Gail Mason, 'Hate Crime Laws in Australia: Are they Achieving their Goals?', *Criminal Law Journal*, Vol. 33 (2009) pp. 326, 328-9.

8 Valerie Jenness, 'The Emergence, Content, and Institutionalization of Hate Crime Law: How a Diverse Policy Community Produced a Modern Legal Fact', *Annual Review of Law and Social Science,* Vol. 3 (2007), pp.141, 143.

9 Shirleene Robinson, 'Homophobia as Party Politics: The Construction of the "Homosexual Deviant" in Joh Bjelke-Petersen's Queensland', *Queensland Review* (forthcoming, March 2010 edition).

10 Victorian Police Service, Gay and Lesbian Liaison Officers, available at http://www.police.vic.gov.au/content.asp?Document_ID=741> (accessed 24 February 2010).

11 Ibid.

CHAPTER 9

Perceptions of Homophobia and Transphobia and Behaviour Modification

One of the most damaging effects of homophobia and transphobia is its impact on LGBTIQ people hiding their sexuality and gender identity. This chapter explores the ways in which LGBTIQ people perceive the need to conceal their sexual orientation and gender identity in different situations based upon their sense of safety and as a risk-reduction strategy. LGBTIQ perceptions of homophobic violence and harassment, discrimination and lack of affirmation impacts on the extent to which they are more likely to conceal their sexual orientation and gender identity in certain venues. This information is useful to agencies that provide assistance to the general and LGBTIQ community, educational institutions throughout Queensland, and employers and unions wishing to create a safe working environment for LGBTIQ employees free from discrimination. This information will also be useful in the fashioning of a strategy of educational initiatives aimed at tertiary educational institutions, governmental initiatives to educate the general populace to change social norms, as well as policing responses and training of police cadets and LGBTIQ liaison officers in Queensland that are contained in some of the recommendations in Chapter 10.

Influence of Past Abuse on Perceptions of Homophobia and Transphobia

As discussed in Chapters 2 and 3, males and females, gay men, lesbian women, transgendered individuals and those classifying themselves as 'other' have encountered differing forms and levels of abuse, harassment and violence. There is a general perception that lesbian women tend to modify their behaviour to avoid being subjected to abuse more than gay males, who tend to be more publicly visible and flamboyant in their younger years and more likely to experience violent physical attacks in public settings, at least in Australia. Transsexual individuals (male to female) are the most likely to experience abuse, harassment and violence. These actual experiences of abuse, harassment and violence would most certainly impact on the way in which LGBTIQ individuals perceive of the risks of homophobic and transphobic abuse, harassment and violence and act on those perceptions of risk in hiding sexual orientation and gender identity.[1] This has been confirmed by the *'You Shouldn't Have to Hide to Feel Safe'* survey from New South Wales, which found that around three-quarters of respondents in that state modified their behaviour in various ways because of concerns about homophobia.[2]

As Gregory M. Herek has pointed out:

> Hiding one's sexual orientation can create a painful discrepancy between public and private identities. Because they face unwitting acceptance of themselves by prejudiced heterosexuals, gay people who are passing may feel inauthentic, that they are living a lie, and that others would not accept them if they knew the truth. The need to pass is likely to disrupt longstanding family relationships and friendships if lesbians and gay men feel they must distance themselves from others to avoid revealing their sexual orientation. Passing also creates considerable strain for gay partnerships.[3]

Although concealing one's sexual orientation or gender identity places a considerable strain on many individuals, a number of respondents from this Queensland study recounted experiences that had caused them to modify their behaviour.

One of the members participating in the Rockhampton focus group, X, a male-to-female transsexual, recounted how physical violence from a family member, as well as abuse and harassment in the workplace, revived traumatic memories of a violent physical attack she experienced at the age of 19 (outlined in Chapter 2) and induced fear of physical violence, abuse, and harassment in the future:

> In 2007, my stepfather found out I was transsexual, he kicked me out of the house I was renting off him and did this with a beating ... I worked in 2008–2009 for a newsagent where I trained a man [who] clearly had issues with me ... and one night trashed the inside of the van, writing a note calling me a faggot and having a clear spaz attack over other issues so minor ... not worth mentioning. I immediately called the manager yet nothing was done about it and the verbal abuse continued and was reported to [the] manager at [the] time ... Still nothing happened and I eventually resigned from my position ... and

[ultimately] left the company ... disappointed in management handling of the matter. I say this was a minor incident as I was not physically hurt by it, but it did strike fear into me knowing he hated me
purely because I was proud of who I was/am, and brought up memories of the earlier [incident of severe physical violence by my stepfa-
ther].

Thus, the personal life experiences of LGBTIQ individuals impact on
their perceptions of the future risk of homophobic and transphobic abuse,
violence and harassment and can result in some individuals concealing
their sexuality or gender identity.

Influence of Media on Perceptions of Homophobia and Transphobia

Other factors, such as the way in which LGBTIQ people are portrayed in
the media, can affect perceptions of risk. Some LGBTIQ people believe that
media visibility is more likely to increase the likelihood of LGBTIQ individuals being subjected to homophobic or transphobic abuse. Others believe
that media visibility is more likely to decrease or have no impact on the
likelihood of LGBTIQ individuals being subjected to homophobic or transphobic violence or harassment. This topic is one that has also been the subject of considerable academic debate.[4] Of the 944 respondents to the
question, 66% of respondents to this Queensland survey — a clear majority — believed that there has been an increase in the visibility of LGBTIQ
persons in the mainstream media, including in news reports and as characters on television shows, in the past two years. Fourteen per cent did not
agree there had been greater visibility in the past two years. Nineteen per
cent said that they did not know. These data and the corresponding raw
number of respondents are given in Table 9.1.

For those 626 people who specified there has been increased visibility
of LGBTIQ people in the mainstream media in the past two years, 45%
felt such media portrayed or represented them in a mostly positive way.
Ten per cent felt LGBTIQ people were portrayed in a mostly negative
way. Forty-two per cent specified LGBTIQ people were represented in
equally positive and negative ways and 2% said none of the above. Six
individuals did not respond to this question. Table 9.2 presents these statistics in greater detail.

As highlighted in Table 9.3, of the 859 respondents to the question,
46% thought the increased visibility decreased the likelihood of LGBTIQ
persons being subject to homophobic or transphobic violence or harassment. Twelve per cent thought the greater visibility increased the likeli-

hood of LGBTIQ individuals being the subject of homophobic or transphobic violence. Forty-two per cent thought it would make no difference. Thus, of those 626 people who specified there had been increased visibil-

Table 9.1
Response to Question, 'In your opinion, in the past two years has there been an increase in the visibility of LGBTIQ Persons in the mainstream media?'

Response	Number	Percentage
Yes	626	66%
No	134	14%
Don't know	184	19%
Respondents	944	

Table 9.2
Response to Question, 'Would you say that the increased visibility of LGBTIQ people in the mainstream media portrays or represents those people in (which of the following ways)?' (For those who specified an increase in visibility)

Response	Number	Percentage
A mostly positive way	282	45%
A mostly negative way	62	10%
In equally positive and negative ways	266	42%
None of the above	10	2%
No response	6	1%
Total	626	

Table 9.3
Response to Question, 'Do you think the increased visibility of LGBTIQ persons in the mainstream media has (had which type of impact on homophobic and transphobic harassment or violence)?'

Response	Number	Percentage
Decreased the risk of LGBTIQ people being subjected to homophobic or transphobic violence and harassment	397	46%
Increased the risk of LGBTIQ people being subjected to homophobic or transphobic violence and harassment	102	12%
Had no impact upon the risk of LBGTIQ people being subjected to homophobic or transphobic violence and harassment	360	42%
Respondents	859	

ity of LGBTIQ people in the mainstream media in the past two years, the overwhelming majority (88%) felt it would either make no difference to the possibility of being the subject of homophobic or transphobic violence in the future, or decrease the likelihood of such violence or harassment occurring in the future. This is important because it demonstrates the potential impact of some of the governmental iniatives suggested in Chapter 10 about deploying media campaigns to help shape social norms in Queensland so that sexual diversity increasingly comes to be celebrated as a virtue rather than viewed negatively. It might also encourage LGBTIQ individuals to be more open regarding their sexuality.

The perceptions outlined above affect LGBTIQ people in several ways, such as encouraging concealment or modification of their behaviour to conform to the heterosexual norm as a protection mechanism, as well as their level of openness about sexuality or gender identity, depending upon their perceptions of safety to be out at certain venues. One transsexual woman in one of the regional focus groups observed that:

> Another point was made by many of us at the focus group about behaviour modification, either at work or everyday lives, acting non-camp or manly to dissolve suspicions that we might be found out, and the replications of this, etcetera, the school teacher being fired, my own personal bashing and rape may both have been from letting down the guard.

Concealment of Sexual Orientation and Gender Identity

LGBTIQ individuals are most likely to conceal their sexual orientation or gender identity while in public, at work or while attending a social/community function. This is followed closely by doing so when accessing services, attending religious events, at an educational institution or with family members. These findings are summarised in Table 9.4.

Understandably, over three-quarters (77%) of individuals never conceal their sexual orientation or gender identity while at home. This intuitively makes sense because individuals in most instances are more likely not to feel the need to conceal their identities in the safety of the home environment, even if they are experiencing difficulties in their relationship with same-sex partners. The almost quarter of respondents who did conceal their sexuality at home may very well still live with their parents or housemates. This was mentioned by some participants in a few of the focus groups.

Table 9.4
Response to Question, 'In the past two years have there been situations where you concealed your sexuality or gender identity for fear of violence or harassment?' (For all survey respondents)

Concealed sexual orientation or gender identity	Never	Occasionally	Usually
At work	29%	37%	25%
At home	77%	14%	9%
With family members	54%	28%	18%
At an educational institution	48%	33%	19%
When accessing services	41%	40%	20%
At religious events	44%	19%	37%
At social/community events	38%	46%	16%
In public	27%	53%	21%
Other	74%	15%	11%

Concealment in Public Places

Seventy-four per cent of respondents occasionally (53%) or usually (21%) concealed their sexual orientation or gender identity for fear of violence or harassment while in public. This corresponds to the locations in which LGBTIQ individuals experienced homophobic or transphobic violence. Specifically, 58% of the respondents experienced some form of abuse, harassment or violence within the past two years in public places. As explored in Chapter 3, 68% of individuals reported experiencing their most recent incident of abuse, harassment or violence in a public place.[5]

One of the lesbian participants at the Toowoomba focus group stated that 'Even if I am walking down the street, I probably hesitate to hold hands'. A young gay male in the same focus group who felt safer in larger communities such as Brisbane stated: 'With public displays of affection ... if I feel safe I will kiss my partner but I'm not someone to walk down the street holdings hands, it's just not something that I do'. Another young lesbian woman who had recently moved to Toowoomba from a town of 10,000 people stated: 'I was born and raised in Goondiwindi which is two and a half hours [away] and I just moved here a couple of months ago and in Goondi I would not feel safe ... too many people know me'. A lesbian in the Brisbane focus group expressed concerns over being judged while in public places. She said, 'You get looked up and down and it is harassment because people just don't want to stay next to you because you [are] kind of just [like a] freak. You know, it's something wrong with you'. A gay male in the Brisbane focus group stated: 'It's a safe[ty] issue'. A lesbian in the group responded: 'It takes the enjoyment out of holding their hands because you're constantly thinking about people just staring at you', and a gay male accurately pointed out: '[heterosexual people] get affirmed if a young couple hold [hands]. And young couples feel that, but young gay couples ... [might] get a look of disgust'.

A transsexual from a regional focus group explained:

> I would say in actual fact I do hide it because I do not tell people who I am and remember, I walk into the ladies toilets every day of the week you might say. I am a female in my mental state. My body is male, except for the operations I've had which has removed all my male sexuality ... but that still doesn't make me look like a female as such. So I have to come across as an ugly looking woman, or that's the way I feel about it, so I am always on the defensive that someone will say something to me like, 'You shouldn't be in here', 'You're a fellow' or 'You're a man'. So I'm always ready to sort of go defensive, because if you try and say, look, I'm sorry, but I'm a transsexual, you start the bunfight. So you have to say, do you mind, my grandchildren would tell you otherwise.

Concealment at Social/Community Events

Sixty-two per cent of respondents occasionally (46%) or usually (16%) concealed their sexual orientation or gender identity while at social/community events. Just 3% of LGBTIQ individuals experienced their most recent incident of abuse, harassment or violence at or near a lesbian/gay or non-lesbian/gay community event. There could be other factors influencing their behaviour, such as concerns when attending such events with their children or with family members, particularly at events, such as weddings or when attending large sporting events in which heterosexual men are drunk and under the influence of alcohol.

Concealment at Work

Sixty-two per cent of respondents occasionally (37%) or usually (25%) concealed their sexual orientation or gender identity while at work. As considered in chapter 3, 12% indicated their most recent experience of abuse, harassment or violence took place at work. In addition to this, fear of discrimination in the workplace is a factor affecting the concealment of sexual orientation or gender identity at work.

In one of the rural focus groups, an individual expressed perceived difficulty in securing employment because she had been vocal in the local newspaper about the way in which LGBTIQ rights were being dealt with at a particular university:

> ... maybe I have not been getting a job because they saw me on the front page of the Chronicle. I don't know. Has my name in their memory that much as someone to blacklist ... I don't know what motivates people.

This participant added that she placed on her CV her experience in gay and lesbian community service:

> I've been looking [for a job], I'm studying community development, and I finish in November, very soon, and I've got a public relations degree and a media degree. I am not an unqualified person ... I was applying for a lot of jobs that I was perfectly qualified for and I have just been shut down. I get promised feedback, I've made contact with them and spoken to the people and they say 'Great, well we'll be in touch, we've got a lot of things' and then nothing. This one in particular, it was a youth worker based in schools and a lot of schools in [this rural community] are private, religious ... a lot of my community experience is in the lesbian and gay community so I think putting that in my cover letter was probably maybe a mistake on my part but not something I regret because I don't want to work for them if they're going to be like that.

A participant in the Toowoomba focus group who worked in a hospital kitchen stated: 'I am not gay at work but I am with my family and friends but I would never be at work ... I would be hung out dry at work if they found out ... I wouldn't ever tell them'. Another participant in the same focus group stated: 'I get a lot of [homophobia] at work but not directed at me, just general homophobia. This one guy thinks all gays should die and it's a choice'.

Similarly, in the Brisbane focus group a younger lesbian explained:

> I would not come out at work and say, "Yeah, I'm gay, I've got a girlfriend", because it's a boys' club. It's really hard for a woman that is not gay to actually ... get a manager's position, and manager on the floor is a man — they're all men. So if I want to come out and say, I'm gay, there will be gossip and my chances of progressing will be lower.

Another lesbian added:

> I think for girls, if everyone around you, like all of the managers, everyone that is a boss is a male, and you are in the beginning of your career, you kind of have to hide because even if you are confident with your sexuality or whatever, you still need to prove yourself, like because I think being a girl you're already discriminated in some sense, so you have to prove yourself harder, and being gay, you want them to

look at you for your skills. So if they know you're gay, the first thing they'll look at you and say — well, all they're going to talk about is you being gay.

Another lesbian observed that 'I think it actually could make it worse ... "You're a gay girl, oh you haven't met the right man". Like, you know, you obviously had a bad experience'.

A gay male pointed out:

... that speaks to the issue of heterosexism. That's the main issue, not just homophobia, but heterosexism. That's an enormous problem in the workplace, and the unions refuse to tackle it.

In some of the focus groups, participants spoke of instances of discrimination and loss of jobs when the employers discovered the sexual orientation or gender identity of their LGBTIQ employees. Thus, the compelling need to conceal in the workplace is not unfounded. Coming out in the process of applying for jobs or the workplace environment can have dramatic ramifications for career development and advancement.

Nonetheless, some individuals have chosen jobs in which their sexuality is considered in a positive light. One member of the Sunshine Coast focus group actually found his sexuality a bonus in his line of work:

My sexuality is actually a bonus at the adult shop. It's a massive boost at the adult shop and mainly because I am treated like royalty down there because my director, the director of the company has been trying to tap into the gay market ... it's a massive asset to be there and I have always chosen roles which have been where my lifestyles and my ideas have been a contributing factor to my job and not a hindrance.

Concealment When Accessing Services

Sixty per cent occasionally (40%) or usually (20%) concealed their sexual orientation or gender identity when accessing services. In several focus groups and written responses to survey questions, the authors learned of instances of discrimination in the provision of legal services, medical services, dental services, massage therapists and even restaurant service. Some of these incidents have been included in previous chapters. One respondent indicated they altered their behaviour or dress for fear of violence or harassment when accessing disability services, and when dealing with banks and government departments.

Concealment While Attending Religious Events

Fifty-six per cent occasionally (19%) or usually (37%) concealed their sexual orientation or gender identity while attending religious events. As outlined in Chapter 1, a majority (57%) of the respondents to this survey do not believe in any religion. Twenty-three per cent of the respondents to this survey identify with the following religions: 13% Catholic; 8% Anglican; and 2% Christian. Given the prohibition in mainstream religions, including Catholicism, against non-procreative sexual activity, it is understandable individuals identifying with them would perceive it necessary to conceal their sexual orientation or gender identity while attending religious events.

A Catholic gay male in the Brisbane focus group stated that 'the Catholic system … [is] on [a] witch hunt at the moment. If you're gay, you're on target.'

A former Catholic gay male in the group stated:

> … in terms of discrimination there's a process within a religious order and the assumed position is that if you're celibate, you're heterosexual, it's not a consideration that you're gay. The default position is you're a heterosexual celibate. There's no acknowledgment that you're a celibate gay, and there is no room for that discussion to take place … That's a huge degree of discrimination. The amount of closet gays in Catholic religious orders is enormous and the amount of mental health disease in religious orders is enormous. They're not all queer. I'd say 72%.

This helps explain why more than half of the respondents would occasionally or usually conceal their sexual orientation or gender identity while attending a religious function.

Concealment at an Educational Institution

Fifty-two per cent occasionally (33%) or usually (19%) concealed their sexual orientation or gender identity at an educational institution. This percentage is understandable given 58% of respondents to this survey are attending an educational institution full-time while 38% are attending part-time (see Chapter 1). Also, presumably some of the respondents to this survey were teachers and academics. A female participant in the Sunshine Coast focus group stated:

> Because I go into a lot of high schools … I have to be very, very careful. It is not something I bring up at all … Because, you know, it just takes one parent to get upset and it's enough to become a big issue sort of thing.

A lesbian participant in one of the focus groups stated:

> It also happens in a tertiary situation … I work in a university and I know of a few staff members who go out of their way to protect their

identity because there are students that will rebel against that and use that against them. I do know of one place where that has happened.

At one university in Queensland, the student equity officer was seconded to another position at the University and the role remained vacant for 18 months. This same university has consistently refused over a 4-year period to create a safe space for LGBTIQ students. Many of the focus groups revealed instances of outright abuse and harassment of staff and students in the primary, secondary and tertiary school educational setting on the basis of sexual orientation and gender identity. (See Chapter 2 and discussion under Recommendation 11, Chapter 10.)

Concealment With Family Members

Forty-six per cent occasionally (28%) or usually (18%) concealed their sexual orientation or gender identity with family members. This is comprehensible as many LGBTIQ individuals have had negative experiences when coming out to their family members. For some who inform their families, they are removed from the will. A gay male participant in the Brisbane focus group stated:

> I know many adults who their parents are deceased and they've found themselves excluded from the estate because they've come totally out but their elderly parents have discriminated against them in terms of denying them a fair share of the family estate.

Others who have come out to their family members are considered *persona non grata*. A gay male participant in the Brisbane focus group stated, 'I have no relationship with my brother or father. They're incredibly homophobic'.

Other families are totally ignorant of LGBTIQ sexual orientation and gender identity. A young lesbian in the Toowoomba focus group stated:

> The first thing my mum said to me when I told her I was lesbian she said 'Have you got AIDS?' ... It's a stereotype attached to gay and lesbian, if you are gay or lesbian you will have AIDS.

A young gay male in the same focus group said, 'The first thing my dad said to me, "Oh I won't have grandchildren" ... And according to my dad's girlfriend's mother I'm a paedophile because I'm gay'.

A gay male in the Brisbane focus group stated:

> I think there's a high degree of unspoken violence in families if you're going through the process of identifying your sexuality. From my own experience, and those of others I know, their understanding of accepting their sexuality, primarily based on their fears of rejection from

one's family is enormous and high rates of teenage suicide are a direct correlation between families' inability to accept their child's sexuality.

Some families choose to remain in denial or ignorant even if an individual is brave enough to come out to their family. The issue is not to be discussed and family members will intentionally avoid asking LGBTIQ individuals about their personal lives. As one female participant in the Brisbane focus group explained:

> I'm a dominatrix, I've been totally out and always have been ... so Mum and Dad just don't want to know the details, so I don't like to tell them the details.

Another lesbian participant in the Brisbane focus group indicated she was able to come out to her mother but not to her brother. She stated, 'I love him to death, but he was raised in the same society with the same parents to ... dislike gay people, and he would be so disappointed, and he is my little brother'.

Another gay male in the Brisbane group observed: '... no matter who you are, you want to be accepted by your family but some people won't ... the dynamics are going to change. There's no doubt about it. The dynamics change once you out yourself'.

Coming out to family members and having them affirm one's sexual orientation or gender identity is probably one of the key factors in helping overcome internalised homophobia and changing wider social norms over time.[6] A mature-aged lesbian in one of the regional focus groups indicated she spoke with members of her own family who accepted her sexual orientation over time. She believed this would create a ripple effect for others similarly situated. As more and more families accept their children's sexual orientation and gender identity and become more open minded towards other LGBTIQ individuals in the general population, the community as a whole will learn to become more accepting of sexual diversity.

Concealment in Other Contexts

Seventy-four per cent of the respondents who checked the box *Other* indicated they never concealed their sexual orientation or gender identity while 15% indicated they occasionally did so and 11% indicated they usually did so. Write-in responses were received from 48 out of the 66 individuals who checked the box *Other* and *Occasionally* or *Usually* in response to the question: 'In the past 2 years have there been situations where you concealed your sexual orientation or gender identity, for fear of violence or harassment?' Many of these responses could fall under some of the above categories, such as 'Accessing services', 'Attending religious events', or

'While in public, such as sporting events or in shopping centres'. Other places where individuals concealed their sexual orientation or gender identity included when accessing medical services (three cases), everywhere (four cases), conceal/omit around most people (three cases), police (two cases), with partner's peers (one case), friends of family members (one case), neighbours (three cases), attending a predominately heterosexual liquor licensed venue (one case), and in business related matters, such as dealing with banks (two cases), and as a volunteer with a kids charity (one case).

Concealment and Modification of Behaviour and Dress (related to sexuality or gender identity)

Survey respondents were also asked if there had been situations in the past two years where they concealed or modified their behaviour or dress sense for fear of violence or harassment relating to sexuality and gender identity.

As Table 9.5 demonstrates, LGBTIQ individuals are most likely to modify their behaviour or dress due to fear of violence or harassment while in public (58%), at work (48%) or while attending a social/community event (48%). This is closely followed by doing so while accessing services (45%) and attending religious functions (42%). As with the previous survey question, 84% do not conceal their behaviour while at home for the reasons speculated previously.

Table 9.5
Response to Question, 'In the past two years have there been situations where you modified your behaviour or dress for fear of violence or harassment?'

Concealed behaviour or dress	Never	Occasionally	Usually
At work	52%	26%	22%
At home	84%	11%	5%
With family members	67%	21%	12%
At an educational institution	62%	26%	12%
When accessing services	54%	31%	14%
At religious events	57%	17%	26%
At social/community events	52%	34%	14%
In public	42%	40%	18%
Other	85%	7%	8%

Forms of Behaviour Modification

The forms of behaviour modification varied considerably and are summarised in Table 9.6. Of those who modified their behaviour for fear of violence relating to their sexuality or gender identity, this was manifested mostly in three predominant forms:

- limiting or not displaying affection to others of the same sex to whom you would usually show affection;
- avoiding discussion about your personal life; and
- avoid telling people you are LGBTIQ.

This was followed by dressing in a different manner to how one would usually dress, not going out alone, avoid going out at certain times, avoid going out completely, avoiding public transport with 2% indicating 'other.'

Analysing Table 9.6, of the 18 who checked the box 'Other', 17 provided written responses, some of which dealt with fear of discrimination (a theme running throughout written responses to survey questions and in focus groups) as well as violence and harassment. The responses speak for themselves:

- 'I do not stop doing anything because I am gay. However, after being the victim of a gay-hate attack, I do modify my behaviour. I do not walk the streets while drunk, do not dress gay in public limit display of same-sex affection, and am VERY streetwise. For example, I will read the street ahead and cross over and turn into a side street if there is potential for trouble. In public I always say 'mate' a lot to strangers and try to act straight to avoid attacks — sounds like I am paranoid. Maybe I am slightly but I like to think of it as just being careful.'

- 'Sometimes I do not wear my sexuality on my sleeve, not from fear of violence but because of my life long experience of silent discrimination.'

- 'Sometimes of course sexuality isn't pertinent to a subject but sometimes I want to be taken seriously and not dismissed albeit silently because I'm a fag — this mostly applies to the University of _____ the most homophobic institution in the country.'

- 'My behaviour adjustment is not usually for fear of violence or harassment, it is more for discrimination generally (i.e. unapproving looks, losing respect of work colleague). I have only once experienced a violent situation.'

Table 9.6
Response to Question, 'When you have modified your behaviour for fear of violence relating to your sexuality or gender identity, what forms of behaviour modification have you engaged in?'

Response	Percentage
Limiting or not displaying affection to others of the same sex to whom you would usually show affection	44%
Avoiding discussions about your personal life	43%
Avoid telling people you are LGBT	43%
Dressing in a different manner to how you would usually dress	24%
Don't go out alone	13%
Avoid going out at certain times	11%
Avoid going out	7%
Avoid public transport	5%
Other	2%

- 'Steer clear of certain areas of town, such as Logan.'
- Two respondents mentioned that they avoid straight places on nights out or non-LGBTIQ venues and events, only go to gay or mixed venues.
- One respondent said they do not go to heterosexual pubs or clubs due to previous violence. A fourth respondent indicated they generally avoid 'the lower socio-economic prodominantly heterosexually oriented liquor licensed venues'.
- 'Adjusting voice and mannerisms.'
- 'Body jewellery.'
- 'Change what I talk about.'
- 'Avoiding certain areas when dressed to party.'
- Two respondents mentioned avoiding public toilets.
- 'Family doesn't accept me.'
- 'Always.'
- 'Not frequent "gay" activities.'

Daily Life

Four questions relating to the daily life of the 1094 survey respondents were asked in this survey. The results pertaining to these questions are summarised in Tables 9.7 to 9.10 and depicted in Figure 9.1 for clarity. Interestingly, most of the LGBTIQ respondents to the survey were open about their sexuality. An overwhelming 64% considered themselves very or somewhat open about their sexuality. Just 3% considered themselves not open at all about their sexuality. Almost half felt confident or very confident about reporting an incident of LGBTIQ threats, harassment or violence to police LGBTIQ liaison officers. This issue is dealt with in greater detail in Chapter 7 on experiences with the police. Just one third considered their sexuality very or somewhat visible to strangers in public places. This may help explain why 74% of individuals occasionally or usually conceal their sexual orientation or gender identity in public and 58% of respondents occasionally or usually conceal their behaviour and modify their sense of dress in public places. Just 26% are very or somewhat afraid of being subjected to violence, harassment or abuse within the next year.

....

Table 9.7
Rating Response to Question 'How open you are about your sexuality?'

Scale	Percentage
1 = *Most open*	36%
2	28%
3	18%
4	8%
5 = *Not open at all*	3%

....

Table 9.8
Rating Response to Question 'How confident you would be about reporting an incident of LGBTIQ threats, harassment or violence to Police LGBTI liaison officers?'

Scale	Percentage
1 = *Very confident*	31%
2	18%
3	22%
4	12%
5 = *Not confident at all*	9%

Conclusion

As explored in this chapter, one of the most detrimental aspects of homophobia and transphobia is its impact on the willingness of LGBTIQ individuals to express their sexual orientation and gender identity openly. This chapter has delved into the ways in which LGBTIQ individuals perceive the need to conceal their sexual orientation and gender identity in different contexts as a means of reducing their risk of being subjected to homophobic and transphobic abuse, harassment and violence as well as discrimination and lack of affirmation. Personal life experiences are one factor that affect these perceptions. Other factors, such as the way in which LGBTIQ are portrayed in the media, can have an impact on personal perceptions of whether such greater public visibility in the mainstream media and as characters in television programs is more likely to increase, decrease or have no impact on the likelihood of LGBTIQ individuals being subjected to homophobic or transphobic violence or harassment. Eighty-eight per cent of the 626 respondents who specified there had been increased visibility of LGBTIQ people in the mainstream media

....

Table 9.9
Rating Response to Question 'How visible you feel your sexuality is to strangers in public places?'

Scale	Percentage
1 = *Most visible*	14%
2	19%
3	28%
4	20%
5 = *Not visible at all*	12%

....

Table 9.10
Rating Response to Question 'How afraid you are of being subjected to harassment, violence, threats or physical abuse in the next year?'

Scale	Percentage
1 = *Very afraid*	10%
2	16%
3	24%
4	27%
5 = *Not afraid at all*	16%

....

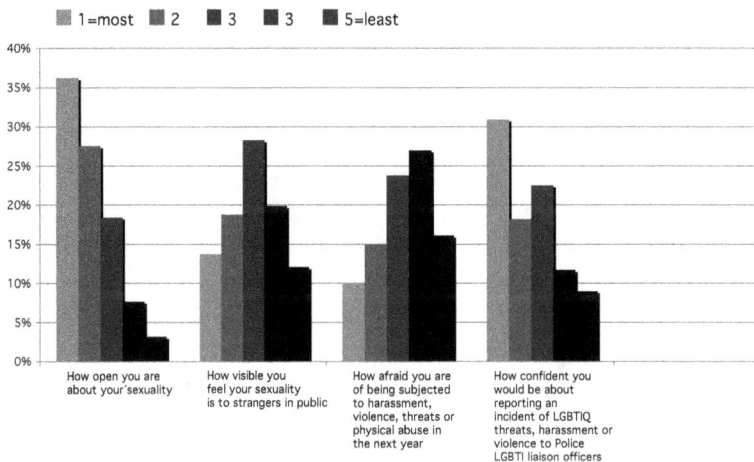

Figure 9.1
Daily life rankings.

in the past two years felt it would either make no difference to the possibility of being the subject of homophobic or transphobic violence in the future or decrease the likelihood of such violence or harassment occurring in the future. This is important because it demonstrates the potential impact of some of the governmental initiatives suggested in Chapter 10 about deploying media campaigns to educate the general populace to change social norms in Queensland so that sexual diversity increasingly comes to be celebrated as a desirable value in a pluralistic multicultural society.

This chapter has found that LGBTIQ individuals are most likely to conceal their sexual orientation or gender identity while in public, at work or while attending a social/community function. This is followed closely by doing so when accessing services, attending religious events, at an educational institution or with family members. This chapter has explored the reasons why LGBTIQ individuals are more likely to conceal their sexual identities in certain contexts, such as while in public places, and less likely to do so in others (e.g. while at home in which 77% never do so).

Survey respondents were also asked if there had been situations where they modified their behaviour or dress sense for fear of violence or harassment in the past two years. This chapter found LGBTIQ individuals are most likely to modify their behaviour or dress sense for fear of violence or harassment while in public, at work or while attending a social/community event. This is closely followed by doing so while accessing services, attending religious functions and to a lesser extent with family members. An overwhelming majority of 84% indicated they do not conceal their behaviour or dress sense for fear of violence or harassment while in the safety of their home environment. The forms of behaviour modification varied considerably with the three main forms limiting or not displaying affection to others of the same sex to whom they would usually show affection; avoiding discussion about their personal life; and avoid telling people they are LGBTIQ. This was followed by dressing in a different manner to how they would usually dress, not going out alone, avoid going out to certain times, avoid going out completely, avoiding public transport with just 2% indicating 'other.' These included 17 responses that demonstrated fear of discrimination or lack of affirmation.

An overwhelming 64% considered themselves very or somewhat open about their sexuality. Just 3% considered themselves not open at all about their sexuality. Just one third considered their sexuality very or somewhat visible to strangers in public places. This may help explain why 74% of individuals occasionally or usually conceal their sexual orientation or gender identity in public and 58% of respondents occasionally or usually conceal their behaviour and modify their sense of dress in public places. Twenty-six per cent are very or somewhat afraid of being subjected to violence, harassment or abuse within the next year.

This information should prove useful to agencies that provide assistance to the general public and the LGBTIQ community, educational institutions throughout Queensland, and employers and unions desiring to create a safe working environment for LGBTIQ employees free from discrimination. Historically, the government and educational sectors and employers have found it difficult to understand the normative impact of approaches to minority groups and minority issues. This information is useful to the construction of educational policies aimed at tertiary educational institutions, governmental initiatives to educate the general populace to change social norms as well as policing responses and training of police cadets and LGBTIQ liaison officers in Queensland that are contained among some of the recommendations in Chapter 10.

Endnotes

1 Gail Mason, 'Violence Against Lesbians and Gay Men', *Crime Prevention Today*, No. 2 (Canberra: Australian Institute of Criminology, 1993), p. 5; Australian Institute of Criminology, 'Crime Victimisation', Australian Institute of Criminology website http://www.aic.gov.au/publications/current%20series/facts/1-20/2008/3z20Crime%20victimisation.aspx (accessed 15 January 2010).

2 New South Wales Attorney General's Department, *'You Shouldn't Have to Hide to be Safe'*: *A Report on Homophobic Hostilities and Violence Against Gay Men and Lesbians in New South Wales* (Sydney: New South Wales Attorney General's Department, Crime Prevention Division, 2003), p.15.

3 Gregory M. Herek, 'Heterosexism and Homophobia' in Robert P. Cabaj and Terry S. Stein, *Textbook of Homosexuality and Mental Health* (Washington: American Psychiatric Press, 1996), p.108.

4 See particularly, F. Fejes and K. Petrich, 'Invisibility, Homophobia and Heterosexism: Lesbians, Gay Men and the Media', *Critical Studies in Mass Communication*, Vol. 10 (1993), and R. Ringer, ed., *Queer Words, Queer Images: Communication and the Construction of Homosexuality* (New York: New York University, 1994).

5 27% of individuals reported experiencing their most recent incident of abuse, harassment or violence on the street, 15% at or near gay and/or lesbian venues, 7% at licensed premises (other than gay or lesbian), 4% at retail premises, 3% at a beach or park (not beat related), 1% at a train station, and 1% at a bus/bus stop.

6 Herek, *Heterosexism and Homophobia*, p.109.

10

From Despair to Hope: Recommendations

In many respects, the quantitative results of the *Speaking Out* survey mirror the findings of other similar surveys such as the 2003 New South Wales survey *'You Shouldn't Have to Hide to Feel Safe'* and the more recent 2008 Victorian study, *Coming Forward*. This study demonstrates the devastating impact of homophobia and transphobia on the LGBTIQ community. The recommendations in this book are informed by the quantitative and qualitative data analysed in this research project. Homophobia and transphobia are perpetuated by a number of interrelated factors, including historical, political, religious and other variables, such as gender, age, education and socio-economic background.[1] The authors firmly believe that if this considerable problem is to be addressed, a multidisciplinary approach must be adopted to help reduce prejudice-motivated abuse, harassment and violence. The authors hope the recommendations in this study will be viewed as an attempt to foster the virtues of diversity and inclusiveness as a source of strength. Diversity, inclusiveness, dignity and autonomy are fundamental aspects of prohibitions on discrimination on the basis of sexual orientation.[2]

The recommendations also reflect the belief that homophobia is a social problem that affects all Australians. As canvassed in Chapter 7, police in other jurisdictions such as Victoria have acknowledged the detrimental impact of prejudice-motivated crimes on the individuals to whom they are directed, the wider group of which they are or perceived to be a member, and society generally.[3] For this reason, the recommendations below are wide-ranging. They reach across several disciplines and include many educational initiatives targeted at all ages and levels of the education system. They also include recommendations that impact on policing, legislative reform and strategies that will encourage victims of homophobic and transphobic abuse, harassment and violence to engage more actively with existing legal mechanisms. These mechanisms include the Queensland Police Service (QPS), the Queensland Anti-Discrimination Commission (ADCQ), and the court system and community support groups.

Recommendations: Law Reforms

Recommendation 1: The Queensland government should introduce legislation prohibiting the introduction of evidence of 'gay panic' and 'non-violent homosexual advance'[4] to sustain the defence of provocation.

Queensland's current common law and legislative approach that permits the use of the 'gay panic' and 'non-violent homosexual advance' defence is outmoded and retrograde. It also reflects, reinforces and perpetuates homophobia.[5] Other Australian states have repealed this form of defence. As early as 1996, the New South Wales Attorney General's Department issued a discussion paper that was harshly critical of the 'non-violent homosexual advance' on the basis that it highlights the perception that 'fear, revulsion or hostility' are justifiable responses to 'homosexual conduct'.[6]

The New South Wales Working Party articulated its belief that the homosexual advance defence may very well have strengthened the 'mythical homosexual male stereotype as 'predator/attacker'.[7] Justice Kirby pointed out in *Green v The Queen* (1997) 191 CLR 334, a case in which the defence of provocation was allowed despite insubstantial evidence of a forceful homosexual advance:

> For the law to accept that a non-violent sexual advance, without more, by a man to a man could induce in an ordinary person such a reduction in self-control as to occasion the formation of an intent to kill, or to inflict grievous bodily harm, would sit ill with contemporary legal, educative, and policing efforts designed to remove such violent responses from society, grounded as they are in irrational hatred and fear ...

> In my view, the 'ordinary person' in Australian society today is not so homophobic as to respond to a non-violent sexual advance by a homosexual person as to form an intent to kill or to inflict grievous bodily harm. He or she might, depending on the circumstances, be embarrassed; treat it first as a bad joke; be hurt; insulted. He or she might react with the strong language of protest; might use as much physical force as was necessary to effect an escape; and where absolutely necessary assault the persistent perpetrator to secure escape ...[8]

This issue has been dealt with in several jurisdictions. In 2003, Tasmania repealed entirely the partial defence of provocation.[9] In 2008, following a Law Reform Commission Report, Western Australia repealed the partial defence of provocation with a proviso under Section 279 (4) of the *Criminal Law Amendment (Homicide) Act 2008* (WA) that 'a person ... who is guilty of murder must be sentenced to life imprisonment unless — (a) that sentence would be clearly unjust given the circumstances of the offence and the person; and (b) that the person is unlikely to be a threat to the safety of the community when released from imprisonment'.[10] One year later, the ACT adopted a partial exclusionary rule prohibiting reliance on 'non-violent homosexual advance' to be used, by itself, as a basis for fulfilling the requirements of provocation.[11] Both the Western Australian and ACT approaches would not ultimately prevent homophobic attitudes from affecting courtroom deliberations, particularly given the multitude of factors taken into account in deciding whether the perpetrator was provoked (ACT) and in deciding if it would be clearly unjust in the circumstances of the offence and the person to impose a term of life imprisonment.[12]

In 2005, Victoria completely abolished the defence of provocation.[13] Victoria ultimately decided to abolish the defence of provocation because a guilty verdict does not necessarily result in a term of life imprisonment. In jurisdictions, such as England and Queensland, where a guilty verdict for murder carries a penalty of life imprisonment, commentators as well as the Victorian Law Reform Commission recommend that the 'non-violent homosexual advance' be removed completely from the ambit of evidence considered in establishing whether the defence of provocation is justified. The authors believe that a similar approach should be adopted in Queensland.[14]

Queensland's Law Reform Commission Report of 2008 acknowledges that the objective test for loss of self-control reflects mainstream heterosexual male social norms. It also cites legal scholars who assert that allowing a 'non-violent homosexual advance' to be considered relevant to the defence of provocation can encourage heterosexual men to construct staged tales of an irrational fear of homosexuality that results in an inability to maintain self-control as evidenced by a violent outburst.[15] Citing the split of opinion between the majority and minority justices in *Green v The Queen* (1997) 191 CLR 334, the Queensland Law Reform Commission Report went so far as to question whether a 'non-violent homosexual advance' could ever justify murder.[16] Indeed, the decision of the majority in *Green* prompted harsh criticism from commentators, noting the decision marshalled in a judicial understanding of the ordinary man as 'a violent homophobe' in which 'non-violent homosexual advances' are revolting and worthy of deadly force as a just punishment.[17]

Adrian Howe, for example, points out the hypocrisy of the reasoning in *Green*:

> Under conditions of masculinist hegemony, such a sexual advance is perceived to be a 'grave' provocation as opposed to a normative or routinised behaviour pattern, such as the unwanted sexual advance made by men towards women on a daily basis ... It matters not that there is no evidence, apart from the dubious statement of the killer, that the alleged sexual advance occurred ... *Green* demonstrates that the uncorroborated and typically far-fetched story told by a young man of a sexual advance by a predatory older man — here a man who was a friend and mentor of his assailant — is one with a great deal of cultural capital under conditions of hegemonic homosexuality ...[18]

Notwithstanding the strong arguments against allowing evidence of 'gay panic' or 'non-violent homosexual advance to be used to establish the defence of provocation, the Queensland Report failed to make any recommendations on this issue.

Despite moves against the concept of a 'gay panic' defence in other states, this defence has been used recently in Queensland. In 2009, two men from Maryborough successfully persuaded a jury that the defence of 'gay panic' was warranted to acquit them from a murder charge, reducing the finding of guilt to a charge of manslaughter. As family law specialist Stephen Page suggested in an editorial in *Q-News*, the facts in this case provide a prime example that allowing evidence to be used to establish the defence of provocation does not even fulfil its purported policy objectives:

> After a night of extremely heavy drinking by the three men, Pearce and Meerdinks alleged that Ruks made a sexual proposition to Pearce, prompting Pearce to start bashing and kicking Ruks. Meerdink then joined in. Pearce claimed he reacted the way he did because he was 'f...ed with as a kid.' Ruk's mother ... is reported to have said that the defence was a 'lie' as her son was not gay.[19]

While the authors strongly advocate the above reform of Queensland's criminal trial procedure in cases involving gay murder, we are also cognisant of the cautionary insights of scholars, such as Stephen Tomsen, who note the limited utility 'of a constant tinkering with criminal trial procedure as a means of addressing a broader injustice ... With regard to gay killings, this means a more general concern with dealing with homophobia outside the seductive drama of the courtroom.'[20] Unfortunately, as was demonstrated in the recent case in Maryborough, the homophobic attitudes underpinning such incidents continue to be reflected in our criminal justice system. Such attitudes need to be addressed.[21]

Policies Served by Hate Crimes Legislation

Hate (or prejudiced-motivated) crimes legislation exists in four jurisdictions in Australia: Western Australia, New South Wales, Victoria and the Northern Territory.[22] Queensland has no substantive hate crime legislation outside the jurisdiction of ADCQ. As explained in Chapter 7, individuals can theoretically be charged under s 131A of the *Anti-Discrimination Act* for severe sexual or gender identity vilification. The recommendations below are based on the belief that Queensland should adopt some form of hate crimes legislation outside the confines of the Anti-Discrimination Act to address non-violent forms of homophobic and transphobic abuse and harassment involving physical threats as well as instances involving actual physical violence.

Statistics previously outlined which state that 53% of the LGBTIQ respondents to this survey have experienced an incident of such harassment or violence within the past two years are troubling. The information gleaned from the written responses to some of the survey questions and the seven focus groups conducted throughout metropolitan, regional and rural Queensland indicate this class of individuals is targeted as a marginalised minority group for discrimination, ridicule, verbal abuse and physical violence, especially transgendered individuals.

There is a widespread unwillingness to engage with law enforcement as reflected in not reporting to law enforcement or seeking professional assistance in 75% of incidents within the past two years. This low percentage of reporting is based partly on personal experiences with police who are understandably reluctant to pursue physical threats as criminal assault because of difficulties with problems of proof. They are also unable to act in instances of verbal abuse (See Chapter 7). Nonetheless, all cadets should be trained to refer instances of verbal abuse to ADCQ because verbal abuse could amount to sexuality or gender identity vilification for which there are remedies under Section 124A of the *Queensland Anti-Discrimination Act* as amended in 1991.

Equally important, all police officers should be instructed to refer all reported incidents of physical threats associated with homophobia or transphobia to ADCQ (in cases where there is insufficient proof to charge an individual with common assault) as there are both civil and criminal penalties available under s 131A of the *Anti-Discrimination Act*. This is despite the fact that the process involved in bringing a charge under s 131A of the *Anti-Discrimination Act* is so complicated that there are no reported instances in Queensland or any other jurisdiction in Australia with similar provisions under which prosecutions or convictions have eventuated[23] (see Chapter 8). Nevertheless, such victims could still seek remedies under s 124A.

Some of the recommendations in this chapter are informed by what could be perceived as the dual failure of police to act on instances of threats of physical violence or verbal abuse, and to refer the victims of such incidents to ADCQ. Many conclusions can be drawn from the non-reporting of incidents, one of which is that both widespread externalised and internalised homophobia continue to persist in Queensland. Prejudice-motivated hate crimes must be placed at the top of the political agenda in Queensland if there is any hope of improving attitudes and awareness among the general population and within the relevant governmental departments about the extent to which members of the LGBTIQ community are subject to ongoing non-violent forms of homophobic or transphobic abuse or harassment and the traumatising effect of such unlawful conduct.

Western Australia has chosen to address the problems of racism and its manifestations by adopting separate hate crimes legislation outside the confines of anti-discrimination legislation. Changes to Victoria's and New South Wales' sentencing legislation are relevant because they were prompted by evidence-based empirical data similar to the data analysed in this survey. All of these states recognised that hate crime laws serve manifold purposes.

Such laws express societal condemnation of crimes committed on the basis of animus towards a particular minority group, which hopefully has the effect of discouraging others from committing such crimes in the future.[24] As canvassed in Chapter 8, social attitudes toward homosexuality in Queensland have undoubtedly improved (if not dramatically then at least incrementally) since male-to-male sexual activity was first decriminalised in 1990.[25]

Recommendation 2: The authors urge Queensland lawmakers to incorporate substantive hate crimes within the Queensland Criminal Code. The authors further recommend that these provisions impose greater penalties for criminal offences against a person or property which are motivated or intended in whole or in part by hostility, intolerance, bias or prejudice of the offender toward the victim on the basis of the actual or perceived LGBTI [sexual][26] orientation or actual or perceived gender identity of the victim.[27] Other jurisdictions, such as the United States, have had hate crimes legislation for almost 30 years.[28] Most of the hate crimes in the United States are state laws enforced by state and local authorities. The federal government prosecutes bias inspired crimes under civil rights legislation over which it retains jurisdiction.[29] The US federal government has had such legislation since the 1980s.[30]

Lawmakers and law enforcement officials should make an explicit acknowledgment that it is possible in the overwhelming majority of instances to distinguish between common crimes, such as assault, and crimes committed on the basis of animus toward homosexual orientation. 79% (459 out of 583 respondents) of those who reported in this study that they had experienced homophobic or transphobic harassment or violence in the past 2 years stated that the incident was preceded or accompanied by homophobic language. Seventy-nine respondents (14%) responded in the negative, while 45 respondents (8%) did not answer this question. This data is consistent with the qualitative data collected in all of the focus groups throughout Queensland and in the written responses to other survey questions. Thus, in the vast majority of cases, it is possible to distinguish common crimes, such as assaults, from violence based on animus toward LGBTIQ sexual orientation and gender identity.[31]

Many scholars in the United States have persuasively reasoned that law enforcement officials initially wrestled with:

> definitional ambiguities related to the parameters of hate crime in general and motive in particular ... political controversies surrounding hate crime and its relationship to political correctness in both law enforcement agencies and communities ... and organisational dilemmas connected to agency structures, resource allocation decision, and workplace culture.[32]

Notwithstanding these obstacles, US hate crimes expert, Valerie Jennes, concludes that hate crime laws are proving successful in achieving their objectives:

> Police officers are being trained to enforce hate crime law, incidents of hate crime are being officially recorded, perpetrators are being arrested, and prosecutors are — on rare occasion — successfully pros-

ecuting hate crimes ... so the implementation of [such laws and the achievement of their policy objectives] is, at least to some degree under way.[33]

Hate crimes legislation also exists in Australia following different models. Western Australia has embraced the penalty enhancement model by increasing penalties for common assault when the assault is provoked in racial circumstances.[34] In 2002, the penalty enhancement model was suggested during an election campaign by the Leader of the State Opposition in New South Wales and quickly dismissed by the State Attorney General at the time.[35] Lawmakers in New South Wales chose to change provisions of sentencing legislation as suggested as an alternative in Recommendation 3.

Recommendation 3: As an alternative to Recommendation 2, the authors urge the passage of legislation providing that [prejudice-motivated] or hate crimes committed on the basis of animus toward gender, LGBTIQ [sexual] orientation or gender identity be recognised as a an aggravating factor in the criminality of the Act, thus justifying the imposition of harsher penalties. This has been referred to as the 'sentence aggravation model.'[36]

Both New South Wales and Victoria have adopted this 'sentence aggravation model'. New South Wales passed legislation in 2003, amending certain hate crimes provisions of sentencing legislation, providing the judge with discretion to consider certain prejudice-inspired crimes as an aggravating factor to be taken into account in determining the appropriate sentence of the offender.[37] In September 2009, Victoria also passed a new law requiring judges, when sentencing offenders who had committed hate crimes, to take into account prejudice or hatred against a particular group as an aggravating factor.[38]

The Victorian Government appointed recently retired Supreme Court Justice Geoff Eames to determine if there is a need for specific hate crimes legislation in that state (aside from considering it as a factor in sentencing) and to examine the nature of the penalties for such crimes to ensure they reflect the seriousness of such prejudice-motivated violence.[39]

The authors suggest Queensland consider this as a viable alternative on the basis that it may have the same general deterrent effect as the passage of hate crimes legislation. However, the authors consider Recommendation 2 to be preferable as it is more consistent with the general development of criminal laws in Australia.

Recommendation 4: The authors urge the passage of a 'Queensland Hate Crimes Statistics Act' to track prejudice-motivated crimes committed, *inter alia*, on the basis of LGBTIQ sexual orientation and gender identity.

Similar legislation has existed in other jurisdictions outside Australia, such as the United States, since 1990. In the United States, both local laws and federal legislation (*Hate Crimes Statistics Act*) assemble such statistics. They both provide for elective or noncompulsory law enforcement agencies throughout the United States to report such crimes to the Federal Bureau of Investigation (FBI) each year. By 2000, 50 states were voluntarily participating in assembling and reporting data on hate crimes to federal authorities.[40] Since 1991, sexual orientation has constituted the third highest category of hate crimes in the United States, according to the statistics released by the FBI.[41]

Other jurisdictions within Australia, such as New South Wales and Victoria, have been gathering and analysing data on gay hate crimes for several years. The authors understand (on the basis of anecdotal evidence) that there is under-reporting in these jurisdictions, at least in part because police officers may not be sufficiently trained to ascertain if the crime was motivated by animus toward sexual orientation or gender identity. This is an ongoing problem in other jurisdictions as well, which must be addressed through the training of cadets and liaison officers about how to determine if a hate crime has been committed. In many states in the United States, laws have been passed which require law enforcement to assemble data on prejudice-inspired crimes as well as require training of law enforcement on how to handle, record and prosecute hate crimes.[42]

The authors understand a newly instituted system known as QPrime has been set up by the QPS since June 2007[43] to, *inter alia*, collect statistical data relating to criminal activity. The authors understand it is possible to use this database to track crimes committed on the basis of animus toward LGBTIQ individuals.[44] Pending the passage of a 'Hate Crimes Statistics Act' in Queensland and/or a 'National Hate Crimes Statistics Act', the authors urge the QPS to release to the public the statistics they have assembled to date and continue to do so on an annual basis so as to promote transparency in enforcing and tracking crimes committed partly or wholly on the basis of prejudice motivated by animus toward LGBTIQ individuals. This will help foster the principles of accountability and enhance confidence in law enforcement (see Chapter 7).

> **Recommendation 5:** The authors recommend that the language in Sections 124A and 131A of the *Queensland Anti-Discrimination Act* be changed to identify LGBTIQ sexual orientation and/or gender identity as the basis of discrimination, and that the grounds covered for vilification and/or severe vilification be extended to include HIV/AIDS.[45] However, the authors recommend that cases not involving severe vilification continue to be dealt with within the jurisdiction of the Anti-Discrimination Commission as currently provided for under Section 124A of the ADA 1991.[46]

The former and Acting Anti-Discrimination Commissioner recently urged a review of the *Queensland Anti-Discrimination Act 1991* (which has not undergone major reform since its enactment) to ensure Queensland returns to being at the vanguard of human rights legislation in Australia.[47] The current language in s 7(1)(1) of the *Queensland Anti-Discrimination Act* prohibiting discrimination on the basis of lawful sexual activity does not foster a positive image of sexual diversity and renders LGBTIQ individuals to positions of invisibility.[48]

The legislation contributes to the creation of a paradigm in which homosexuality is inferior to heterosexuality. Although the language in the legislation appears to be aimed at individuals who identify as LGBTIQ, none of these terms are actually used, thereby relegating existence of such individuals to the 'sexual acts' they may perform, rather than considering them as unique individuals or a community contributing to social and sexual diversity.[49]

> **Recommendation 6:** The authors suggest Queensland consider the passage of separate vilification legislation covering cases of severe vilification on the grounds stated above and make it part of the Criminal Code.

Some commentators have criticised anti-discrimination legislation in various jurisdictions throughout Australia because of the complicated process for bringing prosecutions. It should be noted that the process has proven ineffective as there has never been any convictions in any jurisdiction in Australia for severe vilification resulting in criminal sanctions.[50] The authors suggest the Queensland government should consider whether severe vilification should form part of the anti-discrimination legislation, given the complicated nature of the commencement process. The police are not involved in the process and a request must be made for approval from the Anti-Discrimination Commissioner to commence proceedings (which carry potential criminal penalties) to the Attorney General (AG) or Department of Public Prosecutions (DPP). The authors understand that in many jurisdictions employing a similar process, the AG and the DPP failed to approve the commencement of such proceedings even in the face of substantial evidence.[51]

If this recommendation is adopted, the police will have an obligation to handle the incidents of severe vilification as violations of the general criminal law. This will ensure that victims of hate crimes are not required to deal with the substantial administrative hurdles associated with the current complaint process under the anti-discrimination legislation. More direct criminalisation of this particular conduct will assist in the development of community awareness of both the destructive nature of hate crimes at a societal level and the seriousness with which prejudice-motivated conduct is viewed by the criminal justice system.

Recommendation 7: Alternatively, the authors recommend amending Section 131A of the Act to allow the Commissioner to commence proceedings for severe vilification carrying potential criminal penalties without having to secure approval from the AG or DPP.

Recommendation 8: A legal Service for LGBTIQ communities in Queensland, which provides free legal and referral advice where warranted.

The data collected in this survey indicates there is a dearth of awareness among the LGBTIQ community about their legal rights. The authors are aware that such an initiative is currently underway with the support of the community organisation, the Queensland Association of Healthy Communities (QAHC). The authors wholeheartedly endorse this measure. Hopefully, this Legal Service will advise victims of homophobic and transphobic abuse and violence (as well as discrimination in the workplace) of their rights and remedies that might lead to more active engagement with existing legal mechanisms, such as the QPS, ADCQ and the court system where warranted. If this service becomes operational, the authors suggest the development of an easy to understand booklet similar to the one prepared by the Attorney General's Department of New South Wales in 2009 that will assist LGBTIQ Queenslanders to understand their legal rights.[52]

Recommendations: Educational Initiatives

The education system in Australia is currently undergoing significant review. With this in mind, the recommendations made in this book could be adopted in both Queensland and on a national level.

The Damaging Effects of Homophobia and Transphobia on Students

A 2005 survey of 1745 young individuals aged between 14 to 21 found 38% had experienced unfair and unlawful treatment on the basis of their sexuality at work and school. School was the most conventional venue for abuse, with 60% of young people in this category reporting forms of both verbal and physical abuse and 75% reporting that such abuse occurred in school environments. The researchers conclude school continues to be the most unsafe setting for these types of abuse.[53] These forms of abuse pose damaging consequences for the health of same-sex attracted youth (SSAY) who may resort to substance abuse and greater instances of self-mutilation. These students were also four times more likely to attempt suicide than opposite-sex attracted youth.[54]

Recommendation 9: The authors firmly believe that educational initiatives aimed at all ages and levels of the system must be adopted to avoid the devastating consequences of homophobia and transphobia.

As N, a young gay male, stated in our Gold Coast focus group:

> I think if you put education in primary schools, because as most of us would know with family members [much homophobic abuse, harassment and violence would be minimised]. I have a nephew who I've told that I've been gay since quite young. He's fine with it, he knows my friends and he's like, 'Oh, is this one of your boyfriends', and I'm like, 'Well no but it's a friend'. He doesn't care. His friends don't care either because this is N, whether he's gay or straight or peanut butter — he's still the same person. So I think if you started education from primary school age, they'll grow up knowing that it's a normal thing.

The sentiment expressed by N was a fairly consistent theme arising out of the focus groups because schools serve as a knowledge base for information on sexuality and could be the most ideal starting point for combating homophobic statements and bullying. They can also serve as an important platform from which students can learn about the benefits of living in a pluralistic, sexual diverse society for maintaining a healthy democratic system.

Recommendations: Teaching Sexuality in Queensland Schools

The Queensland Department of Education and Training (QDET) has an Inclusive Education Policy that supports, values, celebrates and responds positively to diversity. This policy provides in pertinent part that teachers 'must be given the opportunity to update and refine their knowledge of issues of ... culture and sexuality in order to respond to diversity and to effectively deliver productive pedagogies'.[55]

Sexual diversity can be covered, but this is not required in the QDET curriculum on sexuality education. Teachers and school officials have discretionary authority about how and at what level such education should be taught. They are not required to issues reports on their approach implemented nor are they required to assess the efficacy of their practices.[56] Parents may opt to have their children removed from the sexuality education part of the curriculum. QDET adopts an across curriculum approach in which such sexual diversity education policy can be included as an optional part of other aspects of the curriculum, such as Health and Physical Education and English.[57]

Recent studies on teaching sex education to SSAY explain not only why it engenders so much controversy but also, more importantly, why such education is 'useless' if it fails to include sexual diversity. Placing sexual diversity aside, sex education has always proven to be fertile ground for controversy because sensitive notions of virtue are enmeshed in the topic and the general public have always been apprehensive about adolescent sexuality.[58]

Concerns over the extent, nature and type of information disseminated to youth have been symptomatic of an underlying anxiety over corrupting the innocence of youth. Despite these concerns, the teaching of sex education in Australia has not yielded the adverse outcomes cited by opponents that have included fears of youths having sex at an earlier age and being more sexually active. Indeed, the reverse has been shown to be the case. Those who are educated about sexual health tend to practise safer sex with fewer partners.[59]

Although schools in Australia are commonly accepted to have an obligation to supply secondary school students with information about safer sex, sexually transmitted diseases and pregnancy, the precise way in which these topics are covered as part of the curriculum, and the age level at which they are taught, is entirely left to the judgment of school officials. This undermines the principles of consistency, transparency and accountability in the teaching of sex education. This usually means the curriculum is based on parental perceptions, which tend to focus on teaching of safer sex as well as reproductive sex in heterosexual relationships rather than the practice of safer sex for SSAY. This effectively means sexual diversity is not included in sexual education classes, thereby depriving up to 11% of SSAY of information on sex education that is pertinent to them.[60]

....

The development of a number of teaching materials, curriculum initiatives and community partnerships in some states for SSAY have in more recent years attempted to foster sexually inclusive education. Nonetheless, these initiatives have encountered resistance and it is highly unclear the extent to which these initiatives have been successful.[61]

A study conducted of sexuality teaching on the Gold Coast in Queensland concluded that:

> School and classroom environments appear to maintain and sometimes reward sexist and homophobic attitudes and behaviours. Several participants questioned Gold Coast schools' ability to adapt sexuality education to reflect cultural diversity. Furthermore, the focus group results indicate limited acceptance of a broad view of sexuality and high levels of uncertainty with regards to appropriate responses to children's expressions of gender, sexual and cultural identity. These findings indicate that diversity and human rights are not always supported in practice. In fact, avoiding concepts that are perceived to be controversial such as pleasurable aspects of sexuality and sexual identities other than heterosexuality contradict these principles.[62]

Recommendations: Bullying in Queensland Schools

QDET has issued a statement to school leaders that currently recognises 'when issues such as racism and homophobia are left unaddressed they can impact significantly on the positive culture of a school and increase the risk of problems including violence'. For this reason, QDET acknowledges it is imperative to maintain an unwavering position that is widely understood by the community that racism and homophobia 'are not tolerated in schools' and that 'decisive action' be taken to 'comprehensively address any issues as they arise'. The statement enumerates some of the steps that can be undertaken to address racism and homophobia.[63]

QDET also has a Responsible Behaviour Plan for Students that prohibits bullying as categorically unacceptable, acknowledging bullying may be related to sexual orientation.[64] Researchers from the Australian Centre for Sex, Health and Society persuasively argue for naming homophobia in anti-bullying policies. These arguments include the widespread view still maintained in much religious writings and practice that persons attracted to the same sex are 'evil, immoral, sick, and abnormal'. These views continue to be widespread among members of the students in schools.[65]

Objecting to homophobic abuse is often much more difficult than is the case with bullying based on other groups such as race or gender. This is in part because teachers in many instances share the same widespread views about individuals attracted to the same sex as the perpetrators of bullying, either because of their firmly held religious views of homosexuality as morally reprehensible, an illness or because of the prior criminality of male-to-male forms of homosexuality in Australia. All these factors may lead to discomfiture with confronting homophobia and transphobia in the school setting. In addition, fear of being branded LGBTIQ by other students could also play a role in an aversion to confronting homophobic bullying. Teachers who lack support from school policies potentially face the possibility of being shamed or disgraced for fostering homosexuality.[66] As one scholar has noted: '... it is recognised that teachers censor their teaching, limiting it to dangers and risks, to protect themselves against charges of promoting sexual activity or 'deviant' behaviours'.[67]

Additionally, SSAY are confronted with the possibility of parental and peer refusal to accept their sexual orientation (particularly if their parents and peers are heterosexual), which places additional hurdles in seeking assistance from these potential systems of support. This lack of assurance of support distinguishes homophobic bullying from bullying of other minority groups, such as race or religion, whose parental membership in the targeted group is most likely the same as that of the bullied student.[68]

Recommendations: Primary and Secondary School

Recommendation 10: The authors urge QDET to adopt both the UNESCO *Guidelines on Sexuality Information* and the *Guidelines for Comprehensive Sexuality Education Kindergarten Through 12th Grade* (3rd Edition) as statewide school policies and practices.

The UNESCO *Guidelines on Sexuality Education* (now in its final version and conference ready, which means it has not yet been officially launched by the United Nations)[69] was jointly authored by Douglas Kirby, a Senior Research Scientist employed by Education, Training and Research Associates, along with Nanette Ecker, the former director of International Education and Training with the Sexuality Information and Education Council of the United States (SIECUS). The international UNESCO *Guidelines* are intended in part to assist educators involved in 'the development and implementation of school-based sexuality education programmes and materials'.[70] The *Guidelines* revolve around 'Relationships; Values, Attitudes and Skills', 'Culture, Society and Law, Human Development', 'Sexual Behaviour', and 'Sexual and

Reproductive Health'.[71] As joint author Nanette Ecker aptly pointed out: 'Maths and science are valued as important for young people to have for their own sake ... A sound sexuality education should be equally valued'.[72] The guidelines are informed by almost 90 studies conducted globally, curricula from 12 countries, and the *Guidelines for Comprehensive Sexuality Education* (3rd Edition) devised by SIECUS that has played a leading role in enhancing sexual health on six continents.[73]

The authors also urge QDET to familiarise themselves with the *Guidelines for Comprehensive Sexuality Education Kindergarten Through 12th Grade* (3rd Edition), prepared by SIECUS to assist educators assess current curricula in an effort to create contemporary sexuality education programs. The latest edition of the *Guidelines* offers particular suggestions to assist teachers 'provide high quality sexual education to young people in their schools and communities'.[74] These guidelines recognise that teachers should begin teaching about sexual diversity at primary school beginning at ages 5 through to 8.[75]

Recommendation 11: The authors recommend that QDET adopt as state-wide school policies and practices, suggested guides, training programs and resources that are used in other jurisdictions, such as Tasmania, New South Wales, South Australia and Victoria, for supporting same-sex attracted students, transgendered students and questioning students and mandatory annual reporting procedures on the outcomes of anti-bullying policies implemented (as currently required in New South Wales and South Australia).

In Victoria, an inclusive approach has been embraced by the Victorian Department of Education and Early Childhood Development on matters concerning sexuality education and sexual diversity. This approach includes a gender identity policy, teaching and learning policies embedded in the curriculum which recognise and support SSAY, student wellbeing procedures, training of principals, and other school leaders, teachers and counsellors to support SSAY, strategies for principals, teachers and parents in responding to homophobic bullying against staff and students, and the role of partnerships between parents and/or carers and schools in supporting sexuality and gender diversity.[76]

Tasmania is considered to have the most progressive policies for sexuality education and government-funded initiatives to challenge homophobia.[77] Based on studies conducted on the percentages of Tasmanians who experience verbal and physical abuse based on sexual orientation, certain benchmarks were set by a Community and Wellbeing committee in the Tasmanian Together Social Plan to: '(a) reduce the incidence of lesbian and gay Tasmanians who experience verbal and physical abuse; (b) increase the percentage of teachers who are educated in harassment and discrimination related to sexuality; (c) reduce the incidents of complaints to the Anti-Discrimination Commission in Tasmania; and (d) increase the percentage of lesbians and gays who feel safe in public spaces'.[78]

A globally recognised authority in providing practical suggestions on ways in which to teach sexual diversity and help overcome homophobia in schools, Daniel Witthaus previously published an educational kit for *Pride & Prejudice* that yielded positive results in educating students on sexual diversity and addressing homophobia in schools.[79] Witthaus' recent book, *Beyond 'That's So Gay': Challenging Homophobia in Australian Schools*, is a practical guide for educators to deal with these same issues in the classroom setting.[80]

As in Queensland, parents of children in schools in Victoria can opt to have their children withdrawn from courses dealing with sexuality education. Anecdotally, the authors understand the number of parents who withdraw their children from sexuality education is very low. Thus, the authors recommend QDET focus its resources on improvements in sexuality education program and curriculum effectiveness. The authors believe that in the rare instances that parents wish to opt their children out of such curriculum, those children may be the students most in need of such education. For this reason, the authors recommend that parents wishing to withdraw their children from sexuality education courses must first be counselled by an appropriate school official to ascertain the reasons for doing so and to advise the parents of the merits of exposing their children to this important part of the curriculum. It may very well be that parental counselling on homophobia and transphobia is needed.

The authors believe that Queensland should specifically address homophobic bullying in their anti-bullying policy and should offer both staff and students protection from homophobic bullying.[81] This, combined with adoption of policies, practices, procedures, and guidelines found in other states, can only serve to assist in overcoming the problem of homophobic bullying and create a safe learning environment that celebrates the values of diversity and inclusiveness.

The authors are aware of the recent report provided to the Queensland government by Dr Ken Rigby (the *Rigby Report*) in February 2010 on issues relating to bullying in schools in Queensland. He has made several recommendations that the authors endorse in other jurisdictions, such as New South Wales and South Australia, mandating schools to report annually on the implementation of their anti-bullying policies. As he accurately states in this report:

> A good deal of useful advice and guidance can and should be provided by QDET and by other educational jurisdictions ... This requires educators to draw on the knowledge and experience derived from the research and associated anti-bullying programs that have become available in recent years ... progress is being made in countries around the world in actually reducing bullying to a substantial degree. This can happen in Queensland.[82]

The authors also note that Queensland Premier Anna Bligh, acting immediately on the recommendations provided in the Rigby Report, announced a new Queensland Schools Alliance Against Violence initiative on 23 February 2010, as this book went to press. The authors consider these moves a proactive first step in dealing with the situation of schoolyard violence and cyber bullying in Queensland schools. This is a very important initiative and the authors acknowledge the willingness of the current Queensland government to commission reports, such as the *Rigby Report* and a willingness to consider adopting 'best practice' models for tackling bullying from other jurisdictions within Australia and globally.[83] The authors urge the Queensland government to act on the recommendations made in this book dealing with homophobic bullying of staff and students in Queensland schools and the impact of homophobia on hiding sexuality in the educational sector, which arose as an issue in many of the focus groups conducted (see Chapters 2 and 9), as well as look to other jurisdictions within Australia for practical teaching materials on training in sexual diversity and confronting homophobia in schools.

M, a middle-aged gay man participating in one of the focus groups, recounted the traumatic experiences of sexual vilification and bullying his partner (a secondary school teacher with 15 years of teaching in various locations in Queensland) experienced in the school setting, which corroborates the findings of the above study. His partner had been subjected to ongoing harassment and vilification for years but was able to deal with the situation until he was transferred from a school in a regional community to a high school in a remote community. The quotations below are from written statements provided by M to the facilitator, written by his partner, P, a middle-aged gay male:

> There have been many incidents relating to my sexual orientation at [this high school], however, none that have been as openly hostile as in the last two to three years. I have had to become thick-skinned during my 15 years as a secondary teacher, regularly being called

degrading and homophobic names either in the classroom or in the playground. This is not uncommon for a teacher and seems to be regarded as part of the job ... for the last four years I was repeatedly subjected to homophobic taunts both verbal and physical from students. I feel that it has gone beyond the stage where this vilification has become unbearable and must stop. It is no longer just schoolyard bullying doing schoolkid antics as indicated by the principal, it has become a school-wide endemic culture of harassment ... Some examples of the harassment and discrimination I have suffered over those four years are as follows:

At the beginning of 1999, I [taught a Human Relationships Education class with about 15 boys]. During those classes, I was constantly called names and harassed with comments such as 'Aren't you the faggot drama teacher?' and so on ... This got progressively worse as the year progressed and eventually reached the point where I was told to 'Fuck off faggot!' in front of the class by two boys. I reported this behaviour to management ... [and] was told by the Principal ... 'These students are only kids P. What can we do?' This name calling spread down to junior level, passed on like an infectious disease. Many Grade 8s, mainly boys, were impressed by this type of homophobic harassment of a teacher and joined in. This group was part of a [larger] group of boys who continued to harass me for the next three years ... The last incident occurred [in 2002] resulted in not only verbal abuse but physical as a [coke] bottle was thrown at me. This was done in front of the students. The boys responsible for this incident have been identified as the same culprits from a previous incident that occurred in [2001] ... So for the last three years until I left the school, I was regularly abused and harassed going to the canteen for lunches and morning teas fulfilling my playground duties and when going to class. I complained to all three managers over the last three years with no significant action or protection. When I finally complained to the Deputy Principal ... in desperation after being abused, yet again, by the same group of boys, she said: 'There is nothing I can do P. Just walk another way' ... I [eventually] contacted the QTU [representative] who claimed that ensuring a safe working environment was one of the many responsibilities of a school principal ... The school representative and I had a meeting with the Principal to attempt to rectify the problem and to discuss the rights of teachers to safety in the workplace. [The Principal] was not sympathetic and questioned if my responses to verbal and physical abuse were reasonable. I suggested they were, due to the expectations the school claimed to have regarding student behaviour and the school-based Behaviour Management Plan. On QTU's advice I had a meeting with a solicitor ... The [Principal] referred me to an Education Queensland psychologist ... I saw her three times. She suggested I was too artistic for teaching and that I was a round peg in a square hole. She recommended I leave teaching and open a coffee shop. I was not impressed ... I feel that the repeated incidents have not been dealt with effectively and have not been offered any solution to the problem. My morale, health and character have suffered due to ridicule and from a lack of school support. I feel isolated and unsafe in the workplace. I will be subjected to the same abuse and harassment and am at a loss as what to do next to protect myself from future harassment when I return to work ...

P has suffered ongoing severe anxiety and depression to the present time and has not been able to return to teaching as QDET dismissed him under Section 28 of the Queensland Public Service Act that said he was no longer fit to undertake duties of a teacher. The above remarks, along with statements made by respondents to the *Speaking Out* survey and participants in several focus groups, reveal a problem of homophobic bullying in Queensland schools. Students and staff are traumatised by these experiences and staff are reluctant to confront such bullying, for reasons previously noted, including lack of support from their peers or management in many instances. While bullying in general has allegedly become more widespread in Queensland (both inside and outside the classroom setting) and has received more intense scrutiny from the government and media, the issue of homophobic bullying seems arguably to have eluded the radar of government. Conspicuous silence in the face of empirical evidence of this as a problem in Queensland, other jurisdictions in Australia and in other countries (such as New Zealand) could be viewed by some as tacit acceptance, if not facilitation, of homophobic bullying.

Recommendation 12: More Queensland government funding to SSAY through media campaigns, such as placards, radio advertisements, directing SSAY and transgendered, intersex and questioning youth to appropriate community support organisations, such as Open Doors and Rainbow Visions (with appropriate contact names and phone numbers). The authors also recommend more government funding for rural, remote and regional areas of Queensland for the above cohort of students where there are no support groups for them in places, such as Townsville.

T, an 18-year-old lesbian in a regional focus group, found it difficult to make meaningful contacts with a group (Rainbow Visions) that meets on an irregular basis. She feels very isolated and frightened without any meaningful support systems, aside from her parents who have embraced her sexual orientation in an extraordinarily positive way. She indicated she had a couple of SSAY friends. However, many of them had mental health problems or issues with drug abuse. The facilitator asked her if she was planning to remain in the area. She indicated she hopes to move to Brisbane (which has a culture that is more socially accepting of LGBTIQ individuals).

Recommendations: Post-Secondary and Tertiary Education

Recommendation 13: The authors recommend all universities in Queensland offering programs to students wishing to become school teachers (K-12) consider requiring such students complete a compulsory course on sexuality education which includes a significant component focused on providing them with a solid understanding of relevant models and approaches to teaching students (beginning in primary school) about sexual diversity so as to build their confidence in teaching sexuality education on a whole of school basis in an inclusive and successful manner.

The authors strongly urge the teachers of these courses to use the International Guidelines on Sexuality Education developed by UNESCO as well as the numerous resources provided by SIECUS, including policy and research resources as well as the *Guidelines for Comprehensive Sexuality Education, Kindergarten Through 12th Grade* (3rd edition) prepared by the National Guidelines Task Force.

Recommendation 14: The authors recommend more courses be offered by tertiary educational institutions in Queensland in queer studies and sexuality studies and/or programs dealing with these issues.

In the Sunshine Coast focus group, one of the participants stated:

It's probably only been about the last three or four weeks that our social work coordinator with whom I get along with very well, that I have been stamping up and down saying something needs to be done about the social work degrees [offered some encouragement] ... I am not doing my Masters until you start putting these sort of criteria in so that I can do my Masters on something [such as sexuality or gender identity].

Recommendation 15: The authors recommend a number of government grants and scholarships be made available to LGBTIQ high school students wishing to enrol in post-secondary and tertiary educational institutions so as to foster the principles of inclusiveness and diversity in the these laboratories of learning.

The promotion and support of higher learning for LGBTIQ students will send a message to secondary school students that LGBTIQ students are valued members of the Australian community, who represent the values of diversity, dignity, autonomy and inclusiveness cherished in our democratic system of government.

Recommendation 16: The authors recommend universities offer scholarship awards to students irrespective of their sexual orientation or gender identity who have demonstrated a commitment to queer issues either through the production of a scholarly piece of work or through their involvement in the LGBTIQ community.

Recognition of merit in LGBTIQ relevant work will serve to raise the public visibility of the LGBTIQ community and queer issues and present them in a positive and rewarding way to the university community.

Recommendation 17: The authors recommend all university equity officers undergo specialised training in sexual diversity and gender identity on a nationwide basis and learn how to implement policies supportive of these principles and of SSAY generally.

There are varying levels of awareness, training, and support provided to SSAY by universities throughout Queensland. A national standardised training framework would help achieve uniformity in the development and implementaton of policies supportive of sexual diversity and gender identity among SSAY.

Recommendation 18: The authors recommend all universities in Queensland establish an ALLY Support Network on their campuses so as to provide opportunities for interested educators to undergo training on handling issues of sexual diversity and gender identity as well as acting as supporters of students struggling with these issues.[84]

An ALLY has undergone a program of training at their University, which is a day-long course at minimal cost to the university, in which they learn about the challenges homophobic and heterosexist attitudes LGBTIQ persons must confront on an ongoing basis.[85] ALLIES are staunch advocates of making the university environment an affirming one in which LGBTIQ people can thrive in a safe, comfortable study and workplace to fully realise their educational potential without having to worry about being verbally abused, physically harassed or otherwise suffer discrimination.

The authors in particular recommend that all managers within the university setting including University Equity and Diversity Officers, Heads of Department, Deans, and relevant Pro Vice-Chancellors and Deputy Vice-Chancellors undergo an ALLY training program as a demonstration of their support for this important initiative aimed at fostering an inclusive tertiary education. The ALLY Support Network has become so popular at some universities that there are waiting lists for people to enrol in the training program. Such initiatives are important. Even post-secondary and tertiary educational institutions rhetorically embracing equity and sexual diversity might be unaware 'why many transgender, bisexual, gay, lesbian or intersex people are not in positions to speak out on their own behalf, or are fearful of being harassed or discriminated against'.[86]

Recommendation 19: The authors recommend a safe space be designated on every post-secondary campus which is easily accessible and highly visible for LGBTIQ staff and students to congregate as they wish.

Some universities have no safe spaces for LGBTIQ students and staff. Others eliminated them once voluntary student unionism legislation was enacted. And even among some of the Queensland universities that do have safe spaces, the facilities are inadequate. A member of one of the focus groups stated:

> We went over [to check out the gay safe place with a guy from one of the community support groups and] it's in the old western campus, in the hall that's been locked up since 2005 and that's where our space is. No-one can access it if they need to and no-one really goes over to the western campus unless they're going to class.

Another member of the same focus group observed: 'You're out in the boondocks'.

Recommendation 20: The authors suggest QDET implement on a mandatory basis a program similar to the ALLY Support Network with compulsory enrolment in such training program by teachers, principals, and other school officials.

Recommendation 21: The authors recommend diversity and equity officers as well as those in positions of higher authority at all universities in Queensland consider initiatives highlighting and celebrating the local queer history of their community and their university and the contributions of the local members of such community to their university.

Such an initiative, the first of its kind in Australia, was held at the University of Newcastle in conjunction with the opening of the 2009 Rainbow Visions Festival (10-18 October). Rainbow Visions-Hunter Inc. is comprised of an alliance of groups and individuals who originate and bolster activities that play a major role in 'making the Hunter region a healthier, more enjoyable, rewarding and culturally rich place for LGBTIQ people'.[87]

Recommendation 22: The authors recommend all universities in Queensland consider adopting enforceable equity policies (where such policies are not already in place) prohibiting homophobic, transphobic or otherwise offensive conduct, verbal abuse or harassment directed towards staff and/or students based upon their actual or perceived sexual orientation or gender identity, both inside and outside the classroom environment, including social networking sites, with the prospect of sanctions, including the potential for expulsion from the university.

There has been an increase of reported cases both in Australia and globally of students propagating intolerance (including toward sexual minorities) in the tertiary educational sector through mass student emails as well as social networking sites, such as Facebook and MySpace. Some universities, such as the University of Birmingham in the UK, have adopted policies prohibiting such conduct which is subject to disciplinary action by the university.[88] On occasions where this type of conduct goes unpunished, intolerance, homophobia and transphobia are further propagated.

Recommendations: Policing Responses

Recommendation 23: The authors recommend that all cadets undergo comprehensive sexual diversity training.

The authors recommend QPS consider adopting aspects of the cadet training programs currently offered by the NSW Police Service and the Victorian Police Service in relation to issues facing sexuality diversity and the functions of their Gay and Lesbian Liaison Officer (GLLO) program. If the issue of offering such training is due to budgetary constraints, the authors recommend the Queensland government grant funds to the QPS specifically earmarked for this training. The authors recommend close collaboration between the policy and curriculum development officials for cadet training in Queensland and the Senior Programs Officer (Gay, Lesbian, and Transgender Issues) for New South Wales and Victoria with a view to incorporating into their cadet training program, the curriculum dealing with sexual diversity and informational seminars surrounding the purposes of the GLLO program.

The NSW Police Service has just begun running a two hour informational seminar to cadets on sexual diversity and the functions of the GLLO portfolio. Victoria has also recently just added a 65-minute session on sexual diversity and information about their GLLO program into their cadet training program. The authors believe exposure to these issues is vital to cadets as the research undertaken for this project indicates there may not be a liaison officer available (as is often the case) in dealing with a situation which arises involving LGBTIQ issues. This is covered in greater detail in Chapter 7.

Recommendation 24: The authors recommend greater publicity of LGBTI liaison officers including colourful posters, placards and signs with accurate up-to-date names and telephone numbers in venues in metropolitan, rural, remote and regional areas of Queensland.

1. Gay and lesbian or queer venues (including in prominent places around the pubs, nightclubs, toilet facilities, etc)

2. Greater prominence be given to the liaison program in the secondary schools in Queensland, with information prominently displayed detailing current names and contact details of LGBTI liaison officers, including annual school visits by liaison officers.

3. Greater prominence at all universities in Queensland with posters placed in prominent places on campuses with relevant names and contact details, including annual visits by liaison officers.

4. Placards and posters placed on major streets, including on streets outside and near all nightclubs (including straight ones), close to bus transport pick up stops and on buses, as well as large signs off the freeway for drivers passing by.

5. Promotion of a revamped liaison program (as outlined below) with the LGBTIQ and mainstream press.

6. Continue to promote the program with community newspapers and magazines, the gay media, gay publications, and LGBTIQ community organisations.

7. A special badge or uniform identifying an officer as a LGBTIQ liaison officer similar to the badges for other liaison officers in the police force. Note this does not mean that the liaison officer must be a member or identify as a member of the LGBTIQ community. (See Chapter 7)

8. LGBTIQ individuals whose cases have been reported to the police and are proceeding to court should be assigned a liaison officer (in addition to the officer in charge of the case).

As canvassed in Chapter 7, 38% of respondents to the *Speaking Out* survey were unaware a liaison program existed. More importantly, only 22 respondents or 4% of the persons who had indicated they had experienced homophobic abuse, harassment or violence in the past two years, had reported their most recent incident to a liaison officer. The suggestions above are intended to raise the profile of the LGBTI liaison program in Queensland as a resource which should be used by the LGBTIQ community.

Recommendation 25: The authors recommend one full-time position is designated for an individual to serve as the Queensland statewide liaison officer.

The Senior Programs Officer (Gay, Lesbian, and Transgender Issues) in New South Wales is a civilian position that overseas program development, policy development, executive advice and support and oversees the training and development of the GLLO training program. Without making any recommendation, the authors suggest the QPS explore the feasibility of splitting the current duties of the state-wide liaison position into two positions, one of which would be civilian and handle the responsibilities for which the Senior Programs Officer is currently responsible in New South Wales and the other one being occupied by a state-wide liaison officer who is a member of the QPS but ensures the policies (e.g., use of QPrime by all officers in the state) are being successfully implemented.

The authors recognise advantages to the approach of New South Wales: (1) There would be less likelihood of high turnover because the position would be an ongoing full-time appointment which would provide a sense of consistency and foster a sense of institutional history and memory, thereby avoiding the problem of cycling state-wide liaison officers on what has become a rotational basis, thereby undermining the purposes for which the liaison program was established in 1997; (2) There would be a clear separation between the police and a civilian employee in the development of policies, executive advice and support and overall responsibility for the development and training of cadets and liaison officers (who might more easily gain the trust and confidence of the LGBTIQ community). At the same time, ensuring the policies developed by the Senior Programs Manager are successfully implemented by the state-wide liaison officer would (if the recommendations made in this book were successfully implemented) be taken more seriously by a member of the QPS than a member of the civilian population. For example, if the use of QPrime is resisted by some members of the Police Service, the state-wide liaison officer could take steps in accordance with the policies of the QPS to ensure such resistance is minimised.

Recommendation 26: The authors recommend specialised training of the Queensland state-wide liaison officer and close coordination with the Senior Programs Officer in New South Wales, and their counterparts, the statewide liaison officers in Victoria and Tasmania.

The authors recommend the QPS consider seconding the current state-wide liaison officer to New South Wales and Victoria to observe how these two states develop programs and policies in relation to the LGBTIQ community; how they develop their training of cadets and liaison officers in relation to the LGBTIQ community; and how they oversee the state-wide liaison program to ensure it is functioning effectively in achieving the goals of the program as enunciated by Commissioner Atkinson and the additional goals outlined in Chapter 7.

Seventy-six per cent of the 835 individuals who answered the relevant survey question reported that the existence of liaison officers increased the likelihood of them reporting an incident of homophobic or trans-phobic abuse to the police. Only 201 respondents (24% of those who answered this question) responded negatively. These statistics demon-strate the survey respondents have an open mind about engaging with a liaison program that fulfils the goals for which it was established.

Recommendation 27: The authors suggest the QPS take advantage of train-ing programs previously designed by the New South Wales Police Force on issues of gay and lesbian liaison and crime prevention and incorporate them into their crime prevention training strategy generally.

The NSW Police have constantly strived to improve greater partnership in crime prevention between members of the LGBTIQ community and law enforcement through 'the design and conduct ... [of] training on a variety of gay and lesbian issues, including violence prevention'.[89] The NSW Police have already provided guidance, support and training on issues of gay and lesbian liaison in other law enforcement jurisdictions both nationally and internationally.[90]

Recommendation 28: In the event Queensland adopts hate crimes legislation (using either the penalty enhancement or sentencing aggravation model), the authors suggest QPS consider drafting separate written guidelines and poli-cies, as well as procedures on training cadets and liaison officers, in applica-tion of the new legislation.

From Despair to Hope: Recommendations

There have been a series of studies undertaken in the United States on the most effective methods for enforcement of hate crime laws. These studies have examined particular approaches successfully undertaken by particular police departments as well as compared approaches in different jurisdictions to help isolate the factors contributing to the relative success of implementing hate crime laws. For example, the Boston Police Commissioner set forth written guidelines implementing a range of novel law enforcement practices 'related to bias-motivated crime (e.g., intensive investigation after an incident, covert surveillance, victim decoys, and cover tests). One of the major empirical findings ... is how law enforcement guidelines and policy prompt change in police practices'.[91] Studies undertaken in 2007 analysed data provided by:

> ... hundreds of California law enforcement agencies and hierarchical linear modelling to reveal that policies do, indeed, increase the rate of official hate crime reporting; moreover, the degree to which law enforcement agencies are integrated into the communities in which they reside and to which they respond amplifies the effect policies have on official reporting.[92]

Also, the exercise of police officer discretion has been mentioned as a crucial factor in many of the studies undertaken. In addition, most of the studies undertaken in the United States emphasise the importance of establishing specialised bias crime units enthusiastically committed to addressing hate crimes because police in such units tend to view their functions in determining if a hate crime has been committed more generally. Certain indicia demonstrate such devotion, such as: (a) formalised training methods describing and applying various factual scenarios to develop an understanding of what constitutes a hate crime so as to encourage a police officer to exercise his/her discretion in accordance with a more expansive view the law; (b) a set of specific principles and; (c) official endorsement by the highest level personnel in the organisation, such as a police commissioner.[93] These units devoted to tackling hate crimes were generally found to be more effective than efforts by law enforcement to address equally serious matters, such as domestic violence.[94]

The authors suggest that QPS adopt similar practices to those outlined above, in particular the establishment of a distinct bias crime policing unit to expose incidents based on prejudice toward LGBTIQ individuals that might have otherwise been regarded as a common crime.

bottom page number229

Recommendation 29: The authors recommend all liaison officers be evaluated by their superiors on the basis of their performance in their roles.

Any reports made over concerns with a liaison officer or complaints received from members of the public should be duly noted in their personnel records and taken into account in their evaluations, including suitability for continuing to serve in the role as well as in their promotions. The authors recommend QPS reconsider the manner in which liaison officers are chosen.

As stated in Chapter 7, the main problems identified with the liaison program in most of the focus groups, included, but were not limited to, the following:

1. Liaison officers, including state-wide liaison officers, cycled through their positions far too often, thereby undermining the ability to develop meaningful relationships with the community and gain their trust and confidence. There have been four or five state-wide liaison officers in the past couple of years.

2. Lack of availability to get timely responses from liaison officers to enquiries from the LGBTIQ community, particularly in rural, regional and remote areas of Queensland. Police officers are in most instances responsive to the calls and the cadets currently have extraordinarily limited training in LGBTIQ issues.

3. Some liaison officers are covering territory far too wide to perform their functions effectively (even those who have garnered the respect of the LGBTIQ community). They are thus unable to respond to calls on a timely basis.

4. There is a perception among some in the LGBTIQ community that members of the police service express a willingness to take on this added responsibility with no real interest in advancing the purposes of the program as evidenced in their failure not only to respond to phone calls but also to attend LGBTIQ functions to which they are invited (and in some instances indicate they will attend) as well as in their failure to respond to enquiries relating to their role as liaison officers on a timely basis. In the Townsville focus group (reiterated to the facilitator in other focus groups), one of the members said: 'That is why they do it actually, it's another step up. In the police, like the army, the more functions you perform, the more bicky points you get'.

5. Lack of effective training of liaison officers.

6. A state-wide liaison officer who is lower in rank (e.g., sergeant) giving orders to the precincts to implement new procedures, such as QPrime, to officers in the precinct of superior rank, such as Inspector. They are less likely to take orders from a state-wide liaison officer of lower rank.

7. Some liaison officers are too high in rank (e.g., Inspector) and, even if well intentioned, their other responsibilities overwhelm their ability to perform their functions as liaison officers.

8. A degree of cynicism has developed among those who have had long-standing dealings with the liaison program and liaison officers about the motives for establishing the program in the first instance. The sceptics feel the program was established so that the QPS could be viewed as progressive when LGBTIQ outreach was viewed as progressive. These same cynics view the liaison program as ineffective to achieve the purposes for which the program was originally established in 1997.

The problems with the liaison program uncovered by this research project might be one of the reasons why only 22 or 4% of individuals who experienced an incident of homophobic or transphobic harassment or violence within the past two years had actually reported the incident to a liaison officer. As Sue Thompson, former Police Gay/Lesbian Client Group Consultant, NSW Police Service convincingly reasons:

> The New South Wales experience has been that without these officers working pro-actively in the gay and lesbian communities and being promoted as skilled and committed individuals who can be asked for by name at a patrol, the violence, harassment and other hate crimes directed against gays and lesbians would remain largely invisible and not be brought to police attention.[95]

As canvassed in Chapter 7, the authors recommend more robust efforts to recruit members from the LGBTIQ community into the QPS through community events, such as Brisbane Pride, Sunshine Coast Pride and Cairns Pride, and through advertisements in the mainstream and LGBTIQ press. This might assist in addressing some of the concerns indentified above with the liaison program.

Recommendation 30: The authors recommend any orders going out to the precincts or local area commands in relation to the liaison program bear the official authority of the Queensland Police Commissioner.

A covering letter commanding all precincts to read and follow the instructions of the state-wide liaison officer will likely be taken more seriously, particularly in the regional, rural and remote areas of Queensland.

Recommendation 31: The authors recommend the government provide more funding to place cameras in areas known to be hotspots of violence in all areas of Queensland, particularly in Fortitude Valley.

See Chapter 7, in which one of the reasons given for not pursuing an incident further was because it occurred in one of the very few areas in the Valley that did not have cameras.

Recommendations: Government Initiatives

Recommendation 32: The authors urge the Queensland government and the national government to launch media campaigns (similar to ones for drug related or domestic violence) which could be both comical, with LGBTIQ icons as actors in the commercials, whilst at the same time conveying the seriousness of homophobic or transphobic abuse, harassment and violence.

Homophobia and transphobia can be combated with the assistance of the media and the political process. Such a media campaign would raise awareness that homophobia and transphobia is just 'not on' in modern Australia. Also, listeners can be warned of the potential ramifications (both civil and criminal penalties for defamation, violating anti-vilification laws, and committing crimes) for verbal abuse, threats of physical violence as well as homophobic or transphobic violence. The research conducted indicates there is a lack of awareness of the existence and functions of the Queensland Anti-Discrimination Commission [ADCQ]. For this reason, the authors also urge the government to provide funding to raise public awareness of the ADCQ and the types of circumstances that warrant reporting an incident to the ADCQ and seeking their professional assistance.

Statistics from this survey indicate that 46% of 859 respondents to a relevant question felt that the increased public visibility of LGBTIQ individuals had actually decreased the risk of LGBTIQ people being subjected to homophobic or transphobic violence and harassment. Forty-two per cent felt it made no difference and a minority of 12% thought it increased the likelihood of such violence and harassment.

The authors firmly believe the portrayal of LGBTIQ individuals in a positive light by the media with inclusive messages to the general population that sexual diversity is something about which Australians should be proud as a source of strength. This can only serve to lessen internalised homophobia and transphobia by LGBTIQ individuals who will feel less at risk of suffering from the traumatising effects of externalised homophobia and its manifestations reflected in prejudice-motivated abuse, harassment and violence. Such positive messages (reinforced by stern warnings of the consequences of undermining such social cohesion by the ugly manifestations of homophobia and transphobia through the criminal justice system and the ADCQ) can only help in shaping Australian social norms in an enlightened way that recognises the importance of celebrating diversity.

Recommendation 33: The authors strongly urge Queensland lawmakers to adopt a holistic approach to addressing prejudice-motivated violence based on animus toward LGBTIQ individuals and in addressing homophobia and transphobia generally.

In this context, we urge Queensland to consider adopting a policy similar to the 'New South Wales Strategic Framework 2007–2012: Working Together Preventing Violence against gay, lesbian, bisexual and transgender people.'[96] This policy would recognise a whole government approach is needed to address homophobic and transphobic violence, including not just the QPS but also other Departments, such as QDET, Queensland Health, the Cities of Brisbane, Sunshine Coast, Gold Coast, Toowoomba, Rockhampton, Mt Isa, Mackay, Townsville and Cairns, the Department of Housing, Department of Communities, Department of Community Safety, and the Department of Justice and Attorney General.

The authors are aware the Queensland government has recently extended an open hand to the LGBTIQ community by inviting them to a BBQ at Parliament House. The authors understand some in the queer community viewed this as an affirming move.

Nonetheless, one participant in the Sunshine Coast focus group who had moved to Queensland from Victoria noted, 'If you look in Victoria and places like that, they have got departments that support the LGBT community ... In Queensland, hello, there's nothing here'. Another participant in the group said, 'That's all we ask is that everybody listens to everybody, it's just a level of common respect and courtesy'. M, a young lesbian woman replied that 'if we had more acknowledgement in our political powers and things like that, so much of this wouldn't be happening'.

Recommendation 34: The authors recommend more government funding that is easily accessible to community support groups in regional, rural and remote communities of Queensland, such as the Anti-Violence Committee in Townsville, the transgender support group in Townsville (Transbridge), and SSAY support groups.

A member of the Townsville focus group explained that an Anti-Violence group was formed after the Townsville office of the Queensland AIDS Council was bombed and has since focussed on preventing violence, including violence against the LGBTIQ community. As one member of the focus group in Townsville stated:

> The trouble is we have no funding; we have no officers who are on standby or anything like this. We have — again, we do a lot of things with a little bit of money, but unless we have some sort of money and some sort of help, we can't do very much ... We have no — we can provide an office, even in our home where it would cost nothing. We have a fax machine; we have a computer, photocopying abilities. We've got email, you name it, but with no funding you are limited in what you can do ... The problem here is this town ...

There is also a transgender group in Townsville that has no access to funding. A member of this group stated:

> Simply we again, [in the] transgender situation, if you come out and you say I've got a problem, you go to the doctor. The doctor says: 'You're a transsexual'. You go to the sexual health, they put you on hormones, they open the door and that's it, you're out. Any problems from there, you figure it out, buddy.

M, a transsexual, explained the dilemma she had when she was fired from her job in the Townsville area because of her sexual orientation and gender identity. She had nowhere to turn except Transbridge, who provided her with temporary shelter and assistance until she was able to move to Cairns.

Recommendation 35: The authors recommend that a full-time position as Policy Advisor or Senior Policy Advisor (depending on the background of the person who fills the position) be created as LGBTIQ Liaison, in the Strategic Policy, Legal and Executive Service of the Queensland Department of Justice and Attorney General.

In 1990, a similar position was created for gay and lesbian issues as a civilian position in New South Wales. The position has been ongoing since that time and has taken a leading role in the Attorney General's Department on issues relating to prevention of prejudice motivated violence based on animus toward the LGBTIQ community. There are now two positions in New South Wales which cover these issues, the Assistant Director General, Crime Prevention and Community Programs and the Senior Policy Officer, Gay & Lesbian Liaison, Crime Prevention Division, NSW Attorney General's Department. Such positions require the occupant to span a variety of disciplines, including law reform, educational initiatives, maintaining links with relevant community support groups, attending educational seminars dealing with LGBTIQ issues and providing advice on matters of crime prevention as it relates to the LGBTIQ community.

Creating such a position in Queensland would demonstrate that this state is committed to tackling some of the most devastating consequences of homophobia and transphobia through the creation of this position. The individual filling this role would take a leading position in the Department of Justice on issues relating to the prevention of prejudice-motivated violence based on animus toward the LGBTIQ community.

Recommendation 36: The authors urge more funding to undertake a national project through an ARC linkage grant or other funding provided by states or the national government which would examine 'best practice' models in relation to the handling and reporting of hate crimes committed on the basis of animus toward the LGBTIQ community which would involve at least three states, including Queensland, Victoria and New South Wales. This smaller Queensland project could lead to a larger project that would canvass a national strategy for addressing homophobia and transphobia generally.

In addition, the authors recommend that benchmarks similar to ones undertaken in Tasmania be set and that a survey addressing issues, such as those identified in this research, be conducted 5 to 10 years after the implementation of any of the above recommendations. This will allow the effect of such reforms to be quantified and will also provide further feedback with respect to the manner in which they have assisted the LGBTIQ community.

Endnotes

1   Alan Berman, 'The experiences of denying constitutional protection to sodomy laws in the United States, Australia, and Malaysia: You've Come a Long Way

Baby and You Still Have a Long Way to Go!', *Oxford University Comparative Law Forum Article 2* (2008) and Alan Berman, 'The Repeal of Tasmanian Sodomy Laws and Homophobia' in Shirleene Robinson (ed), *Homophobia: An Australian History* (Annandale, New South Wales: Federation Press, 2008).

2   Berman, 'The experiences of denying constitutional protection to sodomy laws in the United States, Australia, and Malaysia', citing Scott Long, 'Anatomy of a Backlash: Sexuality and the "Cultural" War on Human Rights', *Human Rights Watch* (2004), pp.3, 17. Available at <http://www.hrw.org/ wr2k5/anatomy /index.htm (accessed 7 January 2010).

3   Victorian Police, 'Preventing Homophobic Crimes' (25 June 2007), available at <http://www. police.vic.gov.au/content.asp?Document ID=308> (accessed 25 February 2010).

4   Distinctions have been drawn between 'gay panic' and 'non-violent homosexual advance' on the basis that the former denotes situations in which evidence is adduced that the defendant's suppressed homosexual inclinations triggered an episode of 'panic' in which the accused reacted with excessive violence after being approached with a suggestion of engaging in homosexual activity. Non-violent homosexual advance refers to violent reactions to homosexual advances by heterosexual men. See Attorney General's Department of NSW, Review of the 'Homosexual Advance Defence', (Discussion Paper 1996); Santo De Pasquale, 'Provocation and the Homosexual Advance Defence: The Deployment of Culture as a Defence Strategy', *Melbourne University Law Review* Vol. 26 (2002), pp 110, 113, cited in Simon Bronitt and Bernadette McSherry *Principles of Criminal Law* (2nd ed), (Sydney: Thomson Law Book Co, 2005), p 276.

5   In 1998, a Working Party set up by the New South Wales government recommended the exclusion of non-violent homosexual advance as a basis for establishing a defence of provocation. See Attorney General's Department of NSW, Homosexual Advance Defence: Final Report of the Working Party (1998), [6.7], available at <http://www.lawlink.nsw.gov.au/lawlink/clrd/ ll_clrd.nsf/ vwPrint1/CLRD_had> (accessed 6 January 2010).

6   Attorney General's Department of NSW, 'Review of the "Homosexual Advance Defence"', (Discussion Paper 1996), p 18, [57] cited by Kirby J in Green v The Queen (1997) 191 CLR 334 at 407 ('Green'). See also Attorney General's Department of NSW, 'Homosexual Advance Defence: Final Report of the Working Party', [6.7].

7   Attorney General's Department of NSW, Review of the 'Homosexual Advance Defence', (Discussion Paper 1996), cited by Adrian Howe, 'Case Notes: Green v The Queen, The Provocation Defence: Finally Provoking Its Own Demise?', *Melbourne University Law Review* Vol 22 (1998), pp.466, 484.

8   Green (1997) 191 CLR 334 at 408-9.

9   *Criminal Code Amendment (Abolition of Defence of Provocation) Act 2003* (Tas) s 4(b), repealing *Criminal Code* (Tas) s 160

10   Law Reform Commission of Western Australia, *Review of the Law of Homicide*, (Final Report 2007), Recommendations 29 and 44 at pp.222 and 317, respectively; available at <http://www.lrc.justice.wa.gov.au/097-FR.html> (accessed 6 January 2010). *Criminal Law Amendment (Homicide) Bill 2008* (WA) cl 12.

11   *Sexuality Discrimination Amendment Act 2004* (ACT), pt 2.1 (commencement date 22 March 2004).

12 Victorian Law Reform Commission, 'Defences to Homicide: Final Report' (Report 2004) p 54 at para 2.90, available at <http://www.lawreform.vic.gov.au/wps/wcm/connect/Law+Reform/Home/Completed+Projects/Defences+to+Homicide/LAWREFORM+-+Defences+to+Homicide+-+Final+Report> (accessed 6 January 2010).

13 *Crimes (Homicide) Act 2005* (Vic) s 3.

14 Victorian Law Reform Commission, 'Defences to Homicide: Final Report', p.55 at para 2.91.

15 Queensland Law Reform Commission, *A Review of the Excuse of Accident and the Defence of Provocation* (2008) available at <http://www.qlrc.qld.gov.au/Publications.htm> (accessed 6 January 2010).

16 Ibid., p.211.

17 See Bronitt and McSherry, *Principles of Criminal Law* (2nd ed), p.277; See also Gail Mason, 'Heterosexed Violence: Typicality and Ambiguity' in Mason and Tomsen, eds, *Homophobic Violence* (Annandale, NSW: The Hawkins Press, 1997).p.26.

18 Howe, 'Case Notes: *Green v The Queen*, The Provocation Defence: Finally Provoking Its Own Demise?', pp.487-490.

19 Stephen Page, 'Maryborough Men Acquitted of Murder: Gay Panic Defence' *Q-News*, date unknown, available at <http://www.qnews.com.au/node/12695/1790> (accessed 6 January 2010); see also Peter Hackney, '"Gay panic defence"cited by alleged murderers', *Queensland Pride*, 7 October 2009 available at <http://qlp.e-p.net.au/news/gay-panic-defence-cited-by-alleged-   murderers-2848.html> (accessed 6 January 2010).

20 Stephen Tomsen, 'Sexual Identity and Victimhood in Gay-Hate Murder Trials', in Chris Cunneen, David Fraser and Stephen Tomsen, eds., *Faces of Hate: Hate Crime in Australia* (Sydney: Hawkins Press, 1997), pp.97, 109.

21 Ibid.

22 *Criminal Code 1913* (WA) ss 77-80, 313, 317-317A, 338B, 444 (as amended by Criminal Code Amendment (Racial Vilification) Act 2004 (WA)); *Crimes (Sentencing Procedure) Act 1999* (NSW) s 21A(2)(h) (as amended by *Crimes (Sentencing Procedure) Amendment (Standard Minimum Sentencing) Act 2002* (NSW)); *Sentencing Act 1991* (Vic) s 5(2) (as amended by *Sentencing Amendment Act 2009* (Vic)); Sentencing Act 1995 (NT) s 6A (as amended by *Justice Legislation (Group Criminal Activities) Act 2006* (NT)). See also Gail Mason, 'Hate Crime Laws in Australia: Are they Achieving their Goals?', *Criminal Law Journal*, Vol 33 (2009), pp. 329-331.

23 Mason, 'Hate Crime Laws in Australia', pp 326, 328-9.

24 Ibid.

25 Berman 'The experiences of denying constitutional protection to sodomy laws in the United States, Australia, and Malaysia', quoting Scott Long, 'Anatomy of a Backlash: Sexuality and the "Cultural" War on Human Rights', p.17.

26 The authors prefer the use of the LGBTIQ orientation rather than sexual orientation which is an impartial term that would offer protection to both sexuality minorities and sexual majorities. As Mason aptly points out, this arguably weakens the policies of hate crime legislation; namely, to protect these disempowered sexual minorities from the legacy of suffering from the devastating

and traumatising consequences of enduring societal heterosexism and homophobia by the dominant majority. See Mason above, n 23.

27 This wording is partly based upon language used in civil rights legislation in the United States of America. See Mason, 'Hate Crime Laws in Australia', p 327, who asserts hate crimes can be largely described as 'crime wholly or partly motivated by, grounded in, or aggravated by, bias or prejudice towards particular groups of people'. The crucial factor is the animus or motivation for the commission of crimes based on bias, intolerance, hostility or prejudice directed at the victim because of the actual or perceived belief that the victim's characteristics render the victim a member of such a group. Most hate crime laws specify the targeted groups offered protection under such laws (e.g., race, religion, disability, ethnic origin, national alienage, homosexual orientation, gender identity, etc.). Hate crimes are common crimes, such as physical intimidation, assault, arson, vandalism, graffiti, and murder; see Federal Bureau of Investigation, Civil Rights, 'Hate Crime — Overview', available at <http://www.fbi.gov/hq/cid/civilrights/overview.htm> (accessed 1 January 2010).

28 The term 'hate crime' first became part of the vocabulary of law enforcement in the US when gangs of individuals sharing a commonality of hatred towards particular groups engaged in a spate of crimes motivated by that bias; see Federal Bureau of Investigation, Civil Rights, 'Hate Crime', <http://www.fbi.gov/hq/cid/civilrights/hate.htm> (accessed 1 January 2010). Hate crime legislation also exists in many other jurisdictions overseas, including the UK, Canada and New Zealand; see Mason 'Hate Crime laws in Australia' (2009), p.327.

29 Federal Bureau of Investigation, 'Civil Rights, 'Hate Crime — Overview' (accessed 1 January 2010).

30 Valerie Jenness, 'The Emergence, Content, and Institutionalization of Hate Crime Law: How a Diverse Policy Community Produced a Modern Legal Fact', *Annual Review of Law and Social Science, Vol. 3* (2007), pp.141, 144.

31 These statistics are similar to those found in studies undertaken in other jurisdictions with smaller sampling numbers. In Victoria, 85% of men reported the incident was accompanied by homophobic language as compared to 87% for women and 75% for transgender and transsexuals. William Leonard and others, *Coming Forward: The Underreporting of Heterosexist and Same Sex Partner Abuse in Victoria* (Melbourne: Australian Research Centre in Sex Health and Society, La Trobe University, 2008), pp.8,37).

32 Quoted from Jenness, 'The Emergence, Content, and Institutionalization of Hate Crime Law', p.151.

33 Ibid.

34 See Mason 'Hate Crime Laws in Australia', p.329, fns 23-27 and accompanying text; see also *Criminal Code 1913* (WA) ss 313, 317-317A, 338B, 444; Geoff Gallop, Premier of Western Australia, *Racial Vilification: Framework for Reform*, (Press Release, 5 August 2004), available at <http://www.mediastatements. wa.gov.au/ArchivedStatements/Pages/GallopLaborGovernmentSearch.aspx?ItemI d=121309&minister=Gallop&admin=Gallop&page=2> (accessed 26 May 2009).

35 Suggestions were made during an election campaign in NSW by the Leader of the Opposition that a coalition government would pass mandatory penalty enhancement legislation for certain crimes due to a rising number of prosecutions involving white women who had been raped by young Lebanese Muslim

males. The suggestion was dismissed by the then NSW Attorney General, Bob Debus, as a derisive move. It could certainly be viewed as an attempt to draw on the prejudices and moral sensitivities of the public at a time when social unity was needed. Subsequently, the government chose to pursue the 'sentencing aggravation model' as proposed as an alternative in Recommendation No. Four. Mason, 'Hate Crime Laws in Australia', pp.333-334; fns 23-27 and accompanying text; see also Stephen Gibbs, 'Move to Add Penalties for Hate Crimes "Dangerous"', *Sydney Morning Herald*, 19 July 2002 available at <http://newstore.smh.com.au/apps/viewDocument.ac?page=1&sy=smh&kw= hate+and+crimes&pb=smh&dt=selectRange&dr=10years&so=relevance&sf=t ext&sf=headline&rc=20&rm=200&sp=nrm&clsPage=1&docID=SMH02071 9ALQPI1NC0CU> (accessed 7 January 2010).

36 Mason, 'Hate Crime Laws in Australia', p 330; fns 33-36 and accompanying text, and p.334. See also *Crimes (Sentencing Procedure) Act 1999* (NSW), s 21A.

37 The minimal amendments to the hate crimes provisions of the sentencing legislation was accompanied by essentially no debate on those provisions except by one member of Parliament who referred to the advantages of these provisions for taking hate into account as an aggravating factor in the criminality of the act, because bias inspired crime amplifies the moral guilt of the criminal in addition to being offensive to the notion of civility in the community and social cohesion. While applauding the new provisions in the sentencing legislation as a welcome reform in terms of the policies underlying anti-discrimination, some commentators implied the amendments were motivated by the same prejudices and moral sensitivities of the public that gave rise to the suggestions of the NSW Opposition Leader in 2002 for mandatory enhanced penalty provisions for particular criminal offences. See Mason, *Hate Crime Laws in Australia*, p.334.

38 Victorian Attorney General, 'Sentencing Act to Recognise Impact of Hate Crimes' (Media Release, 16 September 2009) available at <http://www.premier.vic.gov.au/ component/ content/article/8142.html> (accessed 7 January 2010). See also Victorian Attorney General, 'Sentencing Act to Take Into Account Hate Crimes' (Media Release, 3 June 2009) available at <http://www.premier.vic.gov.au/ compo-nent/content/article/7111.html> (accessed 7 January 2010); Victorian Attorney General, 'New Sentencing Laws To Take Into Account Hate Crime' (Media Release, 24 July 2009) available at <http://www.premier.vic.gov.au/component/ content/article/7625.html> (accessed 7 January 2010).

39 'Hate Crime Law Review Ordered', *Age* [Melbourne], 10 December 2009, available at http://www.theage.com.au/national/hate-crime-law-review-ordered-20091209-kk2m.html (accessed 7 January 2010).

40 See Jenness, 'The Emergence, Content, and Institutionalization of Hate Crime Law', p.146.

41 Federal Bureau of Investigation, 'Hate Crime Statistics', available at <http://www.fbi.gov/hq/cid/civilrights/hate.htm> (accessed 7 January 2010).

42 See Jennes, 'The Emergence, Content and Institutionalization of Hate Crime Law', p.145.

43 'Gay men targets of violence', *Brisbane Times*, 2 November 2008, available at <http://www.brisbanetimes.com.au/news/queensland/gay-men-targets-of-vio-lence/200811/02/1225560616212.html> (accessed 30 January 2010).

44 Ibid.

45 See Mason, *Hate Crime Laws in Australia*, p.330.

46 Ibid.

47 Anti-Discrimination Commission Queensland 'Anti-Discrimination Annual Report 2008-09 calls for comprehensive review of the *Anti-Discrimination Act*', (Media Release, 18 November 2009) available at <http://www.adcq. qld.gov.au/media/09Annual_report.html> (accessed 18 December 2009).

48 Anna Chapman, 'The messages of subordination contained in Australian anti-discrimination statutes' in Mason and Tomsen, eds., *Homophobic Violence*, pp.69-70; Anna Chapman, 'Australian Anti-Discrimination Law and Sexual Orientation: Some Observations on Terminology and Scope', *Murdoch University Electronic Journal of Law*,Vol.3 (1996), paras 4-15.

49 Chapman, 'The messages of subordination contained in Australian anti-discrimination statutes', pp. 69-70.

50 See Mason, *Hate Crime Laws in Australia*, p.330-1.

51 Ibid, p.331.

52 Numerous organisations and individuals contributed to the preparation of the NSW informational booklet including NSW Young Lawyers, Gay and Lesbian Rights Lobby, Inner City Legal Centre, Legal AID NSW, the Gay and Lesbian Immigration Task Force Advocate, Immigration Lawyers and Agents, Attorney General's Department of NSW, ACON, Gay and Lesbian Counselling Service, Professor Jenni Millbank, Yasmin Hunter (Inner City Legal Centre), Paul Boers (Inner City Legal Centre), George Anastasi (Livingstoner and Company Lawyers) and Iain Brady (HIV/AIDS Legal Centre). The NSW booklet is available at <www.lawlink.nsw.gov.au/samesex> (accessed 7 January 2010).

53 L. Hillier, A. Turner and A. Mitchell, *Writing Themselves In Again: 6 Years On — The Second National Report of the Sexual Health and Well Being of Same Sex Attracted Young People in Australia* (Melbourne: The Australian Research Centre in Sex, Health and Society, La Trobe University, 2005) available at <http://www.latrobe.edu.au/arcshs/download_reports.html> (accessed 7 January 2010). See also Jonathon Nicholas and John Howard, 'Same-sex attracted youth suicide: Why are we still talking about it?' (Presentation, 2001) Suicide Prevention Australia National Conference, Sydney, available at <http://www.caps.org.au/assets/site/WSPD06_presentation_J_Nicholas.pdf>.

54 Hillier, Turner and Mitchell, *Writing Themselves In Again*. According to a more recent survey released in 2009 of over 8,000 secondary school students chosen randomly from 96 schools in New Zealand on issues dealing with sexual orientation as well as mental and physical health, more than one third of students identifying as gay or bisexual had thought very seriously about suicide. About half of these same respondents had purposefully harmed themselves in some manner. Same sex attracted youth (SSAY) were found three times more likely to be subjected to bullying in school than opposite-sex-attracted students and experienced a much greater sense of isolation. Over half indicated they had been hit or physically harmed in the past year. They also indicated higher levels of drug and alcohol abuse, sexually transmitted diseases and mental illness. 'Report Shows Gay Youth Face Serious Health Challenges', *Vox News Engine* (New Zealand), 19 October 2009 available at http://www.voxy.co. nz/national/report-shows-gay-youth-face-serious-health-challenges/5/27749> (accessed 16 November 2009).

55 Queensland Department of Education and Training, 'Inclusive Education Statement — 2005' available at <http://education.qld.gov.au/studentservices /learning/docs/inclusedstatement2005.pdf> (accessed 7 January 2010).

56 Elizabeth Barber, 'Positioning sexuality education research on the Gold Coast of Queensland', Australian Association for Research in Education (Discussion paper, 2004) available at <http://www.aare.edu.au/04pap/bar04704.pdf> (accessed 7 January 2010). Lynne Hillier and Anne Mitchell, '"It Was as Useful as a Chocolate Kettle": Sex Education in the Lives of Same-Sex Attracted Young People in Australia', in *Sex Education: Sexuality, Society and Learning,* Vol. 8 (2008), p.211.

57 An across curriculum approach is the first aspect of a whole-school approach to learning that ensures learning occurs: (1) in the classroom (curriculum); (2) in the school environment (through policies, processes, etc- in other words the way a school runs itself, including staff-role modelling); and (3) in school partnerships (with parents and the local community). From a sexual diversity standpoint, it is problematic if a school does not understand family diversity or connect with local gay interest groups.

58 Hillier and Mitchell, 'It Was as Useful as a Chocolate Kettle', p.211.

59 Ibid, p.213.

60 Ibid, p.215.

61 Ibid, p.216.

62 Barber, above n 56.

63 Queensland Department of Education and Training, 'Racism and Homophobia in Schools', available at <http://education.qld.gov.au/actsmartbesafe/ schoolleaders/racism-homophobia.html> (accessed 7 January 2010).

64 Queensland Department of Education and Training, 'Responsible Behaviour Plan for Students', available at <http://education.qld.gov.au/ studentservices/behaviour/bm-plans.html> (accessed 7 January 2010); see Appendix 1, p.12.

65 L. Hillier and A. Mitchell, *Why Homophobia Needs to be Named in Bullying Policy,* Australian Research Centre in Sex Health and Society — La Trobe University (Undated), available at <http://www.latrobe.edu.au/ssay/assets/downloads/Homophobic bullying.pdf> (accessed 7 January 2010).

66 Hillier and Mitchell, *Why Homophobia Needs to be Named in Bullying Policy;* Christian Taylor, 'Time to Target School Bullying', *SameSame,* 2 June 2009, available at <http://www.samesame.com.au/news/local/4090/Time-To-Target-School -Bullying-.htm> (accessed 7 January 2010).

67 Barber, above n 56.

68 See Hillier and others, above n 65.

69 There remains controversy over the timing of the release of these guidelines. The Conference version was presented at the International Sex and Relationships Education Conference in the UK in September 2009. The formal launch was to have taken place at the UN in late October. Apparently, controversy still remains over the timing of the official launch of the Guidelines. Religious and conservative groups have condemned the UNESCO guidelines. The final draft was initially postponed because of opposition from organisations, such as 'Citizens for a Responsible Curriculum', a US group based in Maryland opposed to abortion. It

is not particularly surprising that guidelines on sexuality education have provoked so much controversy and been opposed by certain conservative religious groups. There has existed for many years a coalition of groups that have aligned themselves in the UN over opposition to LGBT rights. This coalition comprises partly non-governmental organisations (NGOs) from the US associated with particular right-wing religious groups. During the Bush administration, there were suggestions by Human Rights Watch, an NGO, that the US was implicitly supporting the position of groups opposed to the recognition of human rights for LGBTIQ individuals. See Berman, 'The experiences of denying constitutional protection to sodomy laws in the United States, Australia, and Malaysia'; Rod Liddle, 'I Know Why The Government Wants to Send Homosexuals Back to Iran To Be Hanged', *Spectator* (UK, 26 March 2008), available at <http://www.spectator.co.uk/the-magazine/features/575491/i-know-why-the-government-wants-to-send-homosexuals-back-to-iran-to-be-hanged.thtml> (accessed 7 January 2010); Scott Long, 'Anatomy of a Backlash: Sexuality and the "Cultural" War on Human Rights', p.13.

70   'New International Guidelines Spell Out What Sexuality Education Needs to Teach', *Gov Monitor*, 31 August 2009, available at <http://thegovmonitor.com/world_news/international/new-international-guidelines-spell-out-what-sexuality-education-needs-to-teach-2751.html> (accessed 7 January 2010).

71   Ibid.

72   Ibid.

73   United Nations Educational, Scientific and Cultural Organisation, 'New International Guidelines spell out what sexuality education needs to teach', (Press Release, 28 August 2009), available at <http://portal.unesco.org/en/ev.php-URL_ID=46306&URL_DO=DO_TOPIC&URL_SECTION=201.html> (accessed 31 December 2009); see also Sexuality Information and Education Council of the United States, 'Leadership & Staff', (2009) <http://www.siecus.org/index.cfm?fuseaction=Page.viewPage&PageId=490&parentID=472> (accessed 27 December 2009).

74   National Guidelines Task Force, 'Guidelines for Comprehensive Sexuality Education (3rd ed)', 'Acknowledgements', p.5, available at <http://www.siecus.org/_data/global/images/guidelines.pdf> (accessed 27 December 2009).

75   Ibid. For example, Topics five and six deal specifically with sexual orientation and gender identity. The developmental messages are concise declarations specifying the precise information young people need to learn about each topic. Their developmental messages are divided into four levels of age. The sub-concept to Sexual Orientation states: 'As people grow and develop they may begin to feel romantically and/or sexually attracted to people of the same and/or a different gender'; Ibid, p.29. At Level 1 (children aged 5-8) the developmental messages are stated as follows: 'Human beings can love people of the same gender and people of another gender; Some people are heterosexual, which means they can be attracted to and fall in love with someone of another gender; Some people are homosexual, which means they can be attracted to and fall in love with someone of the same gender; Homosexual men and women are also know as gay men and lesbians; People deserve respect regardless of who they are attracted to; Making fun of people by calling them gay (e.g., "homo", "fag", "queer") is disrespectful and hurtful'; Ibid, p.29. The developmental messages become more sophisticated at each level. See also Barber, above n 56, who strongly advocates teaching sexuality education at the primary school level but

believes the implementation of such practices would more likely occur if teachers are given a solid understanding during their university studies on the relevant models and philosophies so they feel confident for teaching sexuality education in an inclusive and successful manner.

76 See Victorian Department of Education and Training, 'Safe Schools are Effective Schools: A Resource for Developing Safe and Supportive School Environments', (Melbourne: Victorian Department of Education and Training, 2006), p. 14, available at <http://www.eduweb.vic.gov.au/edulibrary/ public/stuman/ wellbeing/SafeSchoolStrategy.pdf> (accessed 7 January 2010).

77 Rodney Croome, *Rodney Croome Gay Advocate*, available at <http://www.rodneycroome.id.au/weblog> (accessed 6 March 2010).

78 The Summary of Tasmanian Together Social Plan was provided by courtesy of Rodney Croome.

79 Daniel Witthaus, *Pride & Prejudice-Educational Package*, available at <http://www.prideandprejudice.com.au>

80 Daniel Witthaus, *Beyond 'That's so gay!' Challenging homophobia in Australian schools* (Melbourne: Hawker Brownlow Education, 2010); See also http://www.thatssogay.com.au (accessed 6 March 2010).

81 See Victorian Department of Education and Training, 'Safe Schools are Effective Schools: A Resource for Developing Safe and Supportive School Environments', (Melbourne: Victorian Department of Education and Training, 2006), p. 14, available at <http://www.eduweb.vic.gov.au/edulibrary/ public/stuman/ wellbeing/SafeSchoolStrategy.pdf> (accessed 7 January 2010).

82 Ken Rigby, *Report: Enchancing Responses to Bullying in Queensland Schools*, available at <http://education.qld.gov.au/studentservices/behaviour/docs/enhancing-responses-to-bullying-qld-schools.pdf> (accessed 3 March 2010).

83 Jessica Marszalek and David Barbeler 'Group to Tackle School Violence, Bullies', 23 February 2010, available at <http://news.brisbanetimes.com.au/breaking-news-national/group-to-tackle-school-violence-bullies-20100223-osal.html> (accessed 3 March 2010)

84 The University of Newcastle, 'The Role of an Ally' available at <http://www.newcastle.edu.au/service/ally-network/ally-role.html> (accessed 21 December 2009).

85 Ibid.

86 Ibid.

87 See information from Rainbow Visions — Hunter Inc, available at <http://www.rainbowvisions.org.au/> (accessed 7 January 2010).

88 University of Birmingham Social Network Sites (Facebook, MySpace, etc) and Student Issues: Guidelines — January 2008, available at <http://www.as.bham.ac.uk/study/support/sca/Documents/social_networking_guidelines.pdf> (accessed 24 March 2010)

89 NSW Police Force, 'Police Gay & Lesbian Liaison Officers' (Factsheet), available at <http://www.police.nsw.gov.au/__data/assets/pdf_file/ 0011/86393/ GLLO_Fact_Sheet.pdf> (accessed 7 January 2010).

90 Ibid.

91 Quoted from Jenness, 'The Emergence, Content, and Institutionalization of Hate Crime Law', p.152.

92 Ibid.
93 Ibid, pp.152, 154.
94 Ibid.
95 Sue Thompson, 'Hate crimes against gays and lesbians: The New South Wales Police response' in Gail Mason and Stephen Tomsen, eds., *Homophobic Violence* (Sydney: Hawkins Press, 1997), p.135.
96 New South Wales Strategic Framework 2007-2012: Working Together Preventing Violence Against Gay, Lesbian, Bisexual and Transgender People, available at <http://wwwlawlink.nsw.gov.au/lawlink/cpd/11_CPD_strategic_framework> (accessed 10 January 2010).

Appendix 1

Focus Group Questions

Acknowledgment: The following questions were developed by researchers who conducted the New South Wales study, *'You Shouldn't Have to Hide to Feel Safe'*. The Attorney General's Department of New South Wales granted permission for their use in this Queensland study. Ethics permission for their use in a Queensland context was then granted by Bond University and Griffith University.

Questions

1. First a very broad question

    (a) as a lesbian, do you generally feel that you are about as safe from abuse or violence as most other women — or less safe, or more safe?
    Why do you say that?

    OR

    (b) As a gay man, do you generally feel that you are about as safe from abuse or violence as most other men — or less so, or more so?
    Why do you say that?

    (c) What about any bisexual people in the group?

2. (Ask participants to complete *Agree/Disagree* form, then invite discussion.) Do you agree or disagree with each of the following statements? Why is that?

    (a) As a lesbian/gay man/bisexual I feel vulnerable to violence or harassment from people I know.

    (b) As a lesbian/gay man/bisexual I feel vulnerable to violence or harassment from strangers.

    (c) Lesbians/gay men/bisexuals are generally safer if they hide their sexual preference.

    (d) I feel pretty safe in the area where I live.

    (e) Possible anti-gay/anti-lesbian harassment or violence is not much of an issue for me personally.

3. (a) Do you think there are particular situations/locations in which lesbians/ gay men are more likely to be abused or attacked? What situations/locations? Why are they more risky? What issues or situations are of most concern to you personally?

   (b) Just checking again on location or where people live — do you feel that there is more risk of abuse or violence in some areas than others? Which areas are most dangerous, and why?

4. (a) Do you think there are particular types of people who are more likely than others to be the subject of homophobic abuse or attack — for example, in terms of age, gender, race, appearance? Why do you say that?

   (b) [For Indigenous, Asian and Middle Eastern groups] What comments do you have about any homophobic abuse from within your own race or ethnic group, compared with racist or homophobic abuse from other people outside that group?

5. (a) Are different types of people likely to experience different types of homophobic abuse, harassment or violence? In what ways?

   (b) Are some people at risk of abuse or harassment because of their relationship with a lesbian or gay person — for example, a child, other relative, a friend? What is your experience in this regard?

6. **Have you experienced any sort of homophobic abuse, harassment or violence in the past year? If YES:**

   (a) What sort of abuse was involved? What happened? (Ask group:) Have other people had a comparable experience, either in the past year, or at some earlier time?

   (b) What sort of person/people were responsible for that abuse (e.g., gender, age, numbers)?
   (Ask group:) What has the experience of other people been?

   (c) Did you know the perpetrator(s), or know who they were or where they were from? (Ask group:) What about other people's experience in that regard? If you did know the perpetrator(s), what was their relationship to you?

7. What have been the effects for you personally — if any — of experience or concerns relating to anti-gay/anti-lesbian abuse or violence? Have those been shorter-term (how long?) or longer-term effects? What would you say has been the most important or serious effect for you?

8. Are there some things that you do, or avoid doing, because of concerns about anti-gay/anti-lesbian abuse or violence? What sorts of things?

9. And thinking about gay men and lesbians generally — what effects do you think anti-gay/anti-lesbian abuse or violence has on them? What would you say are the most serious or important effects? Are different sorts of people likely to be affected in different ways and, if so, how?

10. When you did/if you did experience an anti-gay/anti-lesbian attack or abuse, whom did you/would you be most likely to go to for help or support? Would it depend on the nature or results of the abuse? In what way?

....

11. (a) How confident would you feel about reporting homophobic abuse or violence to the police if you felt the matter was serious enough?

    (b) Have you ever reported an incident of anti-gay/anti-lesbian abuse, harassment or violence to the police or a Gay and Lesbian Liaison Officer?

    (c) If yes, what were the circumstances? What happened? Were any charges laid relating to the matter(s)?

    (d) How supportive/co-operative did you find the police/GLLOs supportive and cooperative?

    (e) How useful do you feel it was to report the incident in this way?

    (f) Would you recommend that other people go to the police/GLLOs in a similar situation? Why is that?

12. (a) In relation to anti-gay/anti-lesbian abuse or attack, have you ever sought help from other professional people or organisations — for example, a doctor or hospital, counsellor, Lesbian and Gay Anti-Violence Project, a support service at work or at school? In each case:

    (b) What were the circumstances? What happened?

    (c) How supportive cooperative did you find that service/group?

    (d) How useful was it to report the incident or seek help in that way?

    (e) Would you recommend that other people in a similar situation go to that same sort of person/organisation? Why/Why not?

13. If you suffered serious or significant abuse as a lesbian/gay man, are there particular services that you yourself would be:

    (a) likely to use? or

    (b) likely to avoid?

    Why is that?

14. Is there anything else you would like to say about anti-gay/anti-lesbian abuse or violence?

Bibliography

Adam, Barry, *The Rise of a Gay and Lesbian Movement* (New York: Twayne Publishers, 1995).

Anti-Discrimination Commission Queensland, 'Anti-Discrimination Annual Report 2008-09 Calls for Comprehensive Review of the *Anti-Discrimination Act*', (media release, 18 November 2009) <http://www.adcq.qld.gov.au/media/09Annual_report.html> (accessed 18 December 2009).

'Assaults Increase at Queensland Train Stations', ninemsn website, <http://www.news.ninesmn.com.au/national/987218/assaults-increase-at-qld-train-stations> (accessed 17 January 2010).

Australian Bureau of Statistics 2001 Census of Population and Housing Australia, 'Level of Education — Count of Persons Aged 15 and Over With a Qualification', Australian Bureau of Statistics website <http://www.censusdata.abs.gov.au> (accessed 3 March 2010)

Australian Bureau of Statistics, 'Crime and Safety Australia, April 2005' <http://www.abs.gov.au/AUSSTATS/abs@.nsf/productsbyCatalogue/669C5A99 7EAED891CA2568A900139405/> (accessed 2 March 2010)

Australian Institute of Criminology, 'Crime Victimisation', Australian Institute of Criminology website <http://www.aic.gov.au/publications/current%20series/facts/1-20/ 2008 /3%20crime %20victimisation.aspx> (accessed 5 January 2010).

Barber, Elizabeth, 'Positioning sexuality education research on the Gold Coast of Queensland', Australian Association for Research in Education (Discussion paper, 2004) <http://www.aare.edu.au/04pap/bar04704.pdf> (accessed 7 January 2010).

Benjamin, Harry, *The Transsexual Phenomenon* (New York: The Julian Press, 1966).

Berrill, Kevin T. 'Anti-Gay Violence and Victimization in the United States: An Overview', *Journal of Interpersonal Violence*, Vol. 5 (1990), pp.274-294

Berill, Kevin T. and Gregory M. Herek, 'Primary and Secondary Victimization in Anti-Gay Hate Crimes: Official Response and Public Policy' in Gregory M. Herek and Kevin T. Berill, eds, *Hate Crimes: Confronting Violence Against Lesbians and Gay Men* (Newbury Park, California: Sage Publications, 1992).

Berman, Alan, 'The Experiences of Denying Constitutional Protection to Sodomy Laws in the United States, Australia, and Malaysia: You've Come a Long Way Baby and You Still Have a Long Way to Go!', *Oxford University Comparative Law Forum*, Article 2, (2008).

Beyond: *'That's So Gay'*, available at <http://www.thatssogay.com.au> (accessed 6 March 2010).

Chapman, Anna, 'Australian Anti-Discrimination Law and Sexual Orientation: Some Observations on Terminology and Scope' *Murdoch University Electronic Journal of Law* Vol 3 (1996).

Blumfield, Warren J. ed., *Homophobia: How We All Pay the Price* (Boston: Beacon Press, 1992).

Bronitt, Simon and Bernadette McSherry *Principles of Criminal Law* (2nd Edition), (Sydney: Thomson Law Book Co, 2005).

Comstock, G.D., *Violence Against Lesbians and Gay Men* (New York: Columbia University Press, 1991).

Connell, R. W., *Masculinities* (Crow's Nest, New South Wales: Allen and Unwin, 2003).

Couch, M., M. Pitts, H. Mulcare, S. Croy, A. Mitchell and S. Patel, *TranZnation: A Report on the Health and Well-being of Transgender People in Australia and New Zealand* (Melbourne: Australian Research Centre in Sex, Health and Society, La Trobe University, 2007).

Crimes (Homicide) Act 2005 (Vic).

Crimes (Sentencing Procedure) Act 1999 (NSW).

Criminal Code 1913 (WA).

Criminal Code Amendment (Abolition of Defence of Provocation) Act 2003 (Tas)

Criminal Law Amendment (Homicide) Bill 2008 (WA)

Croome, Rodney, *Rodney Croome Gay Advocate*, available at <http://www. rodney-croome.id.au/weblog> (accessed 6 March 2010).

Croteau, J.M., 'Research on the Work Experiences of Lesbian, Gay, and Bisexual People: An Integrative Review of Methodology and Findings', *Journal of Vocational Behaviour*, Vol. 46 (1996), pp.195-209.

Craig, Elaine, 'Trans-phobia and the Relational Production of Gender', *Hasting Women's Law Journal*, No 18 (2007), pp.137-172.

Davies, M., 'Correlates of Negative Attitudes Towards Gay Men: Sexism, Male Role Norms and Male Sexuality', *Journal of Sex Research*, Vol. 41, No. 3 (2004), pp.259-266.

De Pasquale, Santo 'Provocation and the Homosexual Advance Defence: The Deployment of Culture as a Defence Strategy', *Melbourne University Law Review*, Vol. 26 (2002), pp.110-143.

Dick, Sam, 'Homophobic Hate Crime: The Gay British Crime Survey 2008', *Stonewall* 2008 <http://www.stonewall.org.uk/documents/homophobic _hate_crime__final_report.pdf> (accessed 24 January 2009).

Diversity Figures: A Statistical Snapshot of the Diversity of Queensland's Population; Multicultural Affairs Queensland website <http://www. multicul-tural.qld.gov.au/media/diversity_figures_brochure.pdf> (accessed 2 March 2010).

Federal Bureau of Investigation, Civil Rights, 'Hate Crime — Overview', <http://www.fbi.gov/hq/cid/civilrights/overview.htm> (accessed 1 January 2010).

Federal Bureau of Investigation, Civil Rights, 'Hate Crime', <http://www.fbi.gov/ hq/cid/civilrights/hate.htm> (accessed 1 January 2010).

Federal Bureau of Investigation, 'Hate Crime Statistics', <http://www.fbi.gov/hq/cid/civilrights/hate.htm> (accessed 7 January 2010).

Fejes, F., and K. Petrich, 'Invisibility, Homophobia and Heterosexism: Lesbians, Gay Men and the Media', *Critical Studies in Mass Communication*, Vol. 10 (1993), pp.396-422.

Fitzgerald, Andrew, 'Australia's Criminal Justice System Fails Lesbians and Gay Men', *Murdoch University Electronic Journal of Law* Vol 3 (1996), pp.1-3, <http://www.murdoch.edu.au/elaw/issues/v3n2/fitzgera.html> (accessed 31 December 2009).

Flood, Michael and Clive Hamilton, 'Mapping Homophobia in Australia', The Australia Institute webpaper, <http://www. unilife.curtin.edu.au/ sexualdiversity/documents/MappingHomophobiainAustralia.pdf>(accessed 23 January 2010).

'Gay Couple Wins Landmark Hate Case', *Queensland Pride*, 17 November 2008 <http://qlp.e-p.net.au/news/gay-couple-wins-landmark-hate-case-2318.html> (accessed 15 January 2010).

Gallop, Geoff, Premier of Western Australia, 'Racial Vilification: Framework for Reform', (Press Release, 5 August 2004), <http://www.mediastatements.wa.gov.au/ArchivedStatements/Pages/GallopLaborGovernmentSearch.aspx?ItemId=121309&minister=Gallop&admin=Gallop&page=2> (accessed 26 May 2009).

Garnetts, Linda Gregory M. Herek and Barrie Levy, 'Violence and Victimization of Lesbians and Gay Men: Mental Health Consequences', *Journal of Interpersonal Violence*, Vol. 5 (1990), pp.366-383.

Garnets, Linda, Gregory Herek and Barrie Levey, 'Violence and victimization of lesbians and gay men: Mental health consequences', in Gregory Herek and Kevin Berill, eds, *Hate Crimes: Confronting Violence Against Lesbians and Gay Men* (Newbury Park, California: Sage Publications, 1992), pp.207-226.

Gay Men and Lesbians Against Discrimination, *Not a Day Goes By: Report on the GLAD Survey into Discrimination and Violence Against Lesbians and Gay Men* (Melbourne: GLAD, 1994).

'Gay men targets of violence', *Brisbane Times*, 2 November 2008 <http://www.brisbanetimes.com.au/news/queensland/gay-men-targets-of-violence/200811/02/1225560616212.html> (accessed 30 January 2010).

Gettleman, Jeffrey, 'Americans' Role Seen in Uganda Anti-Gay Push' *New York Times*, 3 January 2010, <http://www.nytimes.com/2010/01/04/world/africa/04uganda.html?scp=2&sq=Uganda&st=nyt> (accessed 14 January 2010).

Gibbs, Stephen, 'Move to Add Penalties for Hate Crimes "Dangerous"' *The Sydney Morning Herald*, 19 July 2002, <http://newsstore.smh.com.au/apps/viewDocument.ac?page=1&sy=smh&kw=hate+and+crimes&pb=smh&dt=selectRange&dr=10years&so=relevance&sf=text&sf=headline&rc=20&rm=200&sp=nrm&clsPage=1&docID=SMH020719ALQPI1NC0CU> (accessed 7 January 2010).

Green v The Queen (1997) 191 CLR 334.

Hackney, Peter, '"Gay panic defence" cited by alleged murderers', *Queensland Pride*, 7 October 2009 <http://qlp.e-p.net.au/news/gay-panic-defence-cited-by-alleged-murderers-2848.html> (accessed 6 January 2010).

Harris, Angelique C. 'Marginalization by the Marginalized: Race, Homophobia, Heterosexism and "the Problem of the 21st Century"', *Journal of Gay and Lesbian Social Services*, Vol. 21 (October 2009), pp.430-448.

Harry, Joseph, 'Conceptualizing Anti-Gay Violence' in Gregory Herek and Kevin Berrill (eds), *Hate Crimes* (California: Sage Publications, Inc), p.113-122.

Harry, Joseph, 'Conceptualizing Anti-Gay Violence', *Journal of Interpersonal Violence*, Vol. 5 (1990), pp.350–358.

Heldke, Lisa and Peg O'Connor, *Oppression, Privilege, and Resistance: Theoretical Perspectives on Racism, Sexism and Heterosexism* (New York: McGraw-Hill, 2004).

Herek, Gregory M., 'Heterosexuals' Attitudes Towards Lesbians and Gay Men: Correlates and Gender Differences', *Journal of Sex Research*, Vol. 25, (1988), pp.451-477.

Herek, Gregory M., 'Hate Crimes Against Lesbians and Gay Men: Issues for Research and Policy', *American Psychologist*, Vol. 44 (June 1989), pp.948-955.

Herek, Gregory M., 'Gender Gaps in Public Opinion About Lesbians and Gay Men', *Public Opinion Quarterly*, Vol. 66 (1992), pp.40-66.

Herek, Gregory M., 'Psychological Heterosexism in the United States' in Anthony R. D'Augelli and Charlotte J. Patterson, eds, *Lesbian, Gay and Bisexual Identities Over the Lifespan: Psychological Perspectives* (New York: Oxford University Press, 1995), p.321-346.

Herek, Gregory M., 'Heterosexism and Homophobia' in Robert P. Cabaj and Terry S. Stein, *Textbook of Homosexuality and Mental Health* (Washington: American Psychiatric Press, 1996), p.101-113.

Herek, Gregory M., ed., *Stigma and Sexual Orientation: Understanding Prejudice Against Lesbians, Gay Men, and Bisexuals* (London: Sage Publications, 1998).

Herek, Gregory M., 'The Psychology of Sexual Prejudice', *Current Directions in Psychological Sciences*, Vol. 9, (February 2000), pp.19-22.

Herek, Gregory M., 'Beyond "Homophobia": Thinking About Sexual Prejudice and Stigma in the Twenty-First Century', *Sexuality Research and Social Policy*, Vol. 1, No. 2 (April 2004), pp.2-24.

Herek, Gregory M. and J. P. Capitanio, '"Some of my Best Friends": Intergroup Contact, Concealable Stigma and Heterosexuals' Attitudes Toward Gay Men and Lesbians', *Personality and Social Psychology Bulletin*, Vol. 22 (1996), pp.412-424.

Herek, Gregory M., Jeanine C. Cogan and J. Roy Gillis, 'Victim Experiences in Hate Crimes Based on Sexual Orientation' in Barbara Perry, ed., *Hate and Bias Crime: A Reader* (New York: Routledge, 2003), pp.243-260.

Herek, Gregory M., Jeanine C. Cogan, J. Roy Gillis and Eric R. Glunt, 'Correlates of Internalised Homophobia in a Community Sample of Lesbians and Gay Men', *Journal of the Gay and Lesbian Medical Association*, Vol. 2 (1997), pp.17-25.

'Hate Crime Law Review Ordered', Age [Melbourne], 10 December 2009, <http://www.theage.com.au/national/hate-crime-law-review-ordered-20091209 -kk2m.html> (accessed 7 January 2010).

Hill, Robert J., ed., *Challenging Homophobia and Heterosexism: Lesbian, Gay, Bisexual, Transgender and Queer Issues in Organizational Settings* (San Francisco: Jossey-Bass, 2006).

Hillier, Lynn and Lyn Harrison, 'Homophobia and the Production of Shame: Young People and Same Sex Attraction', *Culture, Health and Society*, Vol. 6 (January-February 2004), pp.79-94.

Hillier, Lynne and Anne Mitchell, '"It Was as Useful as a Chocolate Kettle": Sex Education in the Lives of Same-Sex-Attracted Young People in Australia', *Sex Education: Sexuality, Society and Learning*, Vol. 8, (2008), pp.211-224.

Hillier, Lynne, Alina Turner and Anne Mitchell, *Writing Themselves In Again: 6 Years On — The Second National Report of the Sexual Health and Well Being of Same Sex Attracted Young People in Australia* (2005) The Australian Research Centre in Sex, Health and Society — La Trobe University, <http://www.latrobe.edu.au/arcshs/download_reports.html> (accessed 7 January 2010).

Hillier, Lynne and Anne Mitchell, *Why Homophobia Needs to be Named in Bullying Policy* (Australian Research Centre in Sex Health and Society — La Trobe University), (Undated), available at <http://www.latrobe.edu.au/ssay/ assets/ downloads/Homophobic bullying.pdf> (accessed 7 January 2010).

Hopkins, Patrick D., 'Gender Treachery: Homophobia, Masculinity, and Threatened Identities' in Lisa Heldke and Peg O'Connor, eds, *Oppression, Privilege, and Resistance: Theoretical Perspectives on Racism, Sexism, and Heterosexism* (New York: McGraw Hill, 2004).

Howe, Adrian, 'Case Notes: *Green v The Queen*, The Provocation Defence: Finally Provoking Its Own Demise?' *Melbourne University Law Review*, Vol. 22 (1998), pp.466-490.

Irwin, J., *The Pink Ceiling is Too Low: Workplace Experiences of Lesbians, Gay Men and Transgender People* (Sydney: Australian Centre for Lesbian and Gay Research, University of Sydney, 1999).

Janoff, Douglas, *Pink Blood: Homophobic Violence in Canada* (Toronto: University of Toronto Press, 2005).

Jenness, Valerie, 'The Emergence, Content, and Institutionalization of Hate Crime Law: How a Diverse Policy Community Produced a Modern Legal Fact', *Annual Review of Law and Social Science*, Vol. 3 (2007), pp.141-160.

Kantor, Martin, *Homophobia: Descriptions, Development, and Dynamics of Gay Bashing* (London: Praeger, 1998).

Kimmel, Michael S., 'Masculinity as Homophobia: Fear, Shame, and Silence in the Construction of Gender Identity' in Harry Brod and Michael Kaufman, eds., *Theorizing Masculinities* (London: Sage, 1994).

Kite, Mary E., 'Individual Differences in Males' Reactions to Gay Males and Lesbians', *Journal of Applied Social Psychology*, Vol. 22 (1992), pp.1222-1239.

Kite, Mary E. and B. E. Whitley Jr., 'Do Heterosexual Women and Men Differ in Their Attitudes Towards Homosexuality? A conceptual and methodological analysis' in G. M. Herek, ed., *Psychological Perspectives on Lesbians and Gay Issues, Vol. 4, Stigma and Sexual Orientation: Understanding Prejudice Against Lesbians, Gay Men, and Bisexuals* (Thousand Oaks, California: Sage, 1998), pp.39-61.

Kitzinger, C., 'Speaking of Oppression: Psychology, Politics and the Language of Power' in E. D. Rothblum and L. A. Bond, eds., *Preventing Heterosexism and Homophobia* (Thousand Oaks, California: Sage, 1996), pp.3-19.

Kuehnle, Krishten and Anne Sullivan, 'Patterns of Anti-Gay Violence: An Analysis of Incident Characteristics and Victim Reporting', *Journal of Interpersonal Violence,* Vol. 16 (2001), pp.928-943.

Lawlink Crime Prevention Division, *Working Together: Preventing Violence Against Gay, Lesbian, Bisexual and Transgender People — Strategic Framework 2007 — 2012,* <http://www.lawlink.nsw.gov.au/lawlink/ cpd/ll_cpd.nsf/ Pages/CPD_strategic_framework>

Law Reform Commission of Western Australia, *Review of the Law of Homicide,* (Final Report 2007), <http://www.lrc.justice.wa.gov.au/097-FR.html> (accessed 6 January 2010).

Leonard, William, Anne Mitchell, Marian Pitts and Sunil Patel, *Coming Forward: The Underreporting of Heterosexist Violence and Same Sex Partner Abuse in Victoria* (Melbourne: The Australian Research Centre in Sex, Health and Society, La Trobe University, 2008).

Liddle, Rod, 'I Know Why The Government Wants to Send Homosexuals Back to Iran To Be Hanged' *The Spectator* (UK, 26 March 2008), <http://www.spectator. co.uk/the-magazine/features/575491/i-know-why-the-government-wants-to-send-homosexuals-back-to-iran-to-be-hanged.html> (accessed 7 January 2010).

Long, Scott, 'Anatomy of a Backlash: Sexuality and the "Cultural" War on Human Rights' *Human Rights Watch* (2004), <http://www.hrw.org/wr2k5/anatomy/ index.htm> (accessed 7 January 2010).

Marszalek, Jessica and David Barbeler, 'Group to tackle school violence, bullies', 23 February 2010, <http://news.brisbanetimes.com.au/breaking-news-national/ group-to-tackle-school-violence-bullies-20100223-osal.html> (accessed 3 March 2010).

Mason, Gail, 'Violence Against Lesbians and Gay Men', *Crime Prevention Today,* No. 2 (Canberra: Australian Institute of Criminology, 1993).

Mason, Gail, 'Sexuality and Violence: Questions of Difference' in Chris Cunneen, ed., *Faces of Hate: Hate Crime in Australia* (Annandale, New South Wales: Hawkins Press, 1997), pp. 115-136.

Mason, Gail, 'Body Maps: Envisaging Homophobia, Violence and Safety', *Social and Legal Studies,* Vol. 10 (2001), pp.23-44.

Mason, Gail, 'Not Our Kind of Hate Crime', *Law and Critique,* Vol. 12, (2001), pp.253-278.

Mason, Gail, *The Spectacle of Violence: Homophobia, Gender and Knowledge* (London: Routledge, 2002).

Mason, Gail, 'Hate Crime Laws in Australia: Are they Achieving their Goals?' *Criminal Law Journal* Vol 33 (2009) pp.326-340.

Mason, Gail, 'Heterosexual Violence: Typicality and Ambiguity' in Mason and Tomsen, eds, *Homophobic Violence* (Annandale, NSW: The Hawkins Press, 1997), chapter 2, p.26.

Meyer, I., 'Prejudice, social stress, and mental health in lesbian, gay, and bisexual populations: Conceptual issues and research evidence' *Psychological Bulletin,* Vol. 129, No. 5 (2003), pp.674-697.

Miller, B., and L. Humphreys, 'Lifestyles and Violence: Homosexual Victims of Assault and Murder', *Qualitative Sociology,* Vol.3, No.3 (1980), pp.169-185.

Moore, Clive, *Sunshine and Rainbows: The Development of Gay and Lesbian Culture in Queensland* (St Lucia, Queensland: University of Queensland Press, 2001).

Morgan, David L., 'Practical Methods for Combining Qualitative and Quantitative Methods: Applications for Health Research', *Qualitative Health Research*, Vol. 8, No. 3 (1998), pp.362-372.

Morgan, David L., *Focus Groups as Qualitative Research* (Thousand Oaks, California: Sage, 1998).

Nagoshi, Julie L., Katherine A. Adams, Heather K. Terrell, Eric D. Hill, Stephanie Brzuzy and Craig T. Nagoshi, 'Gender Differences in Correlates of Homophobia and Transphobia', *Sex Roles*, Vol. 59 (October 2008), pp.521-531.

National Guidelines Task Force, *Guidelines for Comprehensive Sexuality Education* (3rd Ed) (2004), <http://www.siecus.org/_data/global/images/guidelines.pdf> (accessed 27 December 2009).

'New International Guidelines Spell Out What Sexuality Education Needs to Teach', *The Gov Monitor*, 31 August 2009, <http://thegovmonitor.com/world_news/international/new-international-guidelines-spell-out-what-sexuality-education-needs-to-teach-2751.html> (accessed 7 January 2010).

New South Wales Attorney General's Department, *'You Shouldn't Have to Hide to be Safe': A Report on Homophobic Hostilities and Violence Against Gay Men and Lesbians in New South Wales* (Sydney: New South Wales Attorney General's Department, Crime Prevention Division, 2003).

New South Wales Attorney General's Departmnet, Review of the *'Homosexual Advance Defence'*, (Sydney: New South Wales Attorney General's Department, 1996).

New South Wales Attorney General's Department of NSW, *Homosexual Advance Defence: Final Report of the Working Party* (Sydney: New South Wales Attorney General's Department, 1998), <http://www.lawlink.nsw.gov.au/lawlink/clrd/ll_clrd.nsf/vwPrint1/CLRD_had> (accessed 6 January 2010).

NSW Police Force, 'Police Gay & Lesbian Liaison Officers' (Factsheet), <http://www.police.nsw.gov.au/__data/assets/pdf_file/0011/86393/GLLO_Fact_Sheet.pdf> (accessed 7 January 2010).

NSW Police Force, *Gay, Lesbian, Bisexual and Transgender Issues*, available at <http://www.police.nsw.gov.au>, (accessed 24 February 2010).

Nicholas, Jonathon and John Howard, 'Same-Sex Attracted Youth Suicide: Why are We Still Talking About It?' (Presentation, 2001) Suicide Prevention Australia National Conference, Sydney, <http://www.caps.org.au/assets/site/WSPD06_presentation_J_Nicholas.pdf>.

Norton, Jodie '"Brain Says You're A Girl, But I Think You're A Sissy Boy": Cultural Origins of Transphobia', *International Journal of Sexuality and Gender Studies*, Vol. 2 (1997), pp.139-164.

Office of Economic and Statistical Research, 'Queensland Regional Profiles', <http://statistics.oesr.qld.gov.au/report-viewer/run?__report=qld-reg-profile.rptdesign&sessionid=7C7DE96133B38058E043A18F39298058&__format=pdf> (accessed 6 January 2010).

Office of the Government Statistician, *Crime and Justice Statistics Queensland 1999-2000* (Brisbane: Office of the Government Statistician, 2001).

Page, Stephen, 'Maryborough Men Acquitted of Murder: Gay Panic Defence' QNews, date unknown, <http://www.qnews.com.au/node/12695/1790> (accessed 6 January 2010)

Peel, Elizabeth, 'Violence Against Lesbians and Gay Men: Decision-Making in Reporting and Non-Reporting Crime', *Feminism and Psychology*, Vol. 9 (1999), pp.161-166.

Pharr, Suzanne *Homophobia: A Weapon of Sexism* (Little Rock: Chardon Press, 1988).

Pitts, Marian, Anthony Smith, Anne Mitchell and Sunil Patel, *Private Lives: A Report on the Health and Wellbeing of GLBTI Australians* (Melbourne: The Australian Research Centre in Sex, Health and Society, La Trobe University, 2003).

Plummer, David, *One of the Boys: Masculinity, Homophobia and Modern Manhood* (New York: Harrington Park Press, 1994).

Queensland Association for Healthy Communities, 'Mental Health and Well-Being in Lesbian, Gay, Bisexual and Transgender Communities', QAHL website <http://www.qahc.org.au/files/shared/Mental_Health_LGBT_factsheet-w.pdf> (accessed 3 March 2010).

Queensland Department of Education and Training, 'Inclusive Education Statement — 2005' (2005), <http://education.qld.gov.au/studentservices/learning/docs /inclusedstatement2005.pdf> (accessed 7 January 2010).

Queensland Department of Education and Training, 'Racism and Homophobia in Schools', <http://education.qld.gov.au/actsmartbesafe/schoolleaders/racism-homophobia.html> (accessed 7 January 2010).

Queensland Department of Education and Training, 'Responsible Behaviour Plan for Students', <http://education.qld.gov.au/studentservices/behaviour/bm-plans.html> (accessed 7 January 2010).

Queensland Government, Department of Local Government, Planning, Sport and Recreation, *Queensland's Aboriginal and Torres Strait Islander Population* (Brisbane: Queensland Government, Department of Local Government, Planning, Sport and Recreation, 2006).

Queensland Government, Disability and Community Care Services, 'Disability — A Queensland Profile, 2005', <http://www.disability.qld.gov.au/ informa-tion/documents/disabilities-queensland-profile-2005.pdf> (accessed 28 February 2010).

Queensland Police Service, R Atkinson, Commissioner, 'Working in Partnership' (2009), <http://www.police.qld.gov.au/programs/community/lgbti/equality.htm> (accessed on 14 January 2010).

Rainbow Visions — Hunter Inc, *Rainbow Visions*, <http://www.rainbowvisions. org.au/> (accessed 7 January 2010).

Raja, Sheela and Joseph P. Stokes, 'Assessing Attitudes Towards Lesbians and Gay Men: The Homophobia Scale', *International Journal of Sexuality and Gender Studies,* Vol. 3, No. 2 (April 1998), pp.113-134.

'Report Shows Gay Youth Face Serious Health Challenges', *Vox News Engine* (New Zealand), 19 October 2009, <http://www.voxy.co.nz/national/report-shows-gay-youth-face-serious-health-challenges/5/27749> (accessed 16 November 2009).

Rigby, Ken, *Report: Enchancing Responses to Bullying in Queensland Schools,* available at <http://education.qld.gov.au/studentservices/behaviour/ docs/ enhancing-responses-to-bullying-qld-schools.pdf> (accessed 3 March 2010).

....

Ringer, R., ed., *Queer Words, Queer Images: Communication and the Construction of Homosexuality* (New York: New York University, 1994).

Robinson, Shirleene ed., *Homophobia: An Australian History* (Annandale, New South Wales: Federation Press, 2008).

Robinson, Shirleene 'Homophobia as Party Politics: The Construction of the "Homosexual Deviant" in Joh Bjelke-Petersen's Queensland', *Queensland Review*, forthcoming, 2010.

Scott, Darryl, *Everyone Has the Right to be Able to Walk Safe in Their Community: Valley Walksafe Project* (2004).

Sexuality Discrimination Amendment Act 2004 (ACT).

Sexuality Information and Education Council of the United States, 'Leadership & Staff', (2009) <http://www.siecus.org/index.cfm?fuseaction=Page.viewPage& PageId=490&parentID=472> (accessed 27 December 2009).

Stryker, Susan and Stephen Whittle, eds., *The Transgender Reader* (New York: Routledge, 2006).

Taylor, Christian, 'Time To Target School Bullying', *SameSame*, 2 June 2009, <http://www.samesame.com.au/news/local/4090/Time-To-Target-School-Bullying .htm> (accessed 7 January 2010).

Tomsen, Stephen, 'Sexual Identity and Victimhood in Gay-Hate Murder Trials', in Chris Cunneen, David Fraser and Stephen Tomsen, eds, *Faces of Hate: Hate Crime in Australia* (Sydney: Hawkins Press, 1997), pp. 97-114.

Tomsen, Stephen, 'Hate Crimes and Masculine Offending', *Gay and Lesbian Law Journal*, Vol. 10 (2001), pp.26-42

Tomsen, Stephen, 'Hatred, Murder and Male Honour: Anti-homosexual Homicide in New South Wales, 1980-2000', *Australian Institute of Criminology Research and Public Policy Series*, No. 43 (2002).

Tomsen, Stephen and Kevin Markwell, 'When the Glitter Settles: Safety and Hostility at and around Gay and Lesbian Public Events', *Australian Institute of Criminology Research and Public Policy Series*, No. 100 (2009).

Tomsen, Stephen and Gail Mason, 'Engendering Homophobia: Violence, Sexuality and Gender Conformity', *Journal of Sociology*, Vol. 37 (2001), pp.257-273.

United Nations Educational, Scientific and Cultural Organisation, 'New International Guidelines spell out what sexuality education needs to teach' (Press Release, 28 August 2009), <http://portal.unesco.org/en/ev.php-URL_ID=46306&URL_DO=DO_TOPIC&URL_SECTION=201.html> (accessed 31 December 2009).

The University of Newcastle, 'The Role of an Ally' <http://www.newcastle. edu.au/service/ally-network/ally-role.html> (accessed 21 December 2009).

Valentine, David, *Imagining Transgender: An Ethnography of a Category* (Durham: Duke University Press, 2007).

Victorian Attorney General, 'Sentencing Act to Take Into Account Hate Crimes' (Media Release, 3 June 2009) <http://www.premier.vic.gov.au/component /content/article/7111.html> (accessed 7 January 2010).

Victorian Attorney General, 'Sentencing Act to Recognise Impact of Hate Crimes' (Media Release, 16 September 2009) <http://www.premier.vic.gov.au /component/content/article/8142.html> (accessed 7 January 2010).

Victorian Attorney General, 'New Sentencing Laws to Take Into Account Hate Crime' (Media Release, 24 July 2009) <http://www.premier.vic.gov.au/ component/content/article/7625.html> (accessed 7 January 2010).

Victorian Department of Education and Training, 'Safe Schools are Effective Schools: A Resource for Developing Safe and Supportive School Environments' (Melbourne, 2006), <http://www.eduweb.vic.gov.au/edulibrary/public/stuman/ wellbeing/SafeSchoolStrategy.pdf> (accessed 7 January 2010)

Victorian Law Reform Commission, 'Defences to Homicide: Final Report' (Report 2004), <http://www.lawreform.vic.gov.au/wps/wcm/connect/Law+Reform/ Home/Completed+Projects/Defences+to+Homicide/LAWREFORM+- +Defences+to+Homicide+-+Final+Report> (accessed 6 January 2010).

Victorian Police Force, *Gay and Lesbian Liaison Officers* (GLLOs), available at <http://www.police.vic.gov.au/content.asp?Document_ID=741>, (accessed 24 February 2010)

Victorian Police Force, 'Preventing Homophobic Crimes', <http://www.police.vic. gov.au/content.asp?Document ID=308> (accessed 25 February 2010)

Weinberg, George, *Society and the Healthy Homosexual* (Garden City, New York: Anchor Press, 1972).

Willett, Graham, *Living out Loud: A History of Gay and Lesbian Activism in Australia* (St. Leonards, New South Wales: Allen & Unwin, 2000).

Williamson, Iain R., 'Internalized Homophobia and Health Issues Affecting Lesbians and Gay Men', *Health Education Research*, Vol. 15 (2000), p.97-107.

Witten, Tarynn M., and A. Evan Eyler, 'Hate Crimes and Violence Against the Transgendered', *Peace Review*, Vol. 11 (1999), pp.461-468.

Witthaus, Daniel, *Beyond 'That's so gay!' Challenging Homophobia in Australian Schools* (Melbourne: Hawker Brownlow Education, 2010).

Witthaus, Daniel, *Pride & Prejudice-Educational Package*, <http://www.prideand prejudice.com.au> (accessed 6 March 2010).

Index

....

perceptions of among LGBTQ community, 127, 146-147, 152
prejudice, 147, 176-178

Religion
Homophobia/transphobia and, 23,
24, 171, 172, 191, 216, 238
Reporting homophobic and transphobic
violence
rates of non-reporting, 13, 165
rates of reporting, 3, 146
Rural areas
level of hostility towards LGBTQ
people, 109, 119

Scott, Darryl, 8, 16, 51, 57, 76, 95
Sodomy
repeal of laws, 236, 238, 242
Suicide, 7, 90, 108, 117, 192, 213, 241

Terrell, Heather K., 111
Tomsen, Stephen, 6, 15, 42, 51, 57, 96,
98, 100, 111, 205, 237, 244

Transphobia, 1-9, 11, 13, 14, 32, 33, 42,
48-51, 56, 59, 60, 70-74, 76, 80, 83,
86, 87, 90, 91, 94, 98, 99, 106, 108,
109, 111, 118, 123, 126-128, 133,
135, 157, 166, 173, 182-185, 187,
189, 191, 193, 195, 197-199, 201,
202, 207, 213, 216, 218, 225, 232,
233, 235, 236
Transgender identity, 4-5

Verbal insults, 50
See also abuse
Victorian Police Service, 170, 180, 181,
226

Weinberg, George, 3, 14
Willett, Graham, 14
Witten, Tarryn M., 5, 45

'You Shouldn't Have to Hide to Be Safe'
report, 9, 35, 42, 102, 131

www.ingramcontent.com/pod-product-compliance
Lightning Source LLC
Chambersburg PA
CBHW070352270326
41926CB00014B/2516